PREPARING FOR INCLUSIVE TEACHING

SUNY series, Teacher Preparation and Development
Alan R. Tom, editor

PREPARING FOR INCLUSIVE TEACHING

Meeting the Challenges of
Teacher Education Reform

EDITED BY
Elizabeth Bondy
and
Dorene D. Ross

STATE UNIVERSITY OF NEW YORK PRESS

Published by
State University of New York Press, Albany

For information, address State University of New York Press,
90 State Street, Suite 700, Albany, NY 12207

Production by Diane Ganeles
Marketing by Anne M. Valentine

Library of Congress Cataloging-in-Publication Data

Preparing for inclusive teaching : meeting the challenges of teacher education
    reform / editors, Elizabeth Bondy and Dorene D. Ross.
        p. cm. — (Suny series, teacher preparation and development)
    includes bibliographical references and index.
    ISBN 0-7914-6357-5 (alk. paper) — ISBN 0-7914-6358-3
        (pbk. : alk. paper)
        1. Teachers—Training of—Florida—Gainesville—Case studies. 2. Inclusive
    education—United States. 3. Interdisciplinary approach in
    education—Florida—Gainesville—Case studies. 4. University of Florida.
    College of Education—Case studies. I. Bondy, Elizabeth. II. Ross, Dorene
    Doerre. III. SUNY series in teacher prepartion and development.

LB1716.F6P74 2005
370'.71'1—dc22

                                                                    2004048186

10 9 8 7 6 5 4 3 2 1

This book is dedicated to

Bill, Charlie, Sam, and Molly
Jack, Kate, and Sarah

and the many teachers who work hard every day
to help all children succeed.

Contents

Foreword

Few issues today are more contested than the challenge of preparing high-quality teachers within a research university setting. Although the sweeping federal education bill, No Child Left Behind, focused new attention on this issue, many programs around the country since the formation of the Holmes Group in 1985 (now the Holmes Partnership) have long been concerned with the question of how best to prepare teachers in an environment where teacher education is not the primary mission. Universities that upheld the ideal of preparing thoughtful, reflective, inquiry-oriented teachers who were well grounded in both theory and practice quite often failed to receive the plaudits they deserved, and the challenges they faced were rarely addressed in the teacher education literature.

This book, edited by Elizabeth Bondy and Dorene Ross, is a long overdue contribution to the field in making visible and explicit just how complicated genuine cross-disciplinary collaboration is in teacher education reform. The most striking feature is the authors' willingness to narrate the story of a teacher education program that has been widely recognized as consistently excellent over time, yet one where the faculty were willing to create new models to ensure teachers are ready for the highly diverse, technologically driven, and socially complex classrooms of the future. The Proteach program in the College of Education at the University of Florida is one such program, and the authors paint a vivid picture of how this program was revised in 1995 to create a unified program that combined traditional preparation in elementary education with special education to ensure preservice students would be able to work successfully in inclusive classrooms. While the program contributors do not shrink from sharing candidly the struggles to bridge differences, and the time- and labor-intensive nature of this collaboration, they also acknowledge the rewards of seeing new ideas flourish in a true partnership among colleagues who did not necessarily share the same theoretical orientations and views of appropriate classroom practices. More importantly, the preservice students' recognition that this combined program strengthened their preparation was even more rewarding to program faculty, a fact confirmed by school districts' strong demand for these candidates.

An added bonus was the inclusion of other contributors external to the university who provided a more objective and nuanced perspective on this innovative and collaborative program. They helped raise important questions that will undoubtedly guide future program revisions, and underscored the need for research universities to reconsider the allocation of scarce resources and faculty lines to teacher education at a time of rapidly growing shortages within the profession. Linda Darling-Hammond and others have continually reminded us that high-quality teachers matter in raising student achievement, especially among those children most in need, and all the authors remind us that quality can be achieved, but at an expense of time, commitment, and resources that are all in scarce supply. In a time of rapidly changing, and increasingly demanding expectations, the picture is clouded as to how quality will be sustained.

These are difficult times for teacher educators and colleges of education. Beset on all sides by a disgruntled public that holds them accountable for teachers' performance in the classroom, and by state governments clamoring for more teachers while increasing mandates for accountability and decreasing funds, they must find creative ways to respond without losing the commitment to maintain the levels of quality and excellence that characterize outstanding programs. This book is a testament to the fact that it can be accomplished, and the program authors' experiences should hearten those who believe in the concept of teaching as a profession, and collaboration across disciplines. While the story still remains to be told as to how they will succeed in the future, given the caliber of the participants involved in this work, I have little doubt they will rise to the challenge.

Catherine Emihovich
Dean, College of Education
University of Florida

INTRODUCTION

ELIZABETH BONDY, DORENE D. ROSS,
AND
LINDA BLANTON

In the spring of 1995 the College of Education at the University of Florida initiated an effort to redesign elementary and special education teacher education. Influenced by a variety of forces within and outside of the college, a planning committee of faculty and school-based colleagues began a four-year journey to unify general and special education in a teacher education program for which faculty in all of the college's five departments would have responsibility.

Not surprisingly, the reform journey was characterized by fits and starts, as reflected in the titles and duration of the five phases of the process:

- Phase I: Getting Started (10 months)
- Phase II: First Design-False Start (6 months)
- Phase III: Back to the Drawing Board—The Redesign Teams (7 months)
- Phase IV: Approval of Curriculum (3 months)
- Phase V: Developing the Courses and University Approval (26 months)

Despite the rocky road, the faculty reached the destination of program approval and the first five cohorts of preservice teachers began the Unified Elementary Special Education Proteach program in the fall of 1999.

Of course, program approval and implementation are merely one destination in the ongoing journey of program improvement. What are the students learning? How do we know? What can faculty do to make program experiences more powerful? These are the questions that guide ongoing efforts to prepare teachers for the increasingly diverse classrooms in our state and nation.

1

Preparing for Inclusive Teaching: Meeting the Challenges of Teacher Education Reform tells the story of the reform effort at the University of Florida. Chapters were written after completion of the first year of the three-year program; they provide a glimpse of the program's beginnings. In particular, chapters provide details of program development and description and close examination of several key features such as teaching teams, unique field experiences, and electronic portfolios. Woven through these descriptive chapters are reports of research conducted by faculty during and after the first year of program implementation. These studies and many others like them continue to provide insight into participants' experiences in the program. These insights guide faculty in adjusting courses, field experiences, and other program structures to promote preservice teacher learning of the knowledge, skills, and dispositions needed to teach in a classroom of diverse children.

Although the chapters focus on one reform effort at a large, state university, chapters written by teacher education experts from other institutions help to contextualize the particulars of this reform within the national education and teacher education scenes. The detailed descriptions of local efforts coupled with the external authors' discussions and critiques of those efforts will be informative and thought-provoking for readers who are considering or engaged in teacher education reform.

OVERVIEW OF THE CHAPTERS

In Part One (chapters 1 and 2) of the book, the authors overview the landscape of reform in teacher education, to include the challenges faced by most who engage in this activity. The authors of chapter 1 (Rennert-Ariev, Frederick, and Valli) describe the recommendations for teacher education reform contained in the major reports and documents of national commissions (e.g., National Commission on Teaching and America's Future), institutional partnerships (e.g., Holmes and Renaissance), and national organizations (e.g., National Council for the Accreditation of Teacher Education). The authors analyzed these reports to identify common recommendations that they organized into two categories: Structural Reforms and Conceptual Reforms. Included in their discussion of Structural Reforms are those reforms relating to governance (i.e., quality control of teacher preparation and credentialing), recruitment (i.e., supply of quality teachers), program extension (i.e., time in teacher preparation), and induction (i.e., quality support systems for beginning teachers). The discussion of Conceptual Reforms focuses on the need for teacher preparation programs to include a clear vision (i.e., a common philosophy of teaching and learning to assure more coherent programs); curricula that reflect strong content and pedagogy; clinical experiences anchored in the context of schools, classrooms, and students; and teacher assessments designed to assure teacher competence. The authors close chapter 1 by discussing the factors that influenced reform groups to put their attention on teaching and teacher education: inadequate school performance, population shifts, and economic changes.

Rod Webb follows in chapter 2 with a discussion of the challenges faced by faculty and administrators who engage in teacher education reform. He overviews the context in which research universities exist, weaves in the literature on the change process, then narrows the focus to the University of Florida and describes how faculty and administrators navigated the sociopolitical and institutional contexts to achieve success in their reform efforts.

Part Two (chapters 3 through 7) contains a description of the University of Florida's reform effort, including the nature of the reformed programs (chapter 3), the processes they used to accomplish their work (chapter 4), how faculty partnered with schools and the community (chapter 5), and how teams worked together (chapter 6). This part concludes with chapter 7 by external author Marleen Pugach who pulls out major themes, raises key questions, and discusses lessons learned.

Ross, Lane, and McCallum begin Part Two in chapter 3 by tracing the history of teacher education innovation at the University of Florida to show the reader how earlier reform efforts influenced current efforts at program renewal. These authors draw on the common recommendations of national reports on teacher education reform to show how these recommendations figured into the redesign of Proteach and led to the new Unified Elementary Special Education Proteach program, UESEP. Faculty and administrators adopted inclusive education as the mission of UESEP and Ross, Lane, and McCallum articulate the themes, values, and content associated with this mission. Other program features, such as, content, cohort approach, varied field experiences, performance assessment, and collaboration are also highlighted. In addition, the authors outline the program by providing a description of each semester of UESEP.

The process used to design UESEP is the focus of chapter 4. Authors Correa, Ross, and Webb review the forces that led to the redesign of Proteach, to include the arrival of a new dean and new federal funding to support program revision. The authors walk the reader through the various phases of the development process and show how they made initial progress, encountered setbacks, and got back on track to continue their progress toward program redesign. Perhaps of greatest benefit to the reader is the section that describes the solutions that faculty and administrators developed to overcome the barriers they encountered.

Chapter 5 emphasizes the process used to design field experiences for UESEP. Like the previous chapter, authors Griffin, Fang, Bishop, and Halsall walk the reader through the design and structure of field experiences and describe solutions to the barriers they encountered. Closing this chapter is a section devoted to the reflections of school district personnel on the UESEP program and its field experiences.

Chapter 6 focuses on teaching teams, made up of full and adjunct faculty and graduate students, who were responsible for teaching approximately 210 students each year. Through these teams, program faculty sought to ensure greater consistency in course content across sections. To document the experiences and attitudes of team members, data were collected through focus groups, surveys, and interviews. Findings reported by Webb, Ross, and McCallum offer insight into faculty perspectives on issues related to instructional autonomy, instructional improvement, collaboration strategies, and cost-benefit. The authors' thoughts about these data reveal insights into the tensions faculty face when engaging in teacher education reform at a large research university.

Chaper 7, authored by Marleen Pugach, pulls out three themes from the discussion of UESEP in Part Two: (a) the hard work of reform that must be sustained over time to be successful, (b) changing the culture of the organization, and (c) resources to support reformed teacher education. In addition, Pugach raises three questions that surfaced from her review of Part Two: How are the themes and goals (of UESEP) connected over time? How is diversity addressed? How is inclusive pedagogy defined? Finally, she addresses lessons learned related to (a) resources, (b) professional development schools, and (c) patience.

Part Three (chapters 8 through 12) includes the perspectives of general and special education faculty to make strong points about the importance of teacher education reform being a collegewide effort. Included in this section are several studies conducted by faculty and doctoral students to understand faculty, student, and practitioner responses to reform. External author Renee Clift's response to this section focuses on a number of key questions that, if answered, might form a picture of a unified teacher education program.

The first chapter in Part Three, chapter 8, examines the nature of collaboration in teaching teams comprised of faculty members from general and special education. In contrast to chapter 6, the authors of chapter 8 dig deeply into the process of collaboration. In addition to offering insights into the process of collaboration (e.g., developing a syllabus together), authors Brownell, McLeskey, Ashton, Hoppey, and Nowak discuss the tensions that resulted from the ways faculty from different fields approach their work. The areas on which the faculty differed were (a) approaches used to set time and work priorities, (b) professional autonomy, (c) views of the classroom teacher's role, and (d) perspectives of knowledge. Especially helpful in this chapter are the segments from field notes used to illustrate tensions in each of the areas on which faculty differed.

In chapter 9 Bondy, Adams, and Mallini report the findings of an interview study by using participants in the revised program's first field experience. Students (nine), cooperating teachers (nine), and instructors (two) made up the sample. Results revealed many benefits to learning and teaching in partnerships. For example, students described benefits such as "understand self as a teacher," teachers noted benefits such as "insights into the teacher education program," and instructors pointed out such benefits as "experimenting with unfamiliar teacher education pedagogy." Interviews revealed that the structure of partnerships promoted collaborative reflection, which in turn facilitated learning.

Chapter 10 was written by counselor educators Amatea and Jennie who make the critical point that teacher education reform is a collegewide effort. They developed, then taught a course on the roles of families and communities in education, and teachers' roles with families. Amatea and Jennie provide an overview of their course and the challenges they faced to assure that classrooms are actually collaborative environments. They close their chapter with a discussion of the shifts they made in their own thinking about school counselor preparation, especially because school counselors play such an important role with children, teachers, and families.

The authors (Bondy, Stafford, and Mott) of chapter 11 report another study of program participants, with a focus on student views of their experiences. Retrospective interviews were used with thirty-nine students who had completed the first two semesters of UESEP. Results showed that students valued such things as practical classes, alignment of coursework and fieldwork, and good instructors, and the meanings they attached to these things were examined. Student concerns focused on such areas as irrelevant information and inconvenience of field experiences, among others. The authors provided numerous examples of student comments to enhance the reader's understanding. Finally, Bondy, Stafford, and Mott offer a number of recommendations for teacher education.

In chapter 12 of Part Three Renee Clift provides an overview of and offers her perspectives on the work done by faculty in the UESEP program to examine, continually and openly, the strengths and weaknesses of their program. Throughout this chapter Clift raises questions that surfaced as she reviewed the data, analysis, and interpretations of the University of Florida faculty. She concludes her discussion by addressing three key questions: What can we learn about teacher education from UESEP? What can we learn about teacher education research from UESEP? What can we learn about ourselves as university-based researchers, teacher educators, and citizens?

Part Four (chapters 13 through 15) focuses on the performance assessments built into the reformed teacher education program at the University of Florida. Following an introduction to performance assessment by external author Catheryn Weitman in chapter 13, Halsall and Vernetson, in chapter 14, provide an overview of the ongoing assessments of student outcomes that are used throughout courses and field experiences in UESEP. Although these authors refer to the use of an electronic portfolio, the detailed description of this system is described in chapter 15 by Ring, Foti, and Swain. After discussion of the development and use of the system, the authors address the challenges they faced and how they found solutions.

In Part Five, authors representing special education, general teacher education, and public elementary school, discuss their reactiions to the first 15 chapters. Linda Blanton comments on lessons and recommendations for special education teacher educators and researchers. Alan Tom identifies redesign issues in UESEP and offers design ideas for teacher educators. Diane Kyle and Gayle Moore respond to UESEP from their experience as colleagues in an elementary Professional Development School attempting to strengthen presence and inservice teacher education and student learning.

There are several ways to approach the reading of this book. Some might choose to begin at the beginning and proceed through the epilogue. This approach would take readers through an overview of the national reform agenda in teacher education and a discussion of the barriers to radical reform in the university; description of the Unified Elementary Special Education Proteach (UESEP) program, the process of program development, and key features of the program; examination of faculty and student learning and experience in the first year of the program; and discussion of the assessment of preservice teacher learning in the program. Some readers may choose to begin at the end of the book with the three chapters written from special education, general education, and school-based perspectives. Others may choose to focus their reading on particular topics, such as teaching teams. In this case, the response chapters throughout and at the end of the text will help determine how to proceed.

Many colleagues within and outside of the University of Florida's College of Education participated in the preparation of this book. Chapter authors include faculty and doctoral students from four departments in the College of Education and even, in two cases, students in the UESEP. Today, there would be even more people eager to contribute. Although at the birth of the book many of the newly developed courses and field experiences had yet to be implemented, four classes of UESEP students have now graduated with the master's degree. Faculty and doctoral students continue to discuss and study the program. Their research helps to improve the program and will no doubt help other teacher educators to do the same. We are grateful to our colleagues and friends who agreed to write with us and who share our enthusiasm for doing and studying teacher education.

PART 1

An Introduction to Reform
in Teacher Education

CHAPTER 1

Mapping the Reform Agenda in Teacher Education: The Challenges for Teacher Educators

PETER L. RENNERT-ARIEV, RONA MONIQUE FREDERICK, AND LINDA VALLI

Since the mid-1980s, a variety of major commission and national organization reports have focused on the reform of teacher education. Before that time, school reform literature centered mainly on issues of curriculum content and academic requirements (National Commission on Excellence in Education, 1983). But with a growing appreciation for the value of good teaching, many influential reform documents explicitly have targeted the nature of teacher preparation as an essential prerequisite for the realization of goals such as higher student achievement and the creation of effective schools. These documents come from a variety of sources, reflecting the broad base of stakeholders who are invested in improving teacher quality. Commissions such as the Carnegie Forum, the National Commission on Excellence in Teacher Education (NCETE), the National Commission on Teaching and America's Future (NCTAF), and the American Council on Education (ACE) have attempted to influence state legislatures, departments of education, and boards of education as well as individual teacher education programs. At the same time institutional partnerships such as the Holmes Group, Project 30 Alliance, and the Renaissance Group have provided a forum for educators within universities and schools to strengthen the articulation between the arts and sciences and the professional preparation of teachers. In addition, the National Council for Accreditation of Teacher Education (NCATE) and, more recently, the Teacher Education Accreditation Council (TEAC) have outlined sets of standards and procedures used to accredit teacher education programs. These guidelines catalyze reform efforts at institutions, particularly during accreditation reviews.

These reform proposals vary in their assessment of the quality of teacher education programs as well as in their recommendations of how programs should be changed (Howey & Zimpher, 1989). Given the proliferation of proposals, with each carrying its own set of assumptions and objectives, the body of teacher education reform literature as a whole can appear fragmented and the individual proposals, idiosyncratic. Recommendations advocated by some are ignored or even opposed by others. Some analysts, however, have noted the convergence of opinions expressed in these documents (Fullan, Galluzzo, Morris, & Watson, 1998) and have looked for ways to identify consensus among a seemingly disparate set of proposals (Valli & Rennert-Ariev, 2000).

This chapter describes the most common recommendations for teacher education put forth by the major reform groups. We group these recommendations into two broad categories: structural characteristics and conceptual characteristics. Structural characteristics refer to the organization and length of the program and generally include the governance of teacher education, recruitment of teachers, and induction of beginning teachers. Conceptual characteristics include the philosophical vision underlying teacher education programs, curricular components, and models of candidate assessment (Feiman-Nemser, 1990; Howey, 1996; Tom, 1997). The following analysis provides an overview of these reforms, the context from which they emerged, and some of the resulting challenges facing today's teacher educators. Although the analysis highlights areas of agreement, we also point out key areas of contention and debate.

STRUCTURAL REFORMS

Governance

During the first half of the twentieth century teachers were generally prepared in normal schools. The second half of the century saw the closing of these schools or their transformation into colleges and universities, where most teachers currently receive both their general and professional education. These institutions of higher education have various mechanisms of quality control, including review by external accrediting agencies. In addition, specialized accrediting bodies oversee professional schools. NCATE and TEAC claim accrediting responsibility for teacher education, although that process is voluntary. State governments, which license teachers, regulate public colleges and universities, and approve professional programs, also have a legitimate role to play in teacher education. This creates a governance issue: How do government agencies, institutions of higher education, and professional organizations share oversight of these programs?

Many of the reform groups have grappled with this tension. Some draw a line between regulating programs and regulating the graduates of programs. The Renaissance Group (1996), for example, says that the state should set outcome expectations for program graduates, but that the university should determine the curriculum, standards, and internal policies. One of the 19 postulates of the Center for Educational Renewal is that teacher education programs should be free from curricular regulations imposed by the state (Goodlad, 1990). Others see a shared responsibility—that certification and program approval are state responsibilities in consultation with the profession—and call for strict enforcement of rigorous standards (NCETE, 1985). NCATE's (1995) approach to shared responsibility has been to develop various forms of partnerships in which the state and NCATE mutually agree upon and coordinate their regulatory functions.

The American Council on Education (1999) has claimed that current mechanisms of quality control are still inadequate:

> Measures for assessing the quality and competence of graduates of teacher education programs and for assessing the quality of the programs themselves fall woefully short of accomplishing their objective. Variations in licensure standards among the states are as numerous as the variations in quality and minimum standards among the nation's 1,200 programs of teacher education. (p. 9)

The Council has joined previous groups in calling upon university presidents to strengthen their commitment to teacher preparation. These calls have included assurance that decision-making authority for teacher education is on a par with other professional schools (Goodlad, 1990), that teacher education is an all-campus responsibility (Renaissance Group, 1996), and that the education of teachers is moved to the center of university agendas (ACE, 1999). With questions about governance, shared responsibility, and mission centrality a long way from resolution, these issues are likely to remain in the forefront of the reform agenda.

Recruitment

Multiple factors contributed to concerns about the supply of quality teachers. These factors include the increasing numbers of school-age children, the need to replace the large numbers of teachers who are retiring or leaving the teaching profession, and the current push for smaller class size. Changing demographics are also forcing policy makers to think about recruiting teachers for culturally and linguistically diverse populations. Consequently, the issue of recruitment has become an important reform initiative. Recommended reforms include the recruitment and retention of minority candidates, special programs to attract minority candidates, and jointly sponsored state and federal recruitment campaigns (Holmes, 1995; NCETE, 1985; Project 30, 1991; Renaissance Group, 1996). Simultaneously, reform groups have pushed for more rigorous admission and graduation standards and for the elimination of policies that lower standards in order to ease supply and demand pressures (Goodlad, 1990; NCETE, 1985).

The National Commission on Teaching and America's Future (1997) has outlined one of the most extensive agendas for enhancing the quantity and quality of the preservice teaching pool. For NCTAF the recruitment challenge is to place *qualified* teachers in every classroom. This means that the recruitment issue should not be framed only (or even primarily) as one of quantity. According to Darling-Hammond, Berry, Haselkorn, and Fideler (1999) approximately 11% of newly hired teachers in 1994 entered the field with no license and an additional 16% received a substandard license. More useful than staffing schools with "warm bodies" is to think about recruitment in terms of quality: equipping schools with certified teachers, especially in poor areas, which have a disproportionate share of teachers who lack credentials (NCTAF, 1997).

As part of the recruitment agenda, NCTAF (1996) suggests providing financial support to teacher candidates who are willing to teach in under-resourced environments. Additional efforts should be made to financially assist minority and multilingual teacher candidates throughout their professional preparation. This could include scholarships, financial aid, and/or loan forgiveness. The active push to attract teachers should begin in middle or high school by providing these students with financial resources to encourage them to consider teaching as a profession. Upon graduation there should be direct lines from teacher preparation programs to classrooms by developing cooperative agreements and collaboration between universities and district administrators. In addition, structural changes such as up-to-date electronic databases are needed at the district level to facilitate the hiring process.

All of these recommendations require additional financial resources and collaboration on the part of universities, school districts, and government agencies if they are to recruit and retain sufficient numbers of committed and competent teacher candidates.

Program Extension

Extending the amount of time that preservice teachers spend in formal preparation is another frequently mentioned reform. The twofold rationale for program extension is that

1. Teachers need more than four years to acquire sufficient general education, pedagogical knowledge, and in-depth knowledge of a particular teaching field, and
2. Extending program length will enhance teaching as a profession (Arends & Winitzky, 1996).

Recommendations to extend programs and to offer graduate level preparation beyond the requirements for a bachelor's degree have evoked strong support from reform groups (e.g., Carnegie Forum, 1986; Holmes Group, 1986; Joyce & Clift, 1984; Smith, 1980). An emerging body of research findings suggests that extended programs result in some positive benefits for prospective teachers, including higher retention rates and greater job satisfaction (Andrew, 1990; Armstrong, Burlbaw, & Batten, 1991).

Nevertheless, proposals for extending programs are still controversial, leading some educational scholars to caution against implementing extended programs without more substantive evidence of the link between teacher quality and length of preparation or more convincing evidence that the added costs of extending programs would be justified (Hawley, 1987; Tom, 1997). The Renaissance Group (1996), an association of liberal arts colleges, argues for the integration of general and professional education rather than reserving professional preparation for an extended, fifth year. Furthermore, some studies indicate that the quality of teacher candidates' learning experiences matters significantly more than the amount of time they spend engaged in it. In their study of 4 and 5 year programs, NCRTE (1991) found high-quality examples of both types. Case studies of high-quality programs, sponsored by NCTAF, were similarly mixed. The important variable seemed to be not the length of the program but rather ways in which programs helped teacher candidates integrate and use different kinds of knowledge for teaching (Darling-Hammond, 2000b). Due to the fierce internal debate about program length, a number of reform groups have remained publicly neutral on this issue.

Induction

Another recommended structural reform is to provide high-quality induction experiences for beginning teachers (Holmes, 1995; NCETE, 1985; NCTAF, 1997). Novice teachers face intense challenges as they transition from student teacher to first-year teacher (Berliner, 1986; Veenman, 1984). These challenges include working to maintain classroom order, developing curriculum and appropriate pedagogical strategies, and addressing individual and cultural differences. To add to their transition problems, beginning teachers are frequently placed in settings characterized by poverty, low achievement, violence, and family instability—often with insufficient assistance, support, and guidance (Darling-Hammond et al., 1999).

In response to these challenges, reformers call for the creation of induction programs to increase teacher retention rates and to help equip new teachers with the knowledge and confidence to effectively teach students, especially ethnically diverse and low-income students. As more and more districts and states work to implement induction programs, various models have emerged. One recommended model is the use of mentors to engage novice teachers in collaborative dialogue around instructional issues and student thinking and learning (Feiman-Nemser & Parker, 1992). Other models include support structures to help beginning teachers deal with psychological stress, and professional development in such areas as curriculum, instruction, assessment, and classroom management (Gold, 1992).

The use of induction programs is now relatively widespread. More than half of all public school teachers with less than five years experience report having participated in some form of induction (NCTAF, 1997). But even though most states currently have induction programs, they vary widely in length, quality, and substance. Only 18 states sponsor programs that include all beginning teachers and few are designed to have a strong impact on both teacher retention and teacher learning (National Association of State Boards of Education, 1998). Calls for universities and school systems to share responsibility for induction programs raise additional governance-related issues (ACE, 1999; Renaissance Group, 1996).

CONCEPTUAL REFORMS

Vision

The notion that teacher education programs should create a consensus around a common philosophy of teaching and learning, and that curricular and instructional decisions should be congruent with this philosophy, is reflected in most reform documents. Accrediting agencies (NCATE, 1995; TEAC, 1998) place particular emphasis on the importance of a coherent vision within teacher preparation programs. The rationale most often given is that a common vision serves as a catalyst for meaningful curriculum development and integration, and that it fosters collaboration, helping to break down antiquated and isolating work roles among preK–12 educators and university faculty.

The Holmes Group (1995), for example, argues that a common vision is both a prerequisite for, and a result of, the common language and agenda that is necessary between university and school faculty and staff. Teacher educators, they believe, must be able to collaborate on behalf of student learning. The isolating work roles, which have traditionally defined faculty work in the academy, are unable to support the type of student-centered learning in which teacher candidates need to take part: [Teacher education programs] "need to recognize interdependence and commonality of purposes in preparing educators for various roles in schools, roles that call for teamwork and common understanding of learner-centered education in the 20th century" (Holmes, 1995, p. 14). New collaborative ways of working for teacher educators, based on a common vision, help overcome the specialized and fragmented nature of their work and invite programmatic improvement.

Curriculum

Two curriculum themes come through the reform documents: teaching for understanding and teaching for diversity. Reform groups have expressed widespread consensus in favor of strong disciplinary preparation for teachers that incorporates an understanding of a discipline's core concepts, structure, and tools of inquiry as a foundation for subject matter pedagogy. National commissions and accrediting agencies have repeatedly stressed the importance of in-depth subject matter preparation to prepare competent and knowledgeable teachers. They express a common concern that today's teachers, especially elementary school teachers, have a thin understanding of the subject matter they teach. Schools, colleges, and departments of education, they believe, have done an inadequate job of creating academically demanding undergraduate programs.

Institutional partnerships, such as Project 30 and the Renaissance Group, pay more attention to the quality of such preparation and urge articulation between the methods used to teach subject matter and the way teachers tend to learn it. Though supportive of subject matter preparation, these groups resist the notion that more academic rigor alone is necessary and articulate a more nuanced understanding of the need for disciplinary preparation. This sentiment is supported by an increasing body of research, including the work of the National Center for Research on Teacher Education. NCRTE (1991) notes that teachers need explicit disciplinary focus, but few positive results can be expected by simply requiring teachers to major in an academic subject. Teachers' exposure to the subject matter needs to be rooted in the underlying meanings and connections inherent in the discipline. Those programs that emphasize the underlying nature of the subject matter, rather than discrete bodies of information, are more likely to produce knowledgeable, dynamic teachers.

Many reform proposals have also designated multicultural and inclusive teaching—teaching for diversity—as central principles. The Project 30 Alliance (1991), for example, includes "international, cultural, and other human perspectives" as one of their guiding principles. Teachers, they believe, need in-depth knowledge of other nations, languages, and cultures as well as opportunities to conduct scholarship on issues of race, gender, ethnicity, and cultural perspectives. The Renaissance Group (1996) expresses a similar goal: teacher education programs need to reflect American diversity and prepare graduates to teach in a pluralistic and multicultural society. The Holmes Group, which was initially criticized for a lack of attention to issues of diversity in Tomorrow's Teachers (1986), responded with specific recommendations for multicultural curricular goals including:

- helping students grapple with the complex social and political reasons underlying student failure and success
- drawing on student diversity to make learning dynamic and interesting for all learners (Holmes Group, 1990).

The importance of preparation to teach special needs students has not received the degree of emphasis in recent reform literature as has preparation for cultural and ethnic diversity (Valli & Rennert-Ariev, 1999). Most reform documents, however, do link teaching for diversity to the needs of both multicultural and special needs populations. NCTAF (1996), for example, highlights the knowledge preservice teachers should have about special needs students and ways to address learning differences and disabilities. NCATE (1995) also deals with knowledge of special needs students—though less explicitly—suggesting that a professional teacher should be able to apply effective methods of teaching students who are at different developmental stages, have different learning styles, and come from diverse backgrounds.

Clinical Experiences

Conceptual reforms have also focused on the central role that clinical experiences play in contributing to teacher development. Reform groups of all types strongly encourage teacher education programs to ground teacher preparation in practice and to link it more directly to the context of "real" schools, classrooms, and students. The selection of suitable field sites for teacher candidates has emerged as a critical issue for many teacher education programs. The degree and nature of cooperation between the university and school-based personnel in setting goals, defining roles, and articulating expectations is a key determinant for successful clinical experiences (Cochran-Smith, 1991; Killian & McIntyre, 1986).

A relatively new type of school/university partnership, the "professional development school" (Holmes Group, 1990), "clinical school" (Carnegie Forum on Education and the Economy, 1986), or "professional practice school" (Levine, 1992) represents a collaborative relationship between schools of education and preK–12 schools. These arrangements have attracted the interest of educators and policy makers for the potential they have for improving the quality of preservice teachers' field experiences. Proponents of Professional Development Schools (PDSs) claim that these settings foster a three-part mission:

- to support student learning for understanding
- to support teacher learning in deliberate ways
- to support research and inquiry directed at the continuous improvement of practice (Levine, 1996).

In addition, PDSs are called upon to serve the needs of children of poverty and special needs populations. The Holmes Group (1990), for instance, advocates that in PDSs "teachers and teacher educators will work hard and inventively to stretch the conventional academic spectrum so that it includes children who are severely impaired" (p. 23).

Teacher Assessment

Noting the inadequacy of judgments about teacher knowledge and skill based on accumulated hours of coursework or performance on multiple-choice tests, reformers call for "performance-based assessments" of teacher candidates. These assessments are designed to target the depth of teachers' knowledge, skills, and dispositions in specific teaching contexts. Drawing on the work of the Interstate New Teacher Assessment and Support Consortium (INTASC), reform groups seek to create a licensing process that identifies teacher competence through authentic performance and shapes preparation and practice in ways that support more powerful forms of student learning (NCTAF, 1996).

Treatment of assessment issues in policy-oriented documents suggests that performance-based assessments have gained widespread acceptance as tools for judging a candidate's competency. NCATE (1985), for example, claims that authentic, performance-based assessments ought to be used throughout a candidate's program and tied to systematic procedures and timelines. NCATE offers specific recommendations for the types of data sources that should be used to assess candidates' progress, including the use of portfolios, teacher research, reflective essays, and concept papers. These sources of data, reformers believe, help situate the assessment of teacher learning in as authentic and meaningful a context as possible.

THE NEED FOR REFORM

Reform groups offer a number of reasons for their interest in the preparation of teachers. The underlying reason is their belief in the importance of high-quality teaching and teacher education. Staffing schools with well-prepared teachers, they argue, is more critical than ever before because of three related factors: inadequate school performance, population shifts, and a changing economy.

School Performance

The 1983 publication of *A Nation at Risk* focused attention on a perceived lack of academic rigor in U.S. schools and sent a warning that schools were failing to produce students who were intellectually equipped to compete on a global level. Since that time, students' low test scores have continued to alarm many educators and policy makers. Noting that more than half of U.S. 4th and 8th graders fail to reach the minimal standard on national tests in reading, mathematics, and science, the chairman of IBM claimed that our schools are pushing the country into a dangerous situation (Orrill, 1994). Additional concern comes from the rankings of U.S. students on international comparisons of mathematics and science achievement. According to the U.S. National Research Center for the Third International Mathematics and Science Study (TIMSS), although U.S. 4th graders perform well in the area of science, by the 8th grade students fall substantially behind their international peers (Valverde & Schmidt, 1997). The pattern is similar in mathematics, where 4th graders score above the international mean, 8th grades at the mean, and 12th graders substantially below the mean.

Both the national and international tests highlight another festering problem: the long-standing achievement gap between racial groups. According to the National Center for Education Statistics Fourth Grade Reading Report Card 2000, Black, Latino and Native American children still lag behind their White and Asian American peers. More than half of all Black, Latino and American Indian 4th-grade children scored "below basic" in reading as compared to 27% of their white counterparts (Donahue, Finnegan, Lutkus, Allen, & Campbell, 2001). This racial gap in student achievement in reading has remained relatively unchanged since 1992.

Many believe that the root of the low-achievement problem is the nature of curriculum and instruction in American schools and argue that the overall mediocre performance of American students is due to an unfocused and undemanding curriculum that values breadth over depth (Valverde & Smidt, 1997). The frequent repetition of procedural routines in school subjects has left many students unable to meaningfully connect ideas and build conceptual understandings. Others echo these concerns and add school structure as a contributing factor. Darling-Hammond (1997), for instance, asserts that the factory model of education, in which teachers plan in isolation and students work alone on facts and algorithms, still persists in today's schools. The result is a schooling process that does not prepare students to understand important ideas or produce thoughtful work. Reformers argue that teacher education faculty, many of whom also plan and teach in isolation (Goodlad, 1990), have not done enough to prepare teachers to change outmoded models of teaching and to counteract low student performance.

Changing Demographics

Some researchers link low achievement, and particularly the achievement gap, to the need for teachers to become more skilled at meeting the diverse needs of learners (Irvine, 2000; Ladson-Billings, 1999). As Ladson-Billings (2001) describes, today's diversity is broader and more complex than ever before. Not only are students more likely to be multiracial or multiethnic but there is also increased diversity along linguistic, religious, and economic lines. This is best illustrated by the influx of Latino students into the public school system over the last

20 years. The enrollment of Latinos alone has increased 157% between 1978 and 1998 (ERIC Clearinghouse, 2001). However, those entering teacher education rarely mirror the demographics of the larger student population. Although the overall public school population comprises 63.5% White, 16.1% African-American, 14.4% Latino, 3.9% Asian Pacific and 1.2% American Indian students (Snyder & Hoffman, 2000), the vast majority of teacher candidates are White, monolingual females who attended rural or suburban schools (Cockrell, Placier, Cockrell, & Middleton, 1999).

The inability of teaching institutions to attract and retain culturally diverse students and faculty has serious implications for teacher education (Ladson-Billings, 1999). Kennedy (1992) reminds us that "diversity among teachers may increase both the students' and the teachers' knowledge and understanding of different cultural groups, thereby enhancing the abilities of all involved to interact with different cultural groups" (p. 84). In addition, the lack of diversity in teacher education programs means that students have fewer role models of color. Scholars cite two problems that teacher education programs must work to overcome: the desire of teacher candidates to teach in educational institutions much like the ones they attended rather than in schools that serve poor children of color, and the low expectations many teacher candidates have for these children (Melnick & Zeichner, 1998; Ladson-Billings, 1999). These problems in the recruitment and preparation of beginning teachers can be contributing factors in the persistent disparity in achievement that continues across racial and socioeconomic lines.

Changing Economy

Reformers also point to the needs of a changing economy and the related implications for teacher education. Advocates for school reform claim that the shift from the industrial age to the information age has placed increased pressure on schools to promote levels of literacy, numeracy, and cultural and scientific understandings never before required of the population as a whole. The availability of high-wage jobs for low-skilled workers is disappearing, with jobs requiring technical skills and knowledge expected to constitute nearly half the total available jobs by the year 2010 (Darling-Hammond, 1997; NCTAF, 1996).

Reformers caution that students who graduate from school without the ability to communicate effectively, use new technologies, and solve complex problems will face enormous disadvantages in a modern, global economy. While blue collar jobs made up 50% of the nation's workforce during the 1950s, that figure was projected to be closer to

10% by the start of the twenty-first century and is not expected to increase over time (Drucker, 1994). Carnevale (1999) explained, "More than two-thirds of the jobs being created in the fastest-growing sectors of the U.S. economy—office jobs (including legal, sales, marketing, accounting, managerial and editorial positions), health care jobs and teaching positions—now require at least some college" (p. 10).

Many argue that there will be increasingly fewer unskilled, manual labor jobs for school drop-outs and that school achievement gaps, which continue to correlate with race, ethnicity, and social class, will create even more social strain and disruption. The persistent racial and class segregation in U.S. schools, coupled with the isolation of poor and minority students into lower academic tracks (Oakes, 1990), contributes to these fears. Schools and teachers must be better prepared to meet the educational needs of all students, regardless of race or social class.

CHALLENGES TO TEACHER EDUCATORS

Many challenges emerge from the reform literature. We focus on the three we regard as most salient to the profession of teacher education: resources, consensus, and research.

Resources

Inadequate funding represents one of the greatest challenges facing teacher educators. In general, as compared to professional programs in other fields, education programs are funded well below the average (NCTAF, 1997). Greater financial resources are needed to:

- Provide meaningful internships with highly skilled teachers
- Develop stronger curricular requirements
- Recruit and retain racially and linguistically diverse faculty and students
- Model and integrate computer technology into classroom practice (ISTE, 1999).

In addition, the commitment of time on the part of teacher educators is essential to improving the education of prospective teachers. Teacher educators must engage in ongoing professional development, collaborate with diverse faculty members (across discipline areas), conduct research on teacher education practices that successfully prepare teachers, and build connections between university faculty and teacher colleagues working in schools. Time constraints for teacher educators represent a particularly acute problem given the research, teaching, and clinical supervision responsibilities that teacher educators are frequently asked to undertake (Ducharme & Ducharme, 1996a).

But these challenges of funding and time are not solely the responsibility of teacher educators. Support must come from states, school districts, and universities, in the form of rewards and incentives. States can provide teacher preparation programs with incentives for successfully incorporating national professional standards (e.g., NCATE, 1995). In the same vein, universities can provide incentives and rewards to faculty who work toward program renewal and improvement.

Consensus Building

The dilemma for those concerned with teacher education is not a lack of thoughtful recommendations but rather the difficulty of consensus building and coordinated political action needed to generate meaningful reform. As Fullan et al. (1998) note, "We need to figure out how to reduce clutter and increase coordination. The field is badly in need of more partnerships, greater coordination of initiatives and more concentrated political resolve to carry the agenda forward in the face of great inertia" (p. 59). The systematic identification of areas of consensus around teacher education reform is an important first step in this process, but the challenge does not end there. Most reform proposals are conceived within the distinct ideological and political boundaries of their sponsoring organizations. These contexts limit opportunities for reformers to build on shared commitments and to concentrate on reforms likely to engender widespread support.

Overcoming the historical amnesia that has plagued teacher education reformers for much of the twentieth century is a related challenge (Zeichner, 2001). Many so-called "new" reforms (e.g., performance-based assessment) have an extensive track record in the reform literature that is perilously ignored in many current reform efforts. Teacher educators would be well-advised to harvest the lessons of the past as they seek to understand the conditions that underlie successful, and unsuccessful, changes in teacher education.

Research Focus

A final challenge for teacher educators is to continue to develop a multifaceted research agenda that yields an empirical basis for recommended reforms. The historically low status of teacher education within the academy (Schneider, 1987), coupled with limited time and funding for research, has helped cast doubt on the claims made by teacher education scholars and reformers. Current critics of formal teacher education (e.g., Fordham Foundation, 1999) allege a thin empirical basis for the policy recommendations made by national commissions such as NCTAF. Ballou and Podgursky (1999), for example, claim that NCTAF's proposal to standardize teacher-licensing processes is unsupported by evidence that licensed teachers with formal university preparation are more effective than unlicensed teachers.

Reform proposals that are credible and garner support across the ideological spectrum require a sound, comprehensive empirical base. One example of such a study is Darling-Hammond's (2000a) analysis of the relationships between teacher qualifications and student achievement. Data were drawn from four sources: a 50-state survey of policies related to teacher recruitment and preparation conducted by NCTAF, case studies of select states, student achievement scores from the National Assessment of Educational Progress (NAEP) tests, and the 1993–1994 Schools and Staffing Survey (SASS). Darling-Hammond concludes that the percentage of well-qualified teachers (as defined by those with full certification status and a major in their teaching field) was the strongest and most consistent predictor of student achievement.

Teacher educators have a wide variety of available research methodologies to bring to bear on reform questions (Kennedy, 1996; Zeichner, 1999). Over the last 20 years many types of qualitative methods—including case study analyses, conceptual analyses, and narrative and phenomenological inquiries—have been used to shed light on the experiences of teacher candidates, their faculty, supervisors, and mentor teachers, and the social and political contexts in which they work. Quantitative methodologies have also become increasingly sophisticated, enhancing researchers' ability to tease out complex relationships among multiple variables. Continued pursuit of a range of research agendas and methodologies, driven by a deeper understanding of the evidentiary basis for recommended reforms, should help sustain a powerful reform agenda. As Darling-Hammond (2000b) notes:

> Although teacher education has been much critiqued, little research has been done to examine the kinds of learning experiences that help beginning teachers acquire the knowledge and skills that underlie learner centered practice. There is not yet a well-developed knowledge base about how to prepare teachers to meet new standards developed by INTASC and NCATE. (p. v)

CONCLUSION

During the first decade of this century, approximately 2.2 million new teachers will be hired to replace retiring teachers, to handle the influx of new students, and to enable schools to reduce class size (Children's Defense Fund, 2000). The reform documents reviewed in this chapter suggest that schools, colleges, and departments of education can play a vital role in preparing teachers for the challenges ahead. Such teachers would have the capacity to draw from many types of knowledge—including knowledge of their subject matter, pedagogical content knowledge, and knowledge of their students—as they create powerful forms of instruction. They would need to learn to teach responsively a student population that is becoming increasingly diverse. These reform proposals are by no means the only recommendations to improve teacher education. Nor are they without their critics. Nonetheless, these proposals shape public discourse about the preparation of teachers and provide a basis for collaborative dialogue and program renewal.

REFERENCES

American Council on Education. (1999). *To touch the future: Transforming the ways teachers are taught: An action agenda for college and university presidents.* Washington, DC: Author.

Andrew, M. D. (1990). Differences between graduates of 4-year and 5-year teacher preparation programs. *Journal of Teacher Education, 41*(1), 45–51.

Arends, R., & Winitzky, N. (1996). Program structures and learning to teach. In F. B. Murray (Ed.), *The teacher educator's handbook: Building a knowledge base for the preparation of teachers* (pp. 526–556). San Francisco: Jossey-Bass.

Armstrong, D. G., Burlbaw, L., & Batten, C. (1991, February). *Extended teacher education programs: What the literature tells us.* Paper presented at the meeting of the Association of Teacher Educators, New Orleans, LA.

Ballou, D., & Podgursky, M. (1999). Teacher training and licensure: A layman's guide. In M. Kanstoroom, & C. Finn (Eds.), *Better teachers, better schools* (pp. 31–82). Washington, DC: Fordham Foundation.

Berliner, D. (1986). In pursuit of the expert pedagogue. *Educational Researcher, 15*(7), 5–13.

Berliner, D., & Biddle, B. (1996). In defense of schools. *Vocational Education Journal, 71*(3), 36–38.

Carnegie Forum. (1986). *A nation prepared. Teachers for the 21st century. A report of the task force on teaching as a profession.* New York: Carnegie Forum on Education and the Economy.

Carnevale, A. (1999). A college degree is the key: Higher education and the changing workforce. *National Crosstalk, 7*(3), 10–11.

Children's Defense Fund. (2000). *The state of America's children.* Washington, DC: Children's Defense Fund.

Cochran-Smith, M. (1991). Learning to teach against the grain. *Harvard Educational Review, 61*(3), 279–310.

Cockrell, K., Placier, P., Cockrell, D., & Middleton, J. (1999). Coming to terms with "diversity" and "multiculturalism" in teacher education: Learning about our students, changing our practice. *Teaching and Teacher Education, 15,* 351–366.

Darling-Hammond, L. (1997). *The right to learn.* San Francisco: Jossey-Bass.

Darling-Hammond, L. (2000a). Teacher quality and student achievement: A review of state policy evidence. *Educational Analysis Policy Archives, 8*(1), 1–49.

Darling-Hammond, L. (Ed.). (2000b). *Studies of excellence in teacher education: Preparation in the undergraduate years.* Washington, DC: American Association of Colleges for Teacher Education.

Donahue, P. L., Finnegan, R. J., Lutkus, A., Allen, N. L., & Campbell, J. (2001). *The nation's report card: Fourth-grade reading.* Washington DC: U.S. Department of Education.

Drucker, P. F. (1994). The age of social transformation. *Atlantic Monthly, 274* (5), 53–80.

Ducharme, E. R., & Ducharme, M. K. (1996a). Development of the teacher education professorate. In F. B. Murray (Ed.), *The teacher educator's handbook: Building a knowledge base for the preparation of teachers* (pp. 526–556). San Francisco: Jossey-Bass.

Eric Clearinghouse on Urban Education. (2001). *Latinos in school: Some facts and findings.* New York: Author. (ERIC Document Reproduction Service No. ED 449288).

Feiman-Nemser, S. (1990). Teacher preparation: Structural and conceptual alternatives. In W. R. Houston (Ed.), *Handbook of research on teacher education* (pp. 212–233). New York: Macmillan.

Feinman-Nemser, S., & Parker, M. B. (1992). *Mentoring in context: A comparison of two U.S. programs for beginning teachers.* East Lansing: Michigan State University, National Center for Research on Teacher Learning.

Fordham Foundation. (1999). *Better teachers, better schools.* Washington, DC: Author.

Fullan, M., Galluzzo, G., Morris, P., & Watson, N. (1998). *The rise and stall of teacher education reform.* Washington, DC: American Association of Colleges for Teacher Education.

Gold, Y. (1992). Psychological support for mentors and beginning teachers: A critical dimension. In T. M. Bey, & C. T. Holmes (Eds.), *Mentoring: Contemporary principles and issues* (pp. 25–34). Reston, VA: Association of Teacher Educators.

Goodlad, J. (1990). *Teachers for our nation's schools.* San Francisco: Jossey-Bass.

Hawley, W. D. (1987). Doubtful efficacy of extended programs. *American Journal of Education, 95,* 275–298.

Holmes Group. (1986). *Tomorrow's teachers.* East Lansing, MI: Author.

Holmes Group. (1990). *Tomorrow's schools.* East Lansing, MI: Author.

Holmes Group. (1995). *Tomorrow's schools of education.* East Lansing, MI: Author.

Howey, K. (1996). Designing coherent and effective teacher education programs. In J. Sikula, T. J. Buttery, & E. Guyton (Eds.). *Handbook of research on teacher education* (2nd ed., pp. 143–170). New York: Macmillan.

Howey, K. R., & Zimpher, N. L. (1989). *Profiles of preservice teacher education: Inquiry into the nature of programs.* Albany: State University of New York Press.

International Society for Technology in Education. (1999). *Will new teachers be prepared to teach in a digital age? A national survey on information technology in teacher education.* Santa Monica, CA: Author.

Irvine, J. J. (2000). *The critical elements of culturally responsive pedagogy: A synthesis of research in culturally responsive teaching.* New York: McGraw-Hill.

Joyce, B., & Clift, R. (1984). The Phoenix agenda: Essential reform in teacher education. *Educational Researcher, 13*(4), 5–18.

Kennedy, M. (1992). The problem of improving teacher quality while balancing supply and demand. In E. Boe, & D. Gilford (Eds.), *Teacher supply, demand and quality: Policy issues, models and databases* (pp. 65–126). Washington, DC: National Academy Press.

Kennedy, M. (1996). Research genres in teacher education. In F. Murray (Ed.), *The teacher educator's handbook* (pp. 120–152). San Francisco: Jossey-Bass.

Kilgore, K. (1996). *Rationale for PROTEACH II.* Unpublished manuscript.

Killian, J., & McIntyre, J. (1986). Quality in early field experiences: A product of grade level and cooperating teachers' training. *Teaching and Teacher Education,* 2(4), 367–376.

Ladson-Billings, G. (1999). Preparing teachers for diversity: Historical perspectives, current trends, and future directions. In L. Darling-Hammond, & G. Sykes (Eds.), *Teaching as the learning profession* (pp. 86–123). San Francisco: Jossey-Bass.

Ladson-Billings, G. (2001). *Crossing over to Canaan: The journey of new teachers in diverse classrooms.* San Francisco: Jossey-Bass.

Lampert, M., & Ball D. (1999). Aligning teacher education with contemporary K–12 reform visions. In L. Darling-Hammond, & G. Sykes (Eds.), *Teaching as the learning profession: Handbook of policy and practice* (pp. 33–53). San Francisco: Jossey-Bass.

Levine, M. (1992). *Professional practice schools: Linking teacher education and school reform.* New York: Teachers College Press.

Melnick, S., & Zeichner, K. (1995). *Teacher education for cultural diversity: Enhancing the capacity for teacher education institutions to address diversity issues.* East Lansing, MI: National Center for Research on Teacher Learning. (ERIC Document Reproduction Service No. ED 392751).

Melnick, S., & Zeichner, K. (1998). Teacher education's responsibility to address diversity issues: Enhancing institutional capacity. *Theory into Practice,* 37(2), 88–95.

National Association of State Boards of Education. (1998). *The numbers game: Ensuring quantity and quality in the teaching work force.* Alexandria, VA: Author.

National Center for Research on Teacher Education. (1991). *Final Report: The national center for research on teacher education.* East Lansing, MI: Michigan State University, Author.

National Commission on Excellence in Education. (1983). *A nation at risk.* Washington, DC: U.S. Department of Education.

National Commission on Excellence in Teacher Education. (1985). *A call for change in teacher education.* Washington, DC: American Association of Colleges for Teacher Education.

National Commission on Teaching and America's Future. (1996). *What matters most: Teaching for America's future.* New York: Author.

National Commission on Teaching and America's Future. (1997). *Doing what matters most: Investing in quality teaching.* New York: Author.

National Council for Accreditation of Teacher Education. (1998). *Program standards for elementary teacher preparation.* Washington, DC: Author.

National Council for Accreditation of Teacher Education. (1995). *Standards, procedures & policies for the accreditation of professional education units.* Washington, DC: Author.

Oakes, J. (1990). *Multiplying inequalities: The effect of race, social class and tracking on opportunities to learn mathematics and science.* Santa Monica, CA: The RAND Corporation.

Project 30 Alliance. (1991). *Project 30 year two report: Institutional accomplishments.* Newark: DE: Author.

Renaissance Group. (1996). *Recommendation evidence* (On-line). Available from http://www.uni.edu/coe/rengroup/html.

Schneider, B. (1987). Tracing the provenance of teacher education. In T. Popkewitz (Ed.), *Critical studies in teacher education* (pp. 211–241). New York: Falmer Press.

Smith, B. O. (1980). *Design for a school of pedagogy.* Washington, DC: U.S. Department of Education.

Snyder, T., & Hoffman, C. (2000). *Digest of education statistics,* p. 60. Washington, DC: Government Printing Office.

Teacher Education Accreditation Council. (1998). *Prospectus.* Washington, DC: Author.

Tom, A. R. (1997). *Redesigning teacher education.* Albany: State University of New York Press.

Valli. L., & Rennert-Ariev, P. L. (2000). Identifying consensus in teacher education reform documents: A proposed framework and action implications. *Journal of Teacher Education, 51*(1), 5–17.

Valverde, G., & Schmidt, W. (1997). Refocusing U.S. math and science education. In *Issues in Science and Technology* (On-line). Available from http://www.nap.edu/issues/14.2/schmid.htm.

Veenman, S. (1984). Perceived problems of beginning teachers. *Review of Educational Research, 54*(2), 143–178.

Zeichner, K. M. (1999). The new scholarship in teacher education. *Educational Researcher, 28*(9), 4–15.

Zeichner, K. M. (2001, April). *Performance-based teacher education and standard-based reform in U.S. teacher education: An his-*

torical analysis and critique. Paper presented at the meeting of
the American Educational Research Association, Seattle, WA.
Zeichner, K. M., Melnick, S. L., & Gomez, M. L. (Eds.). (1996).
Currents of reform in preservice teacher education. New York:
Teachers College Press.

CHAPTER 2

Barriers to Teacher Education Reform: Lessons from the Literature and from Experience

RODMAN B. WEBB

In the legislative funding season, flocks of university administrators migrate to their state capitals and begin a yearly ritual of budgetary courtship. The dance is predictable—as rituals must be—and requires that dark-suited administrators strut the usual university stuff before an increasingly skeptical legislative audience. Presidents and provosts remind lawmakers that universities enable every social, civic, and economic good that politicians might wish for their constituencies. They argue, with conviction, that university funding is an investment, not an expense, and that modest sums spent on ivied campuses will save monumental sums spent less fruitfully in other venues.

Social scientists love such rituals because they carry within them institutional values, tensions, and contradictions. A little digging into the university funding ritual, for example, reveals some central tensions within and between public-university and state-government cultures and perspectives. Take, for example, the claim that universities are engines of economic and social progress and, as such, serve the public good. Few in academe would challenge that claim, as it is a central faith of the academic church. We rest that faith on what Mark Yudof (2002), President of the University of Minnesota, has called "an extraordinary compact" that a century ago research universities forged with states:

> In return for financial support from taxpayers, universities agreed to keep tuition low and provide access for students from a broad range

33

of economic backgrounds, train graduate and professional students, promote arts and culture, help solve problems in the community, and perform groundbreaking research. (p. B24)

Legislators, for their part, are unsure that traditional university models and compacts efficiently serve state needs (Middaugh, 2001, pp. 157–158). Universities describe themselves as engines of social and economic change, but policy makers are not convinced by such claims. From a state-capital perspective, universities too often seem lumbering, expensive, funding-hungry, and surprisingly slow to reform. Term-limited legislators are particularly impatient with universities that respond ponderously to pressing state needs. If a state requires 16,000 new teachers, legislators wonder why universities do not immediately double or triple their production rates.

The university/state compact is under growing strain and might already have broken. States provide shrinking proportions of university funding and are forcing administrators to make up the deficit from other sources: student tuition, federal and foundation grants, patents, distance education, and private-sector partnerships. These moves make universities increasingly market directed; some have called this form of academic capitalism the "entrepreneurial university" (Burton, 1998; Slaughter & Leslie, 1977). Market-directed administrators in market-directed universities pay close attention to status indicators such as *U.S. News and World Report* rankings and funnel disproportionate resources into status disciplines that will improve those rankings and external funding.

What Robert Reich (2000) has said generally about market-directed individuals today might apply equally to market-directed administrators: "Once, the worst thing that could be said of someone was that he had sold out," Reich wrote in his recent book, *The Future of Success*. "Now the worst thing that can be said is that he's not selling" (p. 157).

Research universities are under great pressure to become more entrepreneurial, nimble, responsive, self-supporting, customer friendly, and open to change (Tierney, 1998). College of education personnel feel these pressures acutely, although they are most sensitive to criticisms aimed specifically at teacher preparation programs. Most pressing among those criticisms are the following complaints:

- Teacher education programs do not produce teachers in sufficient numbers. In Florida, for example, approved teacher education programs graduate 5,600 teachers a year, barely a third of state needs.

- Teacher education programs do not produce enough teachers in acute shortage areas. In Florida, for example, about half of education students are enrolled in elementary education programs, but only a third of state vacancies are for elementary teachers.
- Many teacher education program graduates do not teach in public schools. In Florida, about 40% of such graduates move to other states, teach in private schools, or choose not to teach at all.

Legislators point out that teacher education is expensive. In Florida the state's contribution for each graduate of a state-approved, teacher education program is $20,500. Legislators worry that colleges of education are not increasing their numbers sufficiently, are overproducing in low-need areas, underproducing in high-need areas, and not adequately preparing their graduates for the challenges of real-world classrooms. Thus, as the teacher shortages grow more critical, policy makers in the legislative and executive branches look for solutions that bypass colleges of education.

In this chapter I examine the institutional barriers that frustrate teacher education reform. Those barriers are documented in the organizational change literature, and we confronted them all as we redesigned teacher education programs at the University of Florida (UF).

I use the personal pronoun in the chapter because I am exploring uneven and poorly surveyed terrain. I am not as sure of foot or path as I would like to be on this landscape, and I know that others, near to the Florida experience and removed from it, might analyze the literature, the politics, and our own reform efforts quite differently than do I. My goal is to spell out why reform is so structurally difficult in research universities in general and in colleges of education in particular.

One caveat is in order: The term barrier is widely used in the change literature, usually with negative connotations. Reform-minded authors seldom mention that barriers can serve positive or negative ends. Indeed, how we define a barrier depends on how we define the change it impedes. Bad barriers block changes we support, and good ones protect us from changes we oppose. My goal is not to condemn all barriers to change, merely to describe them and the functions they serve within colleges and universities.

In the interests of full disclosure, I should say that I experienced Proteach planning as a faculty member, and I am writing about it as a short-term administrator. I hope my role shifting lends balance to the chapter, even as it caused identity vertigo in its author.

THE IMPETUS TO CHANGE: PRACTICE-DRIVEN TEACHER EDUCATION AT THE UNIVERSITY OF FLORIDA

The change literature suggests that successful reforms seldom spring from within institutions. The impetus to change more often comes from constellations of external forces that eventually grow too strong to be easily ignored. Those forces usually gather slowly, like storm clouds on the horizon, until they reach a critical mass. Yet, even when the storm breaks and reform signals rain everywhere, the institutional instinct generally is to hunker down and wait for the storm to pass.

A few institutions, what I call *forerunner institutions,* recognize changing conditions earlier than others and lead the reform effort. Such institutions generally have change-sensitive leadership, a critical mass of reform-minded personnel, and a history of successful innovation. That was certainly the case at the University of Florida's College of Education in the mid-1990s.

The conditions that moved reform at UF's College of Education are explored elsewhere in this volume so we need only list several key conditions here:

1. Criticism of teacher education coming from politicians; teachers, school system administrators; liberal and conservative think tank personnel; and, not insignificantly, from among leading professors of education.
2. A growing literature documenting the changing conditions of teaching in America and the changing demographics of the American classroom.
3. A history of teacher education innovation at the University of Florida that dates to the progressive era at the turn of the last century.
4. A growing research and reform literature that called for practice-driven, teacher education.
5. A critical mass of faculty in the college who knew the change literature, contributed to it, specialized in teacher education reform or school reform, and worked across departments to build programs and research projects.
6. The installation of a new and energetic dean, Rod McDavis, who was impatient with the status quo.
7. Funding from the BellSouth Foundation supporting our reform effort.

THE UNIVERSITY CONTEXT

Autonomy and Regulation

The public research university is as complex an institution as exists in modern society and, unlike more agile institutions in the private sector, it is slow to react to external demands or executive decisions. As James Dudenstadt, President Emeritus at the University of Michigan, has pointed out, "Pity the poor administrator" who, with the slip of a misplaced metaphor, likens her university to a corporation, its professors to workers, or its students to products (Dudenstadt, 2000, p. 162). Academics reserve deep levels of Dante's hell for those who sin so grievously.

Many academics enter the professorate to escape the "command-and-control" structures of business and government (Dudenstadt, 2000, p. 161). They gravitate, instead, to the "creative anarchy" of academe and jealously guard what they most value: classroom autonomy, research autonomy, and the time and assistance needed to pursue both. They protect these values behind a proud tradition of consensual governance, committee structures, and university procedures. They protect an academic ethos that sets high productivity expectations for those who wish to advance their salaries or careers, and put few limits on others (Middaugh, 2001). In a zero-sum reward system it is in every professor's interest to have some department colleagues who in mid-career opt out of the research rat race and focus exclusively on teaching and service. They are wary of administration and do what they can to limit the power of university managers (Bowen & Shapiro, 1998).

Faculty members generally view regulation and management as a threat to their autonomy and, like Greta Garbo in a different age, wish only to be left alone. Government, however, controls more by regulation than by reward and when universities do not respond quickly to state needs policy makers respond with more regulation (Dudenstadt, 2000, pp. 241–248).

State regulations are especially onerous in teacher education, where government calls for innovation have been most insistent. Faculty argue that reform grows best from within universities, not from without, and that state regulations inhibit rather than encourage program improvement. Government officials retort that tighter regulations are needed precisely because teacher-educators have responded so slowly and ineffectually to state needs. Regulators are moving ever deeper into previously sacrosanct areas such as program requirements, course content, and student assessment.

In Florida, for example, the state dictates almost the entire curriculum in teacher education. Colleges of education must document that state-defined competencies are taught, identify where those competencies are taught, identify how students demonstrate those competencies to their instructors, provide the rubric against which each competence is measured, and identify the remediation opportunities they offer students who fail to meet that competence.

Colleges of education are used to such regulation and have accepted increasing intrusions rather passively. Central administrators have generally ignored regulations that govern teacher education, but when they spot such regulations elsewhere on campus, they quickly recognize what is at stake. As Dudenstadt (2000) noted, "The increasing intrusion of state and federal government in the affairs of the university, in the name of performance and public accountability, can trample on academic values and micromanage many institutions into mediocrity" (p. 239).

Specialization and Integration

Departments are the basic organizational unit in the university. They are generally configured around disciplines or constellations of related disciplines. Degree programs attach to departments and generally include a discipline in their title. Faculty, as we will see later, identify most strongly with their disciplines and then, with lessening degrees of commitment, with their program or programs, department, college, and university.

The Dutch sociologist, Anton Zijderveld (1970), called the drift to specialization "intellectual Taylorism" and thought it an almost irresistible consequence of modernity:

> Specialization . . . cuts reality into little pieces, each piece being the domain of a relatively small group of experts. These experts discuss their theories within their own little group where they apply their own "secret language."
>
> By cutting reality into small pieces, the [academic] is in danger of losing all sense of reality. Sooner or later, many specialties and subspecialties are doomed to be exhausted. The specialist is then compelled to focus on the refinement of existing theoretical models and methods, or to do research for the sake of research without actually adding much to the existing body of knowledge within the field. (pp. 76–77)

Zijderveld goes on to suggest that specialization invites experts to view their segment of knowledge as not simply as important or useful, but rather "as the final reality." From this immodest vantage point, the specialist takes on all comers who might threaten his corner on reality. Yet, that same vantage point makes our expert a "naïve spectator in all matters that happen to transcend his little world" (p. 77).

If specialization is a consequence of modernity, then universities are cultural carriers of the specialization impulse. Robert Zemsky and William Massy, in a 1990 article in *Change Magazine*, attributed "intellectual Taylorism" to what they called the "academic ratchet."

> [The academic ratchet is] a term to describe the steady, irreversible shift of faculty allegiance away from the goals of a given institution, toward those of an academic specialty. The ratchet denotes the advancement of an entrepreneurial spirit among faculty nationwide, leading to an increased emphasis on research and publication, and on teaching one's specialty in favor of general introduction courses, often at the expense of coherence in an academic curriculum. Institutions seeking to enhance their own prestige may contribute to the ratchet by reducing faculty teaching and advising responsibilities across the board, thus enabling faculty to pursue their individual research and publication with fewer distractions. (Middaugh, 2001, p. 2)

The academic programs we offer students may include coursework in several disciplines, but instructors generally do not try to cross disciplinary boundaries in their classes. Thus, universities offer few vibrant interdisciplinary degree programs. Such programs exist, of course, but they struggle for funding, faculty, and legitimization (The Boyer Commission, 1998, p. 23).

Students must declare a major early in their university careers and programs typically require some complementary coursework in related disciplines. Few instructors attend the needs of students from other majors, however, and do little to link the vocabulary, theory, and methods of their own discipline with those of another. Indeed, students are expected to make such connections on their own, although few do successfully.

At the heart of every discipline is a collection of theories that explains why things work as they do. The more advanced the discipline, the more unified and elegant those theories tend to be. Theory is where the academic action is, and it is where self-respecting professors wish to hang out and be noticed. It is also where most professors wish to take their students. Students, however, generally have other destinations in mind. They want to know what a discipline can do for them and how it might guide their professional actions and choices. They value practice and would willingly trade a pound of Piagetian theory for an ounce of practical classroom advice. Faculty battle this vocational mindset, arguing that there is nothing as practical as a viable theory, and they are correct. They have more difficulty than they like to admit, however, making the theory-to-practice connection for and with their students. The Boyer Commission (1998) made the point:

> Many students graduate having accumulated whatever number of courses is required, but still lacking a coherent body of knowledge or any inkling as to how one sort of information might relate to others. And all too often they graduate without knowing how to think logically, write clearly, or speak coherently. The university has given them too little that will be of real value beyond a credential that will help them get their first jobs. And with larger and larger numbers of their peers holding the same paper in their hands, even that credential has lost much of its potency. (p. 6)

The point here is that university structures value specialization and theory over integration and practice. Yet, the professional education literature suggests that we should reverse those priorities, or at least get to specialization and theory by way of integration and practice. Career-conscious faculty are pulled away from undergraduate teaching (a terrain left largely to junior faculty, adjuncts, and graduate students) and toward graduate instruction (where they gather dedicated labor for their grant work). The Boyer Commission (1998) again made the point:

> An undergraduate at an American research university can receive an education as good or better than anything available anywhere in the world, but that is not the normative experience. Again and again, universities are guilty of an advertising practice they would condemn in the commercial world. Recruitment materials display proudly the world-famous professors, the splendid facilities and the groundbreaking research that goes on within them, but thousands of students graduate without ever seeing the world-famous professors or tasting genuine research. Some of their instructors are likely to be badly trained or even untrained teaching assistants who are groping their way toward a teaching technique. (pp. 5–6)

Attending to the reform literature, UF's College of Education set out to create a practice-driven program that was unified, cross-departmental, and interdisciplinary. We set out to measure not only what students know, but also what they learn to do while in the program. We knew at the outset that developing a practice-driven program would be difficult, though we did not anticipate just how difficult it turned out to be. We confronted all of the barriers that the organizational change literature identifies and did what we could to maneuver around them.

BARRIERS TO TEACHER EDUCATION REFORM IN MARKET-DRIVEN RESEARCH UNIVERSITIES

Competition for Status and Resources

Colleges of education have a difficult time competing for resources within market-driven universities because education is, relatively speaking, an easy access and low-status profession. Education borrows knowledge from other disciplines and, although the greatest minds in the western tradition have studied the subject, no educator, philosopher, scientist, politician, critic, or crank has solved its deepest riddles or settled even one of its perennial debates. It is painfully prone to ideological tiffs and political side taking. Our research generally feeds those debates, but does not settle them.

Market-driven universities aspire to "excellence" (Readings, 1996, pp. 21–43) and what David Brooks has called the "power to consecrate" (Brooks, 2000, p. 151). High-status universities, those at the top of yearly rankings, not only enjoy prestige, they profitably confer it to their faculty, students, and graduates. Brooks goes further, "Institutions at the top of each specialty have the power to confer prestige and honor on favored individuals, subjects, and styles of discourse." Thus, market-driven universities exploit every opportunity to move themselves up the rankings (Twitchell, 2002), including hiring insider consultants who know the ranking process and the ever-changing formulae that assure that rankings will change, if only modestly, each year. Again, the Boyer Commission makes the point most sharply:

> The standing of a university is measured by the research productivity of its faculty; the place of a department within the university is determined by whether its members garner more or fewer research dollars and publish more or less noteworthy research than other departments; the stature of the individual within the department is judged by the quantity and quality of the scholarship produced. Every research university can point with pride to the able teachers within its ranks, but it is in research grants, books, articles, papers, and citations that every university defines its true worth. (p. 7)

Within universities, disciplines have their own status hierarchy. Generally, universities value disciplines in the order of their theoretical rigor, level of abstraction, and entrance requirements. Thus, astro-physics, neurology, and constitutional law rank toward the top of the status ladder, and landscape architecture, building construction, and teacher education toward the bottom. Status-sensitive professors in low-status disciplines might be forgiven for emulating the methods and mindsets of high-status counterparts and emphasizing theory over prac-tice. What Peter Berger said of sociology might apply as well to educa-tion: "Little sociologists want to be as much as possible like their big brothers in physics" (Berger, 2002, p. 28).

Universities ascend status lists by improving the rankings of their colleges and departments. Not all disciplines are created equal, how-ever, and, as a consequence, some have more lift potential than others. A top-50 ranking in physics, for example, will lift a university's stand-ing higher than a top-25 ranking in education. That is to say, status disciplines, like status universities, have their own power to consecrate. Colleges of education do not have such power, or at least not enough of it to win funding battles.

What colleges of education offer universities in lieu of status, of course, is profit. Colleges of education generally earn more for their universities than they cost, allowing central administrators to subsidize higher-status programs with dollars from lower-status programs. When we started revising the Unified Elementary Special Education Proteach (UESEP) program, the University of Florida had just initiated a budgeting system that rewarded colleges for credit-hour productiv-ity. The College of Education benefited immediately and substantially from the new system, and more expensive and powerful programs took a financial hit. The system was unpopular and weakened the president and provost who soon left office. The new administration won immediate favor with high-status programs when they restored the old budgeting system.

The promise of a productivity funding formula energized our reform effort at the University of Florida. The quick reversion to a tra-ditional funding system reminded us of what we already knew; tradi-tional funding systems limit reform possibility. In education, more than other disciplines perhaps, even exciting reforms will not fly if they increase costs.

Ranking systems also limit reform possibilities. *U.S. News and World Report* rankings use traditional categories to identify programs. Colleges considering interdisciplinary work must consider what effect new configurations might have on their program rankings. Or, moving from the other direction, rank-sensitive deans may be tempted to alter existing department configurations so that they will more closely reflect *U.S. News and World Report* categories.

University Reward Structures

One of the most interesting and anomalous facts of university life is that professors' salaries have little if any connection with their credit-hour productivity. Indeed, one measure of a professor's success is how distant she is from students, especially undergraduates. Most faculty teach, of course, and students rate their teaching at the end of the semester, but respectable ratings come easily and seldom are rewarded. What is rewarded most consistently is research productivity, as measured by the quantity and quality of one's publications.

Faculty understand that salary and promotion decisions are almost totally dependent on their research record. They must publish steadily, in refereed journals, preferably with high circulation numbers and with low acceptance rates (Dudenstadt, 2000, p. 153). Promotion requires that professors establish a positive reputation in their disciplines and that their counterparts at equal or higher status universities know and respect their work. It is essential, too, that others in the field are willing to testify to the quality of that work and see within it a clear and promising research trajectory.

There is more to professorial work than publishing, of course, and there is good evidence that most professors would rather teach than do research. Still, within research universities nothing affects one's salary, promotion, and employment options more powerfully than one's research productivity. Outside funding is also important, especially in market-driven universities, but wise professors understand that funding is not an end in itself, but a way to subsidize and increase their publication productivity.

Colleges of education have their own discipline hierarchies that mimic university status criteria. Here again, theory generally trumps practice, so teacher educators are disadvantaged in status and funding battles. Alan Tom (1997) and others complain, often with justification, that teacher educators teach more students and fewer graduate classes than their counterparts in other departments. Heavy teaching loads, they argue, hamper their research production and career opportunities.

Much can be said for and against the reward system I describe here, but for the purposes of this chapter we need only ask how such systems affect teacher education reform. In a nutshell, reward structures in market-driven universities create market-driven professors

(Clark, 1998; Middaugh, 2001; Slaughter & Leslie, 1997). Such professors understand that university rewards go primarily to those who produce research publications and only secondarily to those who build, maintain, and reform programs.

Program work is necessary, but market-driven professors try to avoid it. They gauge service work in terms of the time it will take away from more profitable activities, and remind those who suggest reform effort that university service offers few rewards and is always voluntary. Time is academe's most precious commodity and, aside from class and office hours, professors' time is pretty much their own. Even attendance at college and department faculty meetings is often a voluntary activity. Like Melville's Bartleby, market-driven professors master the fine art of refusal.

This is not to suggest the faculty do not work hard; there is much evidence they do (Middaugh, 2001). It is to say, instead, that the focus of their work primarily is on research and teaching and only secondarily on programs and reform. When service work cuts into faculty time, it is usually our teaching that suffers.

Identity, Mindset, and Audience

The reward system affects more than a professor's time commitments and service choices; it also affects loyalties, the kind of research undertaken, and the audience to whom a faculty member writes. One of the most intriguing things about universities is that market-driven professors identify more strongly with their disciplines than they do with their institutions (Dudenstadt, 2000, p. 248). Universities are the mere location of their work, not the object of their effort and obligation. University rewards go to those who contribute most obviously and productively to their discipline, not their institution.

Market-driven researchers generally answer theory questions that worry professors, not practice problems that plague practitioners. They generally write for their university peers, not for teachers, principals, or policy makers who complain, with increasing ferocity, that educational research is inaccessible or, worse, irrelevant to teaching and policy making.

There is little in the university reward structure or in typical career trajectories that encourages faculty to attend to program efficacy or improvement. Professors who take on reform projects do so at some career risk. They can limit such risks by making the reform process an object of study, but the time/product ratio calculations encourage professors to follow their own research specialties and avoid reform entanglements.

The Limits of Administrative Authority

The organizational change literature documents the important role leadership plays in institutional reform. Change will not happen if administrators do not support reform, do not give it direction, and do not reward those who do the work. That reform fact of life is as true in university settings as it is in any other organization, but universities face special problems usually not found in other organizations (Bowen & Shapiro, 1998).

I have argued that professors identify most with their disciplines and only secondarily with their programs, colleges, and universities. Such professors are generally suspicious of those who step away from the "real university work" and take on program reform. Such folk seem misguided and, worse, intent upon joining the administration (Dudenstadt, 2000, p. 248).

Leaving research and teaching for administration can separate professors from their disciplines. The longer professors stay in administration, the more they may become removed from their fields, and the more precarious may be their hold on academic legitimacy. Faculty often distrust "career-minded administrators" who moved too quickly (and eagerly) from their academic work before being fully socialized into professorial values. The traditional work of administration is not reform, but protecting professor autonomy and, more often than not, the status quo.

From a faculty point of view, a good university administrator secures abundant resources, and protects the university from meddling legislators, alumni, boards of trustees, government bureaucrats, parents, and citizens (Dudenstadt, 2000, p. 162). A good dean represents faculty interests to higher-ups, garners resources to support faculty work, and protects faculty autonomy. A good department chair argues successfully for college resources and protects faculty autonomy from meddling, reform-minded deans (Bowen & Shapiro, 1998).

Few appreciate the irony in these competing expectations. Faculty want administrators to have unlimited power to influence university higher-ups and limited power to influence faculty behavior within their own college. Professors have built structures and traditions that limit what administrators can compel. Legislators, business partners, school system administrators, and accrediting personnel are surprised to learn that university provosts and college deans have little power beyond that of purse strings and persuasion (Dudenstadt, 2000; Tierney, 1998).

CONCLUSION

The barriers to practice-driven reform are large, deep, and structural. Within market-driven universities, those barriers include discipline-based departments and programs, discipline hierarchies within the academy, reward systems that value specialization and theory over integration and practice, and funding policies that favor high status disciplines over their lower-status counterparts. Heavy teaching loads in teacher education also inhibit reform, as does a university tradition that counts program work as service and service work as voluntary. If professors choose to "serve," they would do better to serve a professional organization that provides valuable contacts and enhances their professional reputation than they would to serve a college reform effort.

Institutional barriers are so powerful, of course, because we believe in them and organize our work and thinking around them. Market-driven professors do research and writing that captures the attention of their academic peers, or at least they try to. They pursue research funding that allows them to write and they are willing, when necessary, to alter their research interests to fit the funding zeitgeist. In research, as in everything else, they who pay the piper select the tune.

We faced all of these barriers during our reform effort and navigated around most of them. We boasted of this fact during a wrap-up meeting with the BellSouth Foundation. A lawyer consultant for the Foundation listened to our report patiently and, when we finished, said, "Yes, very good. But did you eliminate the barriers you describe?" One might as well have asked Newton after he described the laws of gravity, "Yes, but have you discovered how to repeal those laws?" We can move around and among university barriers, but we cannot wish or manage them away (Birnbaum, 2000).

At the university level, the college did not much affect perennial barriers. We have struggled under budget cuts like all other colleges, and tried to align our work with the university's vision. We have argued that the work of the college should tie more directly to public schools, and the university financially supports partnerships with five of Florida's lowest performing high schools. We have not restored credit-hour funding formulas or altered tenure and promotion criteria to reward service to schools or college programs. Such contributions are valued, but are worth little if not augmented by traditional publications, in traditional numbers, in traditional venues.

Internally, we have lowered traditional boundaries, instituted cross-departmental instruction, and increased faculty collaboration. We have increased our college work with public schools and involved schools in the design and delivery of our teacher education programs. We involved more departments in our teacher education programs as well, but for some departments this involvement is modest and does not involve many professors. We are working to define a scholarship of engagement that will encourage research into teacher education and school improvement, address research findings to different audiences, and make our findings more useful to schools and policy makers. We are working more closely with the state department of education and are opening conversations with legislators.

Barriers, I suggested earlier, serve functions within universities and expose university values and contradictions. Those barriers and contradictions exist externally in the university and internally in faculty habits and values. We certainly wished for easier routes to interdisciplinary work in the college, for example, but we balked when administrators suggested organizational alignments that threatened our specialties and disciplinary commitments. We wanted to raise the status of, and support for, teacher education in the college, but not at the cost (literally and figuratively) of our graduate programs.

We saw the need to make faculty research more relevant to practice, but most of us still believed that quality and worth of that research is better judged by narrow discipline communities than by a wider audience of practitioners. We recognized the pressures on universities to become more responsive (Tierney, 1998) and more accountable, but realized that responsiveness can threaten academic autonomy. We valued and respected collaboration in research and teaching, but were unsure that effective collaboration could or should be forced. Still, we were discouraged when some faculty announced that they would work on collaborative teams and share their work with others, but would not bend their methods or content to the will of the group.

Despite the challenges of reform, we accomplished many things. Our accomplishments are described and examined in the chapters of this book. We turn next to the structure and process of our reform efforts.

REFERENCES

Berger, P. L. (2002, October). Whatever happened to sociology? *First Things,* 126, 27–29.

Birnbaum, R. (2000). *Management fads in higher education: Where they come from, what they do, why they fail.* San Francisco: Jossey-Bass.

48   RODMAN B. WEBB

Bowen, W. G., & Shapiro, H. T. (Eds.). (1998). *Universities and their leadership*. Princeton, NJ: Princeton University Press.

Brooks, David. (2000). *Bobos in paradise: The new upper class and how they got there*. New York: Simon & Schuster.

Clark, B. R. (1998). *Creating entrepreneurial universities: Organizational pathways of transformation*. New York: Pergamon Press.

Dudenstadt, J. J. (2000). *A University for the 21st century*. Ann Arbor, MI: University of Michigan Press.

Middaugh, M. F. (2001). *Understanding faculty productivity: Standards and benchmarks for colleges and universities*. San Francisco: Jossey-Bass.

Readings, B. (1996). *The university in ruins*. Cambridge, MA: Harvard University Press.

Reich, R. B. (2000). *The future of success*. New York: Vintage Books.

Ryan, A. (1998). *Liberal anxieties and liberal education*. New York: Hill & Wang.

Slaughter, S., & Leslie, L. L. (1997). *Academic capitalism: Politics, policies, and the entrepreneurial university*. Baltimore, MD: Johns Hopkins University Press.

The Boyer Commission on Educating Undergraduates in the Research University. (1998). *Reinventing undergraduate education: A blueprint for America's research universities*. [Funded by the Carnegie Foundation for the Advancement of Teaching.] Princeton, NJ: Princeton University Press.

Tierney, W. G. (Ed.). (1998). *The responsive university: Restructuring for high performance*. Baltimore, MD: Johns Hopkins University Press.

Tom, A. R. (1997). *Redesigning teacher education*. Albany: State University of New York Press.

Twitchell, J. B. (2002, November 25). The Branding of Higher Ed. *Forbes, 9*, 50.

Yudof, M. G. (2002, January 11). Is the public research university dead? *Chronicle of Higher Education*, B24.

Zemsky, R., & Massy, W. Cost Containment. *Change 22*, 16–22.

Zijderveld. A. (1970). *The abstract society*. Garden City, NY: Doubleday.

PART 2

Reform at the University of Florida

CHAPTER 3

Description of the Unified Elementary Special Education Proteach Program

DORENE D. ROSS, HOLLY B. LANE, AND CYNTHIA MCCALLUM

The University of Florida has had theoretically grounded, innovative teacher education programs since the development in the mid-1970s of the Childhood Education Program, a program grounded in perceptual psychology (Combs, Blume, Newman, & Wass, 1974). In the early 1980s program faculty engaged in a major program restructuring to create one of the first five-year teacher education programs in the country (Ross & Bondy, 1996; Ross, Johnson, & Smith, 1992; Ross & Krogh, 1988). The original inquiry-based Proteach program stressed themes of developing knowledge of content, drawing on research-based knowledge about teaching, and developing reflective practitioners. In addition, faculty modeled an inquiry orientation for students by continually studying the process and impact of the program.

During the '80s and early '90s, feedback from program graduates increasingly indicated graduates' concerns about meeting the needs of a diverse student population, including children with disabilities, children of poverty, and children from diverse cultural backgrounds. In response, faculty altered both content and process in the teacher education program and initiated some pilot teacher education programs that combined elementary and special education (Bondy, Ross, Sindelar, & Griffin, 1995).

In the early '90s, reports about the state of teacher education in America began to detail similar problems elsewhere and to suggest changes necessary to prepare teachers to teach complex subject matter to an increasingly diverse student population (Goodlad, 1990; Holmes, 1995; National Commission on Teaching and America's Future, 1996). In 2000, Valli and Rennert-Ariev statistically compared major reform reports in order to identify agreement or disagreement among them. While teacher education reform reports have been criticized for being fragmented and idiosyncratic, consistency exists among the largest reports. Valli and Rennert-Ariev claim the most prominent organizations (Holmes Group, National Council for the Accreditation of Teacher Education or NCATE, Center for Educational Renewal, and National Education Association's Teacher Education Initiative) have the strongest rates of agreement. These reports recommend that programs emphasize Vision, Content Standards, Extended Programs, Professional Development Schools, Authentic Pedagogy, and Performance Assessment. While reform reports were not the origin of the Proteach design, they provided faculty with background knowledge for designing the program, and program components are aligned with these recommendations.

Many of these changes require that teacher educators learn to work collaboratively with a variety of constituents so that the work of teaching and teacher education represents the multiple relevant perspectives. For example, the literature recommends stronger linkages between general education, special education, and foundations of education faculties (Holmes, 1995; National Council on Teaching and America's Future or NCTAF, 1996) between college of education faculty and liberal arts and sciences faculties (Holmes, 1995), and between teacher education faculty and school faculties (Goodlad, 1990; NCTAF, 1996). In addition, these reports along with new NCATE guidelines stress performance assessment of teacher education graduates, a task that requires collaboration and coordination by teacher education faculty.

However, the current climate of universities, particularly large Research I universities, favors individual rather than collaborative endeavors, making it hard to incorporate multiple perspectives (see chapter 2). The Holmes Group (1995) reports that in a survey of faculty reactions to proposed changes in teacher education, "survey items that projected the creation of complex programs requiring greater levels of collaboration were perceived as a threat to the traditional autonomy enjoyed within research communities" (p. 19).

In the spring of 1995 a faculty committee was appointed to reconceptualize the elementary and special education teacher education programs at the University of Florida to create one program with a dual emphasis on elementary and special education. This chapter provides a description of the results of a 4-year effort to re-create a teacher education program that implements the reforms advocated in the teacher education reform reports.

OVERVIEW OF THE UNIFIED ELEMENTARY SPECIAL EDUCATION PROTEACH PROGRAM

The Unified Elementary Special Education Proteach (UESEP) program prepares teachers with a dual emphasis in elementary and special education. All graduates also are prepared to work with students who are English Speakers of Other Languages (ESOL). The program is designed to serve several key purposes. First, the program prepares teachers who are capable of creating and maintaining supportive and productive classrooms for diverse student populations. Graduates are also prepared to work collaboratively with school personnel, families, and members of the community to develop alternative ways of educating all children, including those who have traditionally been labeled hard-to-teach and hard-to-manage and students who are linguistically diverse. The program also develops a cadre of special education teachers prepared with the knowledge and collaboration skills necessary to serve as effective consultant teachers to elementary teachers.

The need for educators who can serve the diverse needs of students in the elementary population is well documented in the literature (Lilly, 1992; Miller, 2000; Pugach, 1992; Reynolds, Wang, & Walberg, 1987; Stainback & Stainback, 1987). The growth in numbers of students who have special learning needs or are from linguistically and culturally diverse backgrounds has overtaxed the ability of special programs to provide for them. The problem of providing for students who have difficulty in school can no longer be solved with an alternative educational solution, for as Goodlad (1986) noted, "we are running out of organizational and special group type solutions" (p. xi). Clearly, teachers must be prepared to work with the growing number of students in their classes who have problems learning and comporting themselves in socially acceptable ways and with the increasing population of students with limited English proficiency (LEP). The changing character of the U.S. population of school children, the disproportionate representation of minorities in special education, the large number of students with disabilities and/or with limited English proficiency served primarily in general education classrooms, and the potential of inclusive education policy to increase this number prompted the faculty to adopt inclusive education as the mission of its unified elementary education program.

PROGRAM THEMES

To guide program development efforts, faculty attended to the intellectual and professional development of teachers within the context of the educational outcomes a democratic society demands from its preK through 12 teachers. The knowledge, dispositions, skills, and abilities required for democratic citizenship have been detailed by many scholars (see, for example, Dewey, 1916; Fishkin, 1991; Goodman, 1992; Parker, 1996; Ross, Bondy, & Kyle, 1992; Skrtic, 1991; Webb & Sherman, 1989). These scholars agree on the core elements of democratic citizenship. These elements include informed discretion, commitment to equity, effective communication, critical thinking, appreciation of diversity, and the ability to participate in a critical community. Faculty wove these elements into two inter-related themes addressed within the Proteach program.

Democratic values. Teachers within a democratic society must be committed to the value of equity in education and society. They must be able to work collaboratively with colleagues, families, and members of the community to develop alternative ways of educating our diverse population. In addition, teachers must accept responsibility for the learning of ALL children within our schools. Faculty commitment to a broad definition of diversity that includes ethnic and national heritage, disability, gender, sexual orientation, social class, race, and religion drives this program theme. Demonstration of democratic values requires that teachers:

- accept the responsibility to actively accept and promote the values of equity and democracy
- approach teaching as a process of continuous inquiry or reflection necessary to examine critically the aims and outcomes of their practices
- know and hold themselves accountable to professional ethics and professional standards of best practice for teachers.

Knowledge of content and inclusive pedagogy. Teachers must have a thorough understanding of subject matter. One simply cannot teach what one does not know. Because in today's world content knowledge is constantly changing and expanding, teachers increasingly will be asked to make decisions about what and how to teach. Our aim in our teacher education program is to help preservice teachers develop an understanding of the structure of the disciplines they will teach and strategies for acquiring new information and evaluating sources of information. They need to know this structure well enough to select appropriate content and integrate content across disciplines. In addition, they need to know the professional standards for the content areas well enough to identify common objectives and instructional strategies and their application within an integrated curriculum.

Teachers are more likely to make good decisions about what and how to teach if they develop sound pedagogical knowledge. To do this teachers must use relevant knowledge of content and teaching strategies to study students' learning. This type of comprehensive assessment enables teachers to plan differentiated instruction that is responsive to the diversity in students' needs and backgrounds. We strive to prepare teachers who:

- are prepared to help establish and to participate fully in a learning community
- demonstrate knowledge of subject area content knowledge to identify and organize appropriate content for elementary instruction and to develop appropriate inclusive pedagogy in order to differentiate both instruction and assessment in ways that will facilitate all students' learning
- understand that effective communication is essential to both democracy and education and have the necessary skills to communicate effectively and promote effective communication in the classroom.

Highlighted Program Features

The UESEP program is a five-year initial licensure program (see appendixes A and B for a description of the course framework for the program). During the freshman and sophomore years, students complete their general education requirements and three prerequisite introductory courses to prepare them for program entry. During the junior and senior years, students experience a common curriculum designed to prepare an elementary teacher with an emphasis in special education. During the graduate year, students may elect the dual certification track (Elementary/Special Education) and complete coursework leading to certification in special education and elementary education. Or they may elect the elementary certification track, which confers elementary certification with a 12-credit advanced specialization in one of three areas: Elementary Interdisciplinary, ESOL Specialist, or Elementary Specialist (Literacy, Math/Science, or Technology). All program graduates receive an ESOL endorsement. The next sections summarize some of the key elements of the program. After the description of key elements, we present a brief semester-by-semester summary to provide a clearer picture of the program as experienced by students.

Program content. The program is designed to prepare teachers who are able to work effectively with diverse student populations and who understand and can use research-based practices. The content of the program provides students with breadth of knowledge about teaching and learning and opportunities to develop depth of knowledge in specialized areas. The following sections provide a brief overview of the core content for all students.

Foundations of education. The foundations of education courses provide a context for understanding of and reflection about teaching and learning processes. Students take "Child Development for Inclusive Education" early in their junior year to acquire foundational knowledge about typical and atypical child development. Because students often find the concepts in social foundations courses to be abstract and disconnected from the practical realities of teaching, this course is taught in the graduate year when students will have a stronger background of knowledge and experience. Assessment content is introduced within the context of each methods course and then addressed more comprehensively during the graduate year in a course focused on assessment issues and practices.

Core pedagogical knowledge. Several program courses and experiences emphasize the core pedagogical knowledge needed to teach in a diverse classroom. These present the themes of the program, various models of instruction (e.g., direct instruction, cooperative learning, inductive approaches), skills and strategies of classroom management, (e.g., establishing a classroom community, basic routines and procedures, functional behavioral assessment) and introductory knowledge about the history of special education and of teaching English as a second language. Course content reflects theories and practices of teaching and learning related to the diverse needs of children in contemporary society. Strategies for designing inclusive classroom environments for students with and without disabilities are infused throughout the courses.

Inclusive methods. During the program students take methods coursework in science, math, technology, social studies, reading, and language arts. These inclusive methods courses present content relevant to elementary teachers and integrate theoretical and practical knowledge about elementary content teaching with knowledge of special education and ESOL. Within methods courses, particular emphasis is placed on instructional strategies, classroom-based assessment, and adaptations for children with mild disabilities and limited English proficiency. In addition, content courses taught by faculty outside the College of Education help to build a richer content base for teaching. To help build content knowledge, students take 19 credit hours of coursework in core content areas (i.e., science, social science, composition, and mathematics) through the College of Liberal Arts and Sciences and in areas such as health, music, art, and speech. Coursework in each methods area is also accompanied by relevant field experiences.

Knowledge of technology. Skills in technology are taught explicitly through two technology courses and implicitly within many courses where technology is integrated into course pedagogy. In addition, knowledge of technology is applied as students implement lessons and develop electronic portfolios to document their learning related to the Florida Accomplished Practices (see chapter 15 for more about electronic portfolios).

ESOL foundations and pedagogy. ESOL performance standards are addressed within two dedicated courses and infused throughout other required courses in the UESEP program. In the two courses, students are introduced to five core areas: applied linguistics/language acquisition, cross-cultural communication, practical applications in curriculum, practical applications in materials, and practical applications in assessment. These two courses, along with the infused content in other required courses, prepare teachers to work with LEP students in inclusive elementary classrooms.

Student cohort groups and block scheduling. Students are organized into cohorts of 25–35 during each semester of the program. A cohort group has a common schedule for three or four key program courses each semester. Cohort groups change at the end of each semester, so students get to know and interact with a variety of students across the program. In addition, key program courses are "blocked." That is, students must take all courses in a designated block and blocks must be taken in sequence. The use of blocked courses has facilitated the development of a coherent program sequence. In addition, scheduling cohorts of students in blocks facilitates scheduling and monitoring of field experiences. For example, in the second semester of the junior year, all students in a cohort of 30 are placed in 10 classrooms (in triads) in one school for three hours per week. Three blocked courses taken by all members of the cohort link to this field experience (e.g., observations of lessons and classroom management strategies, implementation of lesson plans, observation of students). By controlling the schedule and placements, two graduate students are able to monitor this early field experience for 150 students in a semester. In addition, students in cohorts report that they feel more empowered to make suggestions and become involved in decision making about the program, that cohorts encourage collaboration among students, that cohorts contribute to their academic success, and that cohorts have allowed them to develop professional relationships that will serve as resources during their professional lives.

It is important to note, however, that cohorts are a mixed blessing. Although the majority of students and faculty report overall satisfaction with the use of cohorts, students are much more positive about them than faculty. Students and faculty report that cohorts can encourage the development of cliques, and escalate minor student concerns. In addition, in some instances cohorts can lead to an us/them division between a faculty member and a cohort of students. There are several alternative ways that this can happen. For example, students who take multiple courses together develop "insider" stories and understandings, leaving a faculty member as the "outsider." One or two vocal students in a cohort can escalate a real or an imagined concern by convincing other students of the significance of the problem. When this happens, communication about problems is more difficult. Faculty and students are working to resolve these problems.

Early and continuous field experiences. The value of field experiences in the development of preservice teachers is well established (Aiken & Day, 1999; Buck, Morsink, Griffin, Hines, & Lenk, 1992; Harlin, 1999; Wiggins & Follo, 1999). Fieldwork in this program begins early and extends throughout the program. During their freshman and sophomore years, students engage in several observation/participation activities in classrooms during prerequisite coursework. These experiences expose students to children and schools and help them decide whether teaching is a profession they wish to pursue. Beginning in the junior year, students have required fieldwork each semester of the program. Specific information about the field component for each semester follows in the semester-by-semester program description.

Performance assessment. The program includes a systematic focus on assessment with performance outcomes specified for students at key points throughout the program. During the first semester of their junior year, students are introduced to an electronic portfolio system in which they document their progress toward mastery of the 12 Florida Accomplished Practices (similar to the Interstate New Teacher

Assessment and Support Consortium standards). Each course in the program targets a small number of standards that may be demonstrated through class assignments during that semester. Students select two pieces of evidence that document a beginning level of mastery for each Accomplished Practices from course assignments or from activities completed during practicum experiences. In most cases students accomplish this by providing less that 24 separate pieces of evidence as one source of evidence can document several Florida Educator Accomplished Practices. (See chapter 15 for more information about the electronic portfolio.)

In addition, we have worked with Educational Testing Service (ETS) to match the Pathwise Classroom Observation System (Dwyer, 1994) to the Florida Accomplished Practices. All university supervisor observations are completed using Pathwise, which provides performance data about preservice teacher performance in planning, establishing, and maintaining the learning environment, instruction, and teacher professionalism (see chapters 13 and 14 for more about performance assessment).

Collaboration. A key to successful implementation of the UESEP program is collaboration. Throughout the design process, collaboration across departments and colleges and with local and distant school personnel was essential. This collaboration has taken many forms.

Collaborative teaching teams. Collaborative teaching teams are used as a strategy to increase program coherence and program integrity. Almost every program course was designed and is taught by a team. Teaching teams include faculty, graduate students, and adjunct faculty (often classroom teachers or administrators). Many course teams include instructors from at least two departments within the college. Each team of five people is responsible for the instruction of approximately 150 students. Teams work together to plan syllabi, to be certain that core course competencies are addressed, to develop primary course assignments, to select course readings, and in many cases, to plan each class session. Although the teams plan together, on most teams each team member teaches one section of the course. That is, teams plan and evaluate together but do not team-teach. The inclusion of teachers or administrators from elementary classrooms on course teams keeps courses focused on classroom realities within the context of educational research and theory (for more information about course teams see chapters 6, 7, and 8).

Collaboration with school partners. Collaboration with school partners has been a key element in the development, delivery, and evaluation of the UESEP program. Several major collaborative efforts with school partners have guided this program.

Alachua County is the program's "home base." The University of Florida has a long history of collaboration with Alachua County schools. In the development of this program, administrators and teachers from the district served on planning committees, reviewed drafts of plans, and participated in planning retreats. In addition, School Partners mini-grants were funded with support from the BellSouth Foundation. These mini-grants provided funds for staff development to prepare teachers to model specific teaching strategies, provided resources for substitute teachers so teachers could participate more actively in planning, funded teachers to coteach courses with university faculty, and purchased materials needed to enrich the school- based experiences of teacher education students. Teachers and administrators also worked with college faculty to develop and revise field experiences and the performance evaluation system used to evaluate school experiences. Commitment to collaboration is also evident in the participation of school partners on teaching teams, on the UESEP Coordinating Committee, and on search committees for new university faculty (see chapters 5 and 10 for more on school/university partnerships).

With the program's focus on educating diverse student populations in inclusive environments came the need to locate additional sites for field experiences. Local schools offered somewhat limited diversity, and inclusive practices were not widely implemented. College of Education faculty worked with personnel from numerous school districts throughout Florida to design the structure and operating processes for a distant internship program. Distant internships were piloted in five school districts. At this point, students have had distant internship experiences in 37 districts and the number of interested students and districts increases each year. University supervisors for distant internships also use the Pathwise Observation System to evaluate student performance

Collaboration with liberal arts and sciences faculty. The existence of cohorts of students who need an appropriate content course to accompany each methods course has created a context for conversation and collaboration among colleagues in the Colleges of Education and Liberal Arts and Sciences. For example, colleagues from the Department of English have developed a course in writing for professional communication. Colleagues in geography, ecology, and entomology have developed content courses that address science or social science content with an interdisciplinary focus appropriate for elementary teachers. Each semester more opportunities for collaboration emerge.

A PICTURE OF THE PROGRAM

During their freshman and sophomore years, students complete 60 hours of coursework primarily in liberal arts and sciences. This coursework has been designated by the state to ensure that students have the content background necessary to teach the elementary Sunshine State (content) Standards. Students are admitted to the UESEP program in their junior year. The following sections describe the focus of each semester in the program and the companion field experience(s) (see appendixes A and B).

Introduction to Teaching, Families, and Children in a Diverse Society

During the first semester of the junior year, blocked courses include Child Development for Inclusive Education, Teachers and Learners in Inclusive Schools, Family and Community Involvement in Education, and Children's Literature in Childhood Education. Students are introduced to program themes, explore their entering perspectives about teaching, learn about typical and atypical child development, and are introduced to the multiple factors that influence school success for children in our diverse society. Coursework introduces a multicultural and social justice orientation to schooling. This emphasis is extended into the fieldwork for this semester during which students read to children in family day care homes and mentor a child in a public housing neighborhood. Both field experiences are linked to the courses in this block. For example, one assignment in the Family and Community Involvement course requires students to interview the caregiver of a child to whom they are assigned.

An Introduction to Pedagogy

During the second semester of the junior year, blocked courses include Core Teaching Strategies, Core Classroom Management Strategies, and Emergent Literacy. All students also must take ESOL Language and Culture, though this course is not part of the "block" of courses taken by each cohort. In this semester, students are taught several alternative instructional strategies (e.g., direct instruction, cognitive strategy instruction, inductive instruction, cooperative learning) and the learning theories that support each strategy. At the same time, they study the processes of the development of reading skills and abilities and learn to apply instructional strategies in the area of reading. They also learn how to structure a classroom community, how to establish the routines and procedures important to good classroom management, and strategies for understanding and dealing with difficult student behavior. During this semester, students work in an elementary classroom in triads for one morning a week. Triads observe lesson and classroom management strategies, interview their teacher, design and teach lessons, and complete literacy assessments. In a field experience for their ESOL class, students participate one hour per week in an ESOL classroom or with a language partner from UF's English Language Institute to increase their knowledge of the role of culture in learning.

Extending Knowledge About Teaching: The Methods Year

During the senior year students take methods courses in five key areas and gradually increase their practical experience with elementary students. In their first semester, blocked courses include Elementary Science Methods for the Inclusive Classroom, Teaching Mathematics in the Inclusive Classroom, and Integrating Technology into the Classroom. Students also take (or have taken) one content course in mathematics and one in science. Faculty in this semester have worked closely to integrate course and field experiences. Because it has been hard to ensure that all students have the opportunity to observe and participate in both science and technology experiences in classrooms during an early field experience, faculty worked to structure three weeks of model field experiences in informal settings. For example, UF preservice teachers work with Alachua County students and district personnel in a district-owned camp, Camp Crystal. Preservice teachers and students collect and analyze water samples from the lake and download the data into computers that the UF students bring to the site. Preservice teachers then design a series of math and science lessons that can be done using the data when the elementary students return to their classrooms. In this way UF students have concrete experiences integrating math, science, and technology in ways that are linked to the learning of elementary students.

In the second semester of the senior year, blocked courses include Language Arts for Diverse Learners, Writing for Professional Communication, Social Studies for Diverse Learners and Integrated Teaching in Elementary Education (this course is a 15-hour per week field placement). Students also take (or have taken) one social science content course. College of Education faculty coordinate their coursework with school faculties and with colleagues in Liberal Arts and Sciences. For example, students learn about the writing process both in

Writing for Professional Communication and in Language Arts. Students learn about the revision process using their own writing from the Professional Communication course. In addition, students integrate lessons in language arts with those in social studies and implement them in their classroom placements. In these placements two students are placed in one elementary classroom where they design lessons and plan, implement, and evaluate accommodations for struggling learners—practicing various models of coteaching. At the current time one faculty/student team is working with a partner school to develop more coherent linkages between university and school contexts. Once they pilot their model, we will begin to expand it to other schools.

Graduate Year: Elementary Certification

During the graduate year all students who elect to earn elementary certification only complete a one-semester full-time graduate internship in an elementary or ESOL classroom (see Appendix B). During the internship semester students take a curriculum course either during or, in the case of distant interns, immediately prior to the internship. In this course students develop and implement a thematic unit and develop an assessment portfolio to document and analyze student learning, which provides an academic framework for the internship experience.

Every effort is made to place students in schools with inclusive classrooms and where teachers model best practice. To increase the probability of finding excellent placements we place students in 37 districts in the state. Students may request distant internships or local placements (within 60 miles of Gainesville).

Students complete the graduate internship during the first full semester of their graduate program. This is done for two reasons, one logistical and one academic. There are several logistical reasons for this internship arrangement. First, this schedule means the majority of students complete internships in the fall, whereas the majority of part-time internships (15 hours per week) occur in the spring, thereby reducing the demand for classrooms and enabling more selectivity in placements. Second, high-stakes assessment of elementary children occurs each spring. Therefore, many teachers prefer not to have interns in the spring. In addition, test preparation activities alter the instructional context of classrooms and change the learning experience of interns.

Academically, faculty believe students receive a stronger master's degree when they complete the internship first. Prior to an internship, preservice teachers often believe they "know it all" and are ready to teach. After an internship, many students realize they still have much to

learn and approach their remaining coursework (e.g., social foundations, assessment, ESOL, and a professional specialization) with more
interest and vigor. Additionally, students pursuing single certification
select a 12-hour area of specialization (e.g., technology, literacy,
math/science, interdisciplinary, ESOL). This specialization has more
academic depth when students complete part of it after their internship
and are able to approach the coursework with questions to answer
derived from practical experience. (For more information about professional specializations see Fifth Year Options on the Unified Elementary
Special Education Proteach Web site: http://www.coe.ufl.edu/school/
proteach/index.html.)

Graduate Year: Dual Certification in Elementary/Special Education

Students have the option of completing a dual certification route in
elementary and special education. All students in the program meet the
requirements for elementary certification. To meet state requirements
for certification in special education (Varying Exceptionalities, Mild
Disabilities K–12), they must complete coursework and field experience
that focuses specifically on students with disabilities.

Faculty from the department of special education designed a
sequence of five graduate courses that build on the foundational knowledge of inclusive pedagogy developed during the undergraduate program and are consistent with the knowledge and skills required of
beginning special education teachers (Council for Exceptional Children,
1998). These graduate courses address the (a) characteristics of and services for students with disabilities, (b) collaboration skills necessary for
consultative and coteaching roles, (c) behavior management principles
and practices, and (d) advanced methods in assessment, curriculum and
instruction for students with mild disabilities.

All students in the dual certification track complete a 120-hour
field experience in a special education setting (12 weeks for 10 hours
per week). The placement for this experience is in a classroom where
the student will have extended opportunities to teach children with
either mild or severe disabilities. During this field experience students
apply the specialized knowledge and skills they are developing in their
specialization coursework. These field experiences are accompanied by
practicum seminars. The semester after this practicum experience, dual
certification students complete a one semester, full-time internship in an
inclusive elementary classroom or in a special education resource room.

The master's program for dual certification students also includes coursework in social foundations, assessment and ESOL.

CONCLUSION

This chapter provides a snapshot of the UESEP program as it was initially implemented. The program advisory council meets regularly to identify concerns and consider program revisions. An overview of program changes made since the program was implemented in the fall of 1999 is presented in the epilogue.

REFERENCES

Aiken, I. P., & Day, B. D. (1999). Early field experiences in preservice teacher education: Research and student perspectives. *Action in Teacher Education, 21*(3), 7–12.

Bondy, E. Griffin, C. Ross, D., & Sindelar, P. (1995). Elementary and special educators learning to work together: Team building processes. *Teacher Education Special Education, 18* (2), 91–102.

Buck, G., Morsink, C., Griffin, C., Hines, T., & Lenk, L. (1992). Preservice training: The role of field-based experiences in the preparation of effective special educators. *Teacher Education and Special Education, 15*(2), 1–16.

Combs, A.W., Blume, R.A., Newman, A.J., & Wass, H.L. (1974*). The professional education of teachers* (2nd ed.). Boston: Allyn & Bacon.

Dewey, J. (1916). *Democracy and education.* New York: Macmillan.

Dwyer, C. A. (1994). *Development of the knowledge base for the PRAXIS III: Classroom performance assessment criteria.* Princeton, NJ: Educational Testing Service.

Dwyer, C. A., & Stufflebeam, D. (1996). Teacher evaluation. In D. Berliner, & R. Calfee (Eds.), *Handbook of educational psychology* (pp. 765–784). New York: Macmillan.

Fishkin, J. S. (1991*). Democracy and deliberation: New directions for democratic reform.* New Haven, CT: Yale University Press.

Goodlad, J. (1986). Foreword. In E. Cohen, *Designing group work: Strategies for the heterogeneous classroom.* New York: Teachers College Press.

Goodlad, J. (1990). *Teachers for our nation's schools.* San Francisco: Jossey-Bass.

Goodman, J. (1992). *Elementary schooling for critical democracy.* Albany: State University of New York Press.

Harlin, R. P. (1999). Developing future professionals: Influences of literacy coursework and field experiences. *Reading Research and Instruction, 38,* 351–370.

Holmes Group. (1995). *Tomorrow's schools of education.* East Lansing, MI: Author.

Lilly, M. S. (1992). Research on teacher licensure and state approval of teacher education programs. *Teacher Education and Special Education, 15,* 148–160.

Miller, M. J. (2000). *Critical Teacher Shortage Areas 2000–2001.* Tallahassee, FL: Florida Department of Education.

National Commission on Teaching and America's Future. (1996). *What matters most: Teaching for America's future.* New York: Author.

Parker, W. C. (1996). *Educating the democratic mind.* Albany: State University of New York Press.

Pugach, M. (1992). Unifying the preservice preparation of teachers. In W. Stainback, & S. Stainback (Eds.), *Controversial issues confronting special education: Divergent perspectives* (pp. 255–270). Needham, MA: Allyn & Bacon.

Reynolds, M. C., Wang, M. C., & Walberg, H. J. (1987). The necessary restructuring of special and regular education. *Exceptional Children, 53,* 391–398.

Ross, D. D., & Bondy, E. (1996). The continuing reform of a teacher education program: A case study. In K. M. Zeichner, S. L. Melnick, & M. L. Gomez (Eds.) *Currents of reform in preservice teacher education* (pp. 62–79). New York: Teachers College Press.

Ross, D. D., Bondy, E., & Kyle, D. W. (1993). *Reflective teaching for student empowerment.* New York: Macmillan.

Ross, D. D., Johnson, M., & Smith, W. (1992). Developing a PROfessional TEACHer at the University of Florida. In L. Valli (Ed.), *Case studies and critiques of reflective teacher education programs* (pp. 24–39). Albany, NY: State University of New York Press.

Ross, D. D., & Krogh, S. L. (1988). From paper to program: A story from elementary PROTEACH. *Peabody Journal of Education, 65*(2), 19–34.

Skrtic, T. M. (Ed.). (1991). *Behind special education: A critical analysis of professional culture and school organization.* Denver, CO: Love Publishers.

Stainback, S., & Stainback, W. (1987). Facilitating merger through personnel preparation. *Teacher Education and Special Education, 10,* 185–190.

Valli, L., & Rennert-Ariev, P. L. (2000). Identifying consensus in teacher education reform documents: A proposed framework and action implications. *Journal of Teacher Education, 51*(1), 5–17.

Webb, R., & Sherman, R. (1989). *Schooling and society.* New York: Macmillan.

Wiggins, R. A., & Follo, E. J. (1999). Development of knowledge, attitudes, and commitment to teach diverse student populations. *Journal of Teacher Education, 50*(2), 94–105.

CHAPTER 4

Designing the Program: An Overview of the Process

Vivian I. Correa, Dorene D. Ross, and Rodman B. Webb

In early spring of 1995 the dean of the College of Education charged a planning committee to redesign the 10-year-old Proteach teacher education programs in the college by unifying elementary and special education. Proteach, a five-year teacher education program, had been in existence since 1985 and provided separate degrees and certifications in elementary, secondary, and special education (Ross & Bondy, 1996; Ross, Johnson, & Smith, 1992; Ross & Krogh, 1988).

The catalyst for this new reform in teacher education came from multiple sources. Most notably, the catalyst was the arrival of the new dean in the fall of 1995. Additionally, two collaborative teacher education initiatives had been pilot tested through funding from the U.S. Department of Education, Office of Special Education Programs (OSEP). The first initiative was the development and implementation of the Unified Early Childhood program, a joint program to prepare early childhood and early childhood special education teachers for new state certificates in early childhood (see Correa, Hartle, Jones, Kemple, Rapport, & Smith-Bonhue, 1997; Hartle, Jones, Rapport, Kemple, & Correa, 1994; Kemple, Hartle, Correa, & Fox, 1992). Although the Unified Early Childhood program had initially been funded by OSEP in 1992, the experimental program was approved and institutionalized in the college in the fall of 1995.

The second initiative involved another OSEP funded grant, Preparation and Accommodation through Reflective Teaching (Project PART), providing elementary education preservice students with financial incentives to add on a special education mild disabilities certificate (Bondy, Ross, Sindelar, & Griffin, 1995). The Unified Early Childhood program and Project PART were prototypes for the new vision of teacher education at the University of Florida. The enthusiasm, innovation, and successes of those programs served as catalysts for the development of the Unified Elementary Special Education Proteach (UESEP) program in 1995.

Other trends and national reforms influenced the work of the college in the spring of 1995; in particular, a direct call for the creation of supportive, inclusive, effective schools for all children including ethnically and racially diverse students, as well as students with disabilities (Pugach, 1992). Clearly, colleges of education were reexamining the content of their teacher education programs based largely on the changing character of the U.S. population of school children, the disproportionate representation of minorities in special education, the large number of students with disabilities served primarily in general education classrooms, and the potential of inclusive education policy to increase this number (Kilgore, 1996).

Unifying general and special teacher education had begun in earnest at the University of Wisconsin, Milwaukee in 1993. At the time, the unification process had been described as not being simply a matter of renegotiating an existing relationship but instead as "recreating the basic culture of schools, colleges, and departments of education within which teacher education takes place" (Pugach, 1992, p. 258).

The charge by the dean in the spring of 1995 to reform the teacher education programs at the University of Florida thrust the college into a remarkable journey of reform and collaboration across departments in the college. The process of redesigning the teacher education program in elementary, middle school, and special education took over four years. At times the process progressed smoothly; at other times the planning committee encountered major hurdles that threatened the demise of the restructuring effort. This chapter describes the planning process, the challenges encountered, the strategies used to overcome barriers, and the ongoing challenges of implementation. Although the development process was not organized into clear phases, in retrospect there were six phases to the process.

The following sections describe this process, which can be summarized as follows:

- Phase I: Getting Started (10 months)
- Phase II: First Design—False Start (6 months)
- Phase III: Back to the Drawing Board—The Redesign Teams (7 months)
- Phase IV: Approval of Curriculum (3 months)

• Phase V: Developing the Courses and University Approval (26 months)

PHASE ONE: THE CHARGE AND INITIAL ORGANIZATIONAL STRUCTURES

The dean appointed the Proteach planning committee and placed the associate dean of academic affairs in charge of coordinating the reform efforts. The planning committee was asked to reconceptualize the elementary and special education teacher education programs at the University of Florida in order to create one program with a dual emphasis on elementary and special education, to use the reform literature to guide our thinking, and to build the best possible program within specific constraints.

Although the charge to the planning committee was to design the "finest" unified program possible, certain parameters were to be considered. The new plan was to maintain a five-year program, culminating in a master's degree in the College of Education. The bachelor's program would have to be shortened to 120 hours. The new program would have to involve all units in the college, requiring representation on the planning committee from Counselor Education, Educational Psychology, and Education Leadership (traditionally programs with little or no involvement in teacher education). Furthermore, it was expected that the new program would be ready for implementation within 16 months for the start of the 1996 fall semester.

Over the next eight months, the committee brainstormed ideas for the redesign of the program, invited a consultant to advise the group on the process, and developed an initial curriculum design. The committee understood that the redesign work would require a new culture of communication and collaboration among faculty and across departments related to the teacher education curriculum. Experts who had attempted similar reforms would assist the college in the process.

Dr. Marleen Pugach was hired as a consultant to describe the unification process used at the University of Wisconsin, Milwaukee. Dr. Pugach's visit was beneficial in providing the planning committee with strategies for unifying the general and special education curricula. However, she advised the committee that undertaking such significant reform would take substantial time and much dialogue.

External pressures from the state legislature also influenced the work of the planning committee. A new state university system (SUS) policy limited all undergraduate programs to 120 credit hours and required a smoother articulation with community college transfer students. The work of the planning committee was organized into three subgroups: (a) general education/ preprofessional requirements (freshman, sophomore years), (b) the professional core/clinical requirements (junior, senior, and graduate years), and (c) the unifying philosophy and assumptions. The general education and professional core subgroups had the difficult task of trimming the undergraduate program from approximately 128 hours to 120 hours while simultaneously blending two stand-alone programs of general education and special education into a single unified program. Additionally, the general education subgroup was asked to design at least three freshman/sophomore courses in education to be offered by the Florida community colleges as part of their Associate of Arts (AA) degree.

The work of the subgroup on philosophy and assumptions developed four major themes: inclusion, diversity, equity, and leadership. The initial mission and program themes emerged from the subgroup (chapter 3 for the revised mission and themes of the program).

Each subgroup brought their work back to the larger planning committee for review. Although the committee included representatives from each unit across the college, time constraints had precluded collegewide discussions about the reform process. Furthermore, in order to get the program ready for implementation by fall 1997, the committee pushed to get a set of courses in place for faculty review in early spring 1996.

PHASE TWO: THE FIRST DESIGN—A FALSE START

Due to time constraints and efforts to preserve many of the courses currently existing in the college curricula, the committee created a side-by-side elementary/special education program. Students would take a set of existing elementary courses and a set of existing special education courses creating an elementary teacher education program with "add-on" special education courses to meet the minimal certification requirements. In February 1996 this initial design of the curriculum framework was presented to the faculty for feedback at a collegewide retreat. During the retreat faculty were asked to work together to identify benefits, concerns/fears, and potential solutions. Although both positive and negative feedback was generated about the design and program, there was an overwhelming apprehension from the faculty about the design of the curriculum framework and the planning process.

Shortly after the retreat, a subgroup of the planning committee did a content analysis of the data from a written survey on the design and the overall process. Faculty reported general support for the concept of unifying the general and special education teacher education programs and supported the inclusion of all departments in the curriculum. However, there was significant concern that the conceptual framework was not sufficiently articulated, and that the program did not reflect a unified curriculum. Faculty also were concerned about the extent to which college resources and support would be given to faculty for developing and teaching courses in the seemingly time-intensive program. Faculty felt that insufficient time had been given to cross-departmental discussions. In the end, faculty requested that (a) the process be slowed-down, (b) the community and school stakeholders be included in the process, (c) a careful analysis of college resources be conducted, (d) faculty development be embedded in the reform process, and (e) the program reflect a more unified and integrated curriculum.

PHASE THREE: BACK TO THE DRAWING BOARD: THE DESIGN TEAMS

Faculty leaders, though somewhat discouraged, were not surprised by faculty feedback about a curriculum design that had only lukewarm support from the planning committee. In an effort to keep the momentum going across the college, a second retreat was scheduled to clarify the mission of the unified teacher education program and articulate guiding themes for the program.

In the summer of 1996, one year and three months after initiating the reform effort, the planning committee decided to rethink the process for designing the new Proteach program. They decided to expand the design process beyond the original committee members. It was clear that they needed to give more thought to the conceptual framework and program themes. The committee worked to create a process that would lessen the sense that the planning committee was trying to dictate a curriculum to the college, and instead provide a structured method for deciding on a curriculum.

Rethinking the process took two forms. First, a writing task force expanded the conceptual framework and revised the program themes consistent with faculty feedback from the previous retreats. Second, four design teams were formed to independently develop model curriculum frameworks.

In August 1996 a redesign mini-retreat was held. The four design teams consisting of faculty volunteers and K-12 teachers and administrators were given their charge: to create a potential design for Unified Elementary Special Education Proteach. Three teams worked independently to develop three separate designs for the elementary/special education program. The fourth team created a design for a Unified Middle School Special Education program.

Six months later, in February 1997, college faculty met in a day-long retreat to analyze the strengths and weaknesses of each of the four designs. After this retreat a faculty group synthesized the work of the three elementary and special education design teams to create one program design that maximized the strengths and minimized the weaknesses of the three designs. Faculty considered this new program design and provided feedback and recommendations that were reviewed by the planning committee, which modified the design to address faculty concerns.

Concurrently, a subgroup of faculty developed and submitted a BellSouth Foundation Special Initiatives grant proposal focused on re-creating colleges of teacher education. In March 1997 the College was awarded $250,000 to support program development and evaluation over a three-year period (see Wisniewski, 2001).

PHASE FOUR: APPROVAL OF THE CURRICULUM BY THE FACULTY

In April 1997 a fourth retreat was organized for the purpose of showcasing the integrated design. It was critically important to present a thorough rationale for the program, the philosophical themes and assumptions, and the new framework of courses in the program. An outside consultant worked with faculty to help them come to consensus on modifications of the proposed curriculum framework. At the conclusion of the retreat, faculty approved the framework pending modifications to reflect faculty feedback. In an effort to recruit new faculty to the reform process, the faculty decided to reconstitute the planning committee that had been chaired by the associate dean. The committee was renamed the Coordinating Committee and was cochaired by one faculty member in general education and one in special education. Two years after initiating the process, a milestone had been reached! The college had agreed on a Unified Elementary and Unified Middle School curricular framework.

PHASE FIVE: DESIGNING THE COURSES AND
UNIVERSITY APPROVAL

The fifth phase of the reform process was the longest. It began in June 1997 and ended 26 months later, in August 1999, when the first cohort of students began courses in the Unified Elementary Special Education Proteach program (UESEP).

This phase of the process required fine-tuning the curriculum framework, developing individual courses, presenting the total package to the college and university curriculum committees, and reaching out to all Florida school districts to showcase the program. Additionally, during these months of rigorous work, the Florida Department of Education mandated that all state teacher education programs include five three-hour endorsement courses in English for Speakers of Other Languages (ESOL) embedded in the program. The ESOL mandate added much stress to the work of the coordinating committee. An additional ESOL course was added to the framework, requiring that an existing course be cut. The committee decided the remainder of the ESOL content would be infused in other course syllabi.

During phases four and five of the process, more than half the faculty in the college worked on program and/or course design teams to develop a program that was substantially different from the first side-by-side program of February 1996. The program required the redefinition of course content and development of syllabi for every course and field-based experience in the program (30 undergraduate and 36 graduate hours) and required that faculty from two or more departments collaborate in the design and delivery of many courses. In addition, the program required that faculty teaching courses within a common semester coordinate academic and field experience expectations. Other faculty development activities focused on the use of technology in teacher education.

In this final phase before implementation, faculty in the college expressed concerns related to collaboration, teaching teams, and faculty workloads. Faculty recognized quickly what administrators are slow to grant, that collaboration is a costly enterprise. Present practices and policies reward those who do not collaborate. Faculty also worried that there were no organizational supports in the college for cross-department collaboration.

As a response to concerns about collaboration, three initiatives were taken. First, faculty were invited to apply for Teacher Education Pedagogy minigrants to experiment with teaching strategies and collaborative structures for working with colleagues in other departments and in public schools. Faculty from six different course teams, most from the first year of the program, received funding for these minigrants. Faculty work on these minigrants suggested several potential ways that collaboration might be structured. Second, a small committee developed models of collaboration to share with faculty (Ross, Correa, & Webb, 1999). The committee drew on the collaborative structures developed in the minigrants and structures currently in use in the college. The six models are described in appendix C.

Third, two of the department chairs developed some basic assumptions about collaboration to help address issues related to faculty load and assignment:

1. Faculty members will be in charge of or lead only one course team each semester in the program.
2. Doctoral students will be integral to the delivery of multiple sections of one course with supervision from targeted faculty leaders.
3. All courses require some kind of cross-departmental infusion especially the courses in special education and elementary education.
4. The faculty member who serves as team leader for a particular semester will receive load credit for this role (.06 FTE for each instructor supervised and .25 FTE for teaching his/her section of the course).

The issues raised during this phase of planning were not new; they had surfaced early in the process. However, as implementation neared, faculty became more nervous about the realities of the reformed program. Although faculty repeatedly expressed concerns, at the same time they showed amazing willingness to become involved in the reform effort, to develop a program consistent with the recommendations in the major reform reports, and to alter their instructional practices (Ross, Correa, & Webb, 1999).

The next section of the chapter will report more specifically on the barriers encountered during the four years of program development and present solutions for overcoming the barriers. Analysis of faculty concerns reveals that the barriers to reform in teacher education lie less in faculty resistance than in university structure (see chapter 2).

BARRIERS ENCOUNTERED AND STRATEGIES TO OVERCOME BARRIERS

The development of this program required almost four years. Sustaining momentum was a recurring challenge and required a continuous process of identifying potential barriers and developing strategies to overcome them. During the development of the program we encountered barriers related to establishing collaborative partnerships with schools, establishing cross-departmental collaboration, responding to outside mandates from the university and the Florida Department of Education, and coping with changes in key administrators during the change process. Each barrier warrants serious discussion and development. However, none of these issues will surprise our colleagues in higher education, for these are the barriers encountered by every reform effort in teacher education. We will briefly describe the barriers we faced as we grappled with each issue. We want to stress that we have not solved any of the problems we encountered. We were, however, able to sustain forward progress. As we describe each barrier, we will also describe one or two strategies that helped us to maintain momentum in the face of the barriers.

Barriers and Solutions Related to Developing School Partnerships

A great deal has been written about the barriers to creating professional development schools. These barriers were similar to the barriers we encountered in developing clinical partnerships with school colleagues. Like others, we found it challenging to establish and sustain collaborative relations with schools for several reasons (see for example Book, 1996; Goodlad, 1993; Paul, Duchnowskil, & Danforth, 1993; Ross, Brownell, Sindelar, & Vandiver, 2000). First, neither K–12 faculty nor university faculty have sufficient time for planning, discussion, and collaboration given the complexity and intensity of their other roles as educators. Second, the reward structures in schools and universities do not support this work. Although university faculty have more flexibility in their schedules, most university tenure and promotion systems reward research and publication first, teaching second, and service to schools last (see chapter 2). Giving substantial time to schools may slow a faculty member's progress toward tenure, promotion, and merit. Finally, the generation of full-time equivalency credit (FTE) is an issue. College budgets—at least at the University of Florida—are determined by FTE generation. Putting faculty in schools, even to supervise student teachers, is not an effective generator of FTE.

To overcome these barriers, several strategies were employed simultaneously. The dean worked with the State Council of Deans to propose to Florida's State University System Board of Regents (replaced in 2002 by individual university boards of trustees) that universities recognize work in schools as part of a faculty member's official load.

Although this never became policy, the discussion led to a pilot "Professor in Residence" program that enables a faculty member to be assigned to a school for 25% of his/her load. Eventually, the tenure and promotion policies were revised to place more emphasis on service to schools, which helped our efforts in school partnership. Additionally, with support from the BellSouth Foundation we provided incentives to school-based faculty and university faculty who participated in planning activities. The most important incentives provided funds to pay substitutes so teachers could attend staff development and planning sessions, funds to provide food at collaborative functions, and most importantly, funds to purchase similar instructional materials for school-based and university-based faculty. The latter was particularly important to the program planning effort.

Although schools and the university had curriculum materials, they often did not have the same materials nor did schools have enough resources (especially books) for their student population and certainly not enough to share with teacher education students. By creating a pool of common materials (e.g., leveled books for beginning readers), college and school faculty found greater opportunities for shared learning.

Barriers and Solutions Related to Establishing Cross-Departmental Collaboration

Issues related to establishing cross-departmental collaboration and collaboration with colleagues in the College of Liberal Arts and Sciences are similar to those in creating collaborative relationships with school colleagues. The culture of a research I university favors autonomy and specialization rather than collaborative endeavors (Holmes, 1995, p. 19). In this context, the higher paid and most respected scholars in colleges of education are those whose work looks most like that of their colleagues in liberal arts and sciences (Stoddart, 1993). This definition of research discourages time-consuming, collaborative scholarship and program development work. Thus, time and reward structures again emerge as barriers to reform. In this reform effort, we were asking faculty to work across departments to design courses. Faculty worried that they were packing too much content into too few hours and that their own disciplines would get short-changed. They also worried that collaborative teaching might undermine their classroom autonomy, lower their teaching ratings, and loosen faculty ties to their disciplines. They worried that subject matter might be watered down or distorted when taught by professors out of their fields.

Although faculty expressed concerns about cross-departmental collaboration, they also found the discussions rewarding and exciting academic work. The most serious concerns (e.g., those about autonomy and course compression) were the most intense during the planning stages of the program. As faculty began to teach the newly designed courses, these concerns diminished and, in some cases, even reversed themselves (see chapters 6 and 8 for more discussion of issues related to teaching teams).

Several strategic solutions helped to support collaboration within the competitive world of a research I university. First, providing tasks, resources, and timelines encouraged faculty to do this work and, as noted, collaboration with colleagues was intrinsically motivating to many faculty. Second, funding from BellSouth supported "minigrants," which enabled faculty to experiment with instructional innovations prior to implementation of the program. Additional funding from the Florida Department of Education supported faculty in the development of performance indicators within courses and an electronic portfolio system (see chapter 14). These grants provided incentives and resources for doing collaborative work. Third, department chairs found ways to provide load credit for leading a teaching team. These three efforts did not remove faculty time pressures, but they did provide concrete acknowledgement that team leadership is a significant instructional responsibility. For a thorough discussion of the barriers involved in establishing teaching teams and the strategies used to overcome these barriers see Ross, Correa, and Webb (1999) and chapters 6 and 8.

Barriers and Solutions from Outside Mandates

During the development of the Unified Elementary and Unified Middle School programs, numerous outside mandates complicated reform efforts. Examples of these mandates include (a) a Board of Regents ruling that no undergraduate program in the university system could exceed 120 hours; (b) a state directive that all teacher education graduates receive the maximum ESOL endorsement (the equivalent of 15 hours of coursework); (c) continuous state conversation about potential changes in certification requirements; (d) a "university bank" budgeting system that fostered competition among colleges and rewarded departments for FTE generation; and (e) a shift in university priorities that rewarded graduate credit generation more than undergraduate credit generation. These latter two were the most significant barriers because they reinforced the cultural context of a research I university and reiterated the importance of individual, competitive work at a time when we were trying to establish a more collaborative culture in the college. At the same time, the shift from undergraduate enrollment targets to graduate enrollment targets created new demands on college resources and discouraged faculty and administrators from investing energy and resources in teacher education.

Outside mandates are inevitable in the world of public education. The work of reform is influenced by outside events that cannot be anticipated or controlled. Outside mandates influence faculty morale and inevitably slow the momentum of reform; however, the University of Florida experience indicates that when college administration and faculty leaders stay focused on the reform effort, they can find ways to sustain faculty efforts despite outside pressures. The most viable strategy available was to work with and around each new and distracting mandate. For example, when asked to add four new ESOL courses (over the one already included in the program) the faculty added one three-hour ESOL course and infused the remaining ESOL competencies in other coursework in the program. Another strategy was to resist when compliance was impossible. For example, meeting the ESOL mandate made it impossible for us to comply with the 120 credit-hour rule. Despite university discouragement, college administrators pushed for an exception that enabled the faculty to lengthen the program by four credit hours. A third strategy was that leaders in the College of Education worked to help faculty view the barriers presented by the pressures as opportunities. The shift in university priorities from undergraduate to graduate education was clearly—and continues to be—a challenge. However, bringing high-quality graduate students with recent classroom experience into graduate programs improved both our graduate and undergraduate programs. When these graduate students teach with our faculty on teaching teams, their knowledge enhances the education of our undergraduate students. Faculty want both high-quality graduate students and high-quality teacher education programs. College leaders tried to help everyone recognize that graduate and undergraduate programs were not necessarily competing priorities.

Conclusion: Last Words on Overcoming Barriers

Leadership is important in any reform effort. The dean of the College of Education initiated this particular reform, although clearly there was faculty support and evidence that faculty were already moving in a similar direction. Without the support of the dean and associate dean it is unlikely that significant reform would have been possible. At the same time, top-down pressure from administration created faculty resistance that caused tension. Although reform efforts require leadership by faculty and administration alike, tension caused by top-down pressure means the reform is vulnerable when leadership changes occur. As faculty restructured the teacher education programs, they experienced a number of personnel changes in key leadership positions, including the dean and the chairs of the two departments most heavily involved in the reform effort. In fact, implementation began—with logistical issues unresolved—under an interim dean and a new chair in a key department. Nevertheless, implementation proceeded and the program was institutionalized in the fall of 1999.

Part of the college's success is attributable to luck; part to planning and support. In searching for people to fill new leadership positions, faculty obviously looked for people who would support the reform effort. The funding provided by BellSouth made faculty responsible for sustaining and documenting progress in the reform. In addition, throughout the effort, leadership included both administrators and faculty members. Broad-based leadership diminishes the impact of one or two key players, but the fact that our dean left just at the point of implementation was problematic. Fortunately, the interim dean had been associate dean during the planning process and had a clear commitment to the reform effort. Had we encountered a dean with a different agenda at that point, the reform effort might have been irreparably harmed. When implementing something radically different, faculty concerns are inevitably at a high point immediately prior to implementation. A change in the commitment of administrative leadership at that key juncture would have been significant.

REFERENCES

Bondy, B., Ross, D., Sindelar, P., & Griffin, C. (1995). Elementary and special educators learning to work together: Team building processes. *Teacher Education and Special Education, 18*(2), 91–102.

Book, C. L. (1996). Professional development schools. In J. Sikula, T. J. Buttery, & E. Guyton (Eds.), *Handbook of research on teacher education* (2nd ed., pp. 194–210). New York: Macmillan.

Correa, V., Hartle, L., Jones, H., Kemple, K., Rapport, M. J., & Smith-Bonhue, T. (1997). The Unified PROTEACH early childhood program at the University of Florida. In L. Blanton, C. Griffin, J. Winn, & M. Pugach (Eds.), *Teacher education in transition: Collaborative practices in general and special education* (pp. 84–105). Denver, CO: Love.

Goodlad, J. (1993). School-university partnerships. *Educational policy,* 7(1), 24–39.

Hartle, L. C., Jones, H. A., Rapport, M. J., Kemple, K. M., & Correa, V. I. (1997). Systems change in the process of unifying teacher education. *Journal of Early Childhood Teacher Education,* 18(1), 75–88.

Kemple, K. M., Hartle, L. C., Correa, V. I., & Fox, L. (1994). Preparing teachers for inclusive education: The development of a unified teacher program in early childhood and early childhood special education. *Teacher Education and Special Education,* 17, 38–51.

Kilgore, K. (1996). *Rationale for PROTEACH II.* Unpublished manuscript.

Paul, J. L., Duchnowski, A. J., & Danforth, S. (1993). *Teacher education and special education,* 16, 95–109.

Pugach, M. (1992). Unifying the preservice preparation of teachers. In W. Stainback, & S. Stainback (Eds.), *Controversial issues confronting special education: Divergent perspectives* (pp. 255–270). Needham, MA: Allyn & Bacon.

Ross, D. D., & Bondy, E. (1996). The continuing reform of a teacher education program: A case study. In K. M. Zeichner, S. L. Melnick, & M. L. Gomez (Eds.), *Currents of reform in preservice teacher education* (pp. 62–79). New York: Teachers College Press.

Ross, D. D., Brownell, M., Sindelar, P., & Vandiver, F. (1999). Research from professional development schools: Can we live up to the potential? *Peabody Journal of Education,* 74(3 & 4), 209–223.

Ross, D. D., Correa, V., & Webb, R. (1999, February). *Teacher education reform through college-wide collaboration.* Paper presented at the meeting of the American Association of Colleges of Teacher Education, Washington, DC.

Ross, D. D., & Krogh, S. L. (1988). From paper to program: A story from elementary PROTEACH. *Peabody Journal of Education,* 65(2), 19–34.

Ross, D. D., Johnson, M., & Smith, W. (1992). Developing a PROfessional TEACHer at the University of Florida. In L. Valli (Ed.), *Case studies and critiques of reflective teacher education programs* (pp. 24–39). Albany, NY: State University of New York Press.

Winsniewski, R. (2001). *Recreating colleges of teacher education: A report on a BellSouth Foundation Special Initiative.* Atlanta, GA: BellSouth Foundation.

CHAPTER 5

The Field Experiences: Teaching
in Partnership with Schools
and Community

CYNTHIA C. GRIFFIN, ZHIHUI FANG, ANNE G. BISHOP,
AND SHAREN HALSALL

The importance of field experiences in the Unified Elementary Special Education Proteach (UESEP) program is unmistakable. Eight field placements have been designed to ensure optimal experiences for university students, cooperating teachers, child-care providers, families, and children in these settings. Organized in schools, after-school programs, museums, nature centers, day-care centers, and subsidized housing communities, the field experiences are characterized by features supported in the literature and by the collective wisdom of the faculty and our school partners. The design, delivery, and evaluation of these experiences became possible by forming important school partnerships with our neighboring school district (i.e., Alachua County), and with districts throughout Florida. Without these collaborative relationships, the field experiences could not possibly provide students with the preparation necessary to learn how to address the needs of children in diverse classrooms, or to work collaboratively with school and community personnel to educate all children.

The design of the field experiences began with the formation of two types of working groups. First, teams of mostly faculty, including some graduate students and school personnel, met on a regular basis to study and plan. These groups drew upon their own expertise, consulted the literature, and explored programs at other institutions to create optimal field experiences in the new UESEP program. At times groups

83

were discouraged by the scant research they found in the literature. McIntyre, Byrd, and Foxx (1996) and Buck, Morsink, Griffin, Hines, and Lenk (1992) have described this dilemma, suggesting further that field experiences in teacher education are often considered the most important part of programs, but what constitutes effective experiences, including student teaching, is not clear. However, some guidance from current research suggests that effectiveness has more to do with whether the student has opportunities to reflect on practice, and less with the length of the experience, particularly if it lacks components of analysis and self-assessment (e.g., Armaline & Hoover, 1989; Nelson, 1999; O'Hair & O'Hair, 1996). Ultimately, the campus-based design groups considered this kind of information as they worked together.

The second type of group consisted of UF faculty and our school and community partners. Like the first groups these also met regularly to discuss the design of the field experiences, but usually met off-campus at a place convenient to all. In particular, these groups dealt with the difficult task of finding, and also creating, inclusive classrooms for students in the new program. The commitment in the UESEP program to inclusive school placements for all preprofessional teachers is indisputable. Although Florida, unfortunately, has lagged behind other states in experimenting with inclusion, pockets of inclusion have emerged throughout the state. The collaborative partnerships have helped make the difference. To date, the number of elementary school placements that include diverse groups of students in general education classrooms (e.g., students with disabilities, students served by Title I programs) has increased considerably, and will no doubt continue to grow.

Through significant effort these groups have carved out field experiences that are characterized by (a) strong linkages between campus coursework and the fieldwork; (b) the use of interdisciplinary experiences (e.g., units of instruction); (c) the utilization of technology; and (d) the modification of the field experience context (e.g., use of cohort groups divided into triads and pairs in single settings). All of these characteristics are viewed by McIntyre, Byrd, and Foxx (1996) as important trends in the design of field experiences. More recent research endorses the use of paired peer placement with peer coaching (Wynn & Kromrey, 2000) and self-evaluation and reflection on practice (Ebby, 2000; Hutchinson & Martin, 1999) in field placements.

We now turn to a brief description of each one of the field experiences in the UESEP program. The descriptions are arranged in chronological order, beginning with the first experiences in the first semester of the junior year (semester five), and ending with the graduate year internship program, for a total of eight experiences completed during five semesters. Some of the descriptions also include a discussion of the challenges faced and lessons learned in the process of creating and implementing these experiences. Then, in keeping with our commitment to school and community partnerships, we offer the perspective of one school district as it worked collaboratively with us in this endeavor. Finally, we conclude with a few thoughts about the future.

DESCRIPTIONS OF FIELD EXPERIENCES

Semester Five (First Semester of the Junior Year)

Bright Futures. Bright Futures (Bondy & Davis, 2001), also known as the Mentoring Project, is a field experience that is tied to EEX 3070 (Teachers and Learners in Inclusive Schools), a course that examines diversity and its impact on students' school experiences. Funded by the U.S. Department of Housing and Urban Development, Bright Futures is a joint initiative of the College of Education at UF, the Gainesville Housing Authority, and the Gainesville Police Department. The objective of this field experience is twofold: (a) to develop prospective teachers' intercultural communicative competence and their commitment to teaching educationally disadvantaged children; and (b) to improve children's social and academic skills. To accomplish these goals, each preprofessional teacher (or "mentor") is assigned to a child (from preschool age through middle school) who lives in one of six local public housing neighborhoods. Each mentor-child pair meets for an hour twice per week for 10 weeks at a community center within the neighborhood. In addition, some mentors take their child on field trips to local sites of interest on weekends and during the evening. The mentor plans lessons and activities for the child with the help of information from the child's classroom teacher and guidance from the field supervisor at the site. Students talk and write about mentoring in EEX 3070 as they draw on course concepts to interpret their observations and experiences in the field. In SDS 3430, Family and Community Involvement in Education, students focus on their children's families and neighborhoods and complete an interview with their children's caregivers. Students write a paper comparing and contrasting experiences, beliefs, and values in their own families and the families of the children they work with in Bright Futures. For Child Development, mentors complete multiple observations of their child's cognitive, social, and motor development.

Booktalk. Project Booktalk (Lamme, 2000), an experience tied to the Children's Literature course (LAE 3005), offers preprofessional teachers an additional opportunity to work with children from low-income environments. A collaborative initiative between the College of Education and the Youth Services Division of the Public Library, Project Booktalk involves preservice teachers in 10 visits to local licensed day care homes. The students, individually or with a partner, sign up for a home with up to five children who can be from birth through age five. Students first visit the local public library to pick up a sack of library books to be used with the children. While at the day care home, students read, show books, and conduct a library story hour in a variety of ways (e.g., talk, dance, sing, puppets, flannelboards) in order to engage children with the literature. They are required to read with children on laps (in the case of toddlers) or cradled in their arms (in the case of infants) and closely observe their responses to literature. Students then leave the books in the home for the day care provider and children to use through the week. At each subsequent visit, students return with a new set of books to replace the previous batch. At the end of the semester, students write a letter to each family explaining how their child has responded to the literature and make recommendations for future reading. Students are also required to maintain a log documenting what they have learned (about books, learning to read, culture) from these visits and how these learning experiences might impact them as future teachers.

Semester Six (Second Semester of the Junior Year)

The second semester of the junior year has a number of field experiences that are tied to four courses. We present the courses here and the field experiences linked to each.

Core Management and Core Teaching Strategies. During semester six, students register for both EEX 3257 (Core Teaching Strategies) and EEX 3616 (Core Management Strategies). Together, these courses share a field experience that includes a three-hour per week placement in an elementary classroom. In this classroom preservice teachers observe, tutor individual students, and teach two lessons using two of the instructional strategies taught in Core Teaching Strategies. Working in groups of three, students plan, teach, and evaluate one lesson using direct instruction and one lesson using cognitive strategy instruction. The content of the lessons must be selected with input from the cooperating teacher and must fall within the expected curriculum for the grade level and school site. These lesson plan assignments give preservice teachers opportunities to practice writing and implementing appropriate lesson objectives, activities, and assessment strategies that are well aligned and engage diverse students successfully in learning.

Field experience assignments for EEX 3616 (Core Management Strategies) allow students to work individually or in groups to complete a teacher interview, a diagram of the classroom, and other projects that assist preservice teachers in noticing classroom routines, rules, and procedures. Additional assignments help preservice teachers attend to the classroom teacher and how he or she manages student work, instructional materials, and instructional time. Preservice teachers also spend a significant amount of time analyzing incidents involving children exhibiting problem behaviors and the teachers' responses to these behaviors. These observations culminate in the development of classroom management plans and intervention plans that include functional behavioral assessments and recommend positive behavioral supports.

Emergent Literacy. Emergent Literacy (EEC 3706) is a course about theory and practice in the teaching of early literacy development. The purpose of the field experience for this course is to give students an opportunity to apply the assessment instruments and teaching strategies discussed in class with children who experience difficulties learning to read. In this field placement, each pair of students was initially assigned a struggling reader in the after-school program at one of the local schools. There were several components to the tutoring experience. Specifically, students conducted formal and informal assessments of the child's reading and writing and interpreted the findings. Next, they identified the child's literacy strengths and weaknesses and set goals for instruction. Based on these goals, preservice students designed and implemented six to eight lessons that built on the child's strengths and addressed his or her needs. Students tutored twice per week for six weeks, with each tutoring session lasting approximately 35–45 minutes. The student pair planned each lesson together, but alternated their instructional leadership. After each tutoring session, each student wrote a reflection paper discussing the successes, challenges, and concerns in the planning and implementation of the lessons. At the end of the semester, each tutoring pair submitted a tutoring log containing assessment reports, lesson plans, reflection papers, artifacts from tutoring, and a summary report detailing the areas of progress that the child has made during the tutoring program and areas of concerns for further work. The goal of the tutoring project was for preservice teachers to learn to assess children's literacy potential and use the assessment data to guide instruction.

Unfortunately, faculty faced considerable challenges when first implementing this field experience. One problem was that many parents took advantage of the after-school tutoring program on an "as-needed"

basis. In addition, some children were enrolled in other federal programs (e.g., America Reads) and school-initiated remediation programs
(e.g., Reading Rescue), or were involved in after-school sports or art
enrichment programs. Consequently, there was no guarantee of children's consistent attendance, thus the progress and even completion of
preservice teachers' course assignments was hindered. Another concern
was the lack of resources for close supervision of preservice teachers,
especially given the number of students in the UESEP program and
their tutoring schedules. Our strategy for solving these challenges was
to revamp the tutoring experience. This was accomplished by integrating the field experience for EEC 3706 with those required of the Core
Teaching Strategies (EEX 3257) and Core Management Strategies (EEX
3616) courses. Currently, students in EEC 3706 are required to complete, in pairs, three field-related projects. The first is an Observation
Report in which students describe literacy lessons over the course of a
day in the elementary classroom where they are placed, and critique
these lessons in light of the guiding principles and best practices discussed in EEC 3706. The second is the Individualized Education Plan
(IEP). In this assignment students assess a struggling reader in the same
classroom using a variety of instruments, identify the child's literacy
strengths and needs, set goals for instruction, and design five sample
lesson plans that address these goals. The third is a reflective teaching
assignment, for which students teach a literacy lesson in the same elementary classroom and write a reflective paper on the planning and
implementation of the lesson. In addition, students are encouraged to
infuse the skills and strategies they learn in EEC 3706 into the teaching
assignments required of them in EEX 3257 and EEX 3616. Two types
of field experiences accompany Language and Culture (EDG 4930), an
ESOL (English Speakers of Other Languages) foundation course that
covers basic concepts about language, language acquisition, and culture, as well as how and why these concepts are relevant to teachers.
For half of the semester, students spend time observing and assisting in
an elementary ESOL classroom for one class period (45–60 minutes)
per week for five weeks. The other half of the semester they meet one
hour per week for five weeks with an adult English learner (called a
"conversation partner") from the English Language Institute (ELI) at
UF. For each experience, students are required to keep a learning log,
noting the date, time, place, activity, and any observations or comments that may be useful in preparing their focus papers. The focus
papers are of two kinds. For a culture focus paper, students write about
their conversation partner's perceptions of certain aspects of U.S. culture and how these are similar to or different from their own home cul-

ture. Students also write about the ways in which the elementary ESOL classroom represents and celebrates students' cultures. The language focus paper requires students to write about their analysis of an oral language sample collected from the adult conversation partner or about the conversation partner's experience learning English. In the case of the elementary ESOL classroom, students can discuss the types of language functions or speech acts observed in a particular learner, or write about the effectiveness of classroom discourse (e.g., how the teacher modifies language to provide comprehensible input or, how the teacher provides opportunities for children to use language productively during the lesson). In sum, through these two types of field experiences, students work toward applying ideas about language and culture with ESL learners, thereby developing a better understanding of how culture influences language learning, communicative styles, value/belief systems, and patterns of interaction/behavior.

Semester Seven (First Semester of the Senior Year)

Mathematics/ Science/ Technology. The Mathematics, Science, and Technology (MST) faculty at UF have created a truly integrated, multidisciplinary field experience for students in the UESEP program. However, MST faculty encountered problems similar to those that occurred in the implementation of the Emergent Literacy (EEC 3706) experience. As a result, the MST faculty completely redesigned the delivery of the field experience after the first semester. The initial design was characterized by a traditional nine-week placement in schools. During the final four weeks of that experience, student triads had teaching responsibilities that were agreed upon by faculty, cooperating teachers, and students, and involved planning and carrying out instruction using resources available at the school. This approach did not last because faculty realized that the kinds of integrated experiences and resources they had envisioned for their students had not materialized in the schools. For example, some schools, in an effort to bolster student achievement, curtailed science and technology instruction so that more time could be devoted to explicit instruction in reading. At other schools, scheduling of science, math, and technology instruction simply did not coincide with course offerings students needed to take on campus. Consequently, the MST faculty used their collective resources and designed a better-quality field experience that met their objectives.

Students enrolled in SCE 4310 (Elementary Science Methods for the Inclusive Classroom), MAE 4310 (Teaching Mathematics in the

Inclusive Elementary Classroom), and EME 4406 (Integrating Technology Into the Classroom) now have a field experience that takes them to museums and nature sites in the local community. Preservice teachers are required to make visits to two of these places and develop virtual fieldtrips that are multidisciplinary and include the use of a "tech tool" such as a calculator or digital camera. In addition, preservice teachers make two visits to a camp for children run by the local school district (i.e., Camp Crystal Lake). In teams of three to four, preservice teachers attend the camp one time with an elementary school teacher and his or her class to conduct activities together, such as water quality sampling and testing. The second visit is an independent experience that gives preservice teachers an opportunity to complete activities about the ecosystem. A field advisor is assigned to attend all of the camp visits to help facilitate the activities.

Semester Eight (Second Semester of the Senior Year)

Integrated Teaching. Integrated Teaching in Elementary Education (EDE 4942) is designed as an intensive experience during the integrated semester in Language Arts for Diverse Learners (LAE 4314) and Social Studies for Diverse Learners (SSE 4312). Students complete the field experience with a partner to develop skills in collaboration to better meet the needs of all students in the elementary classroom.

Integrated Teaching consists of 15 classroom hours a week for the length of the semester with additional time spent preparing and assessing the instruction designed for, and shared with, children. Faculty in Language Arts and Social Studies education work together with Integrated Teaching faculty to design assignments for preservice teachers that combine methods and content areas across general and special education. One key assignment is the development and implementation of an integrated curriculum project (including three to five lessons) in Language Arts and Social Studies. In addition to the content integration, this assignment assists pre-service teachers in the development of modifications and accommodations for diverse learners.

The application and refinement of skills in curriculum development and implementation is one of three important skill areas that are the focus of the Integrated Teaching experience. Students are given opportunities to use these skills in teaching situations with individuals, small groups, and large groups. Preservice teachers are also taught to design instruction that is tailored to the individual learning needs of students. Course objectives related to classroom management and professional development are also important in the Integrated Teaching field experience.

Master's Program

Internship. Once students reach the graduate year, they specialize and enter a dual certification track that confers both elementary and special education certification, or a single certification track that awards elementary certification with a specialization in one of several areas (see chapter 3). Consequently, there are two separate internship experiences depending on the track chosen. Students choosing the single track complete a semester-long internship in Elementary Education (EDE 6948) while students in the dual track register for EEX 6863 Internship in Special Education. Both experiences require an additional course (EDE 6225 or EEX 6786, respectively) offered at the beginning of the semester and then periodically throughout the remainder of the semester. Practices in Childhood Education (EDE 6225) is an elementary curriculum course that focuses on taking responsibility for all children's learning through careful attention to classroom conditions, curriculum, instructional strategies, and assessment practices that enable all students to participate and learn. Transdisciplinary and Transition Services in Special Education (EEX 6786) addresses three distinct, yet overlapping areas, including professional collaboration and consultation, school change, and transition in special education.

Graduate interns spend 12 weeks in their internship classrooms with more than half of that time spent in full-time planning and teaching. These interns gradually take control of the classroom at the beginning of the semester, and then give back planning and teaching responsibilities to the teacher at the end, in the same incremental way. Interns follow the same daily schedules as their teachers, and attend all school meetings (e.g., faculty meetings, parent conferences, IEP meetings). For all interns, regardless of the track chosen (i.e., single or dual), the preferred internship placement is in an inclusive classroom setting. However, as discussed earlier, it is often difficult to find enough inclusive placements in the counties surrounding the university. Consequently, interns who request it are placed in inclusive sites away from campus, but whenever feasible, near the students' home communities. During the internship experience, students complete application assignments for EDE 6225 or EEX 6786 and a variety of activities that help them become familiar with their schools, their responsibilities as teachers, and their students For example, they communicate with parents and design and collect evaluations of their performances from cooperating teachers, families, and when appropriate, from children.

CHALLENGES AND SOLUTIONS

There are inherent challenges in the implementation of any field experience. The challenges faced by faculty in the UESEP program have been numerous. However, these challenges have allowed faculty to develop fairly creative solutions. A discussion of some of these challenges, and the ways they were resolved, follows. Three distinct categories of challenges are presented, including student-centered concerns, placements, and communication and professional development.

Student-Centered Concerns

All of the field placements require a significant amount of preservice teachers' time. Most of these students carry a full course load of 15 credit hours each semester; in addition, many hold part-time jobs to help pay their college expenses. Moreover, students are often required to complete some field-based projects in other courses that require them to spend some time, often brief, in the school or community. As a result, they feel overwhelmed. They feel hurried between courses, having to rush from school sites back to campus before their next class. Hence, students often complain about the heavy workload and the overall intensity of the semesters.

One way faculty have addressed this dilemma is to make explicit connections between the field experiences and courses during the semester. This requires communication among the instructors who teach various courses during the semester. For example, instructors who teach courses during the Bright Futures and Project Booktalk semester now make it evident on their course syllabi how the field experiences can be relevant to and integrated with their courses. For example, the Family and Community Involvement in Education course (SDS 3430) requires a "Caregiver Interview" that can be completed with caregivers in the Project Booktalk day care homes or in the Bright Futures neighborhoods. In the Child Development for Inclusive Education course (EDF 3115), students have observations and other assignments that they frequently complete with their Bright Futures children. In the Core Teaching Strategies (EEX 3257), Core Management Strategies (EEX 3616), and Emergent Literacy (EEC 3706) courses, faculty now use the same field placement for their course assignments. Another strategy for helping students is to communicate field experience expectations and time commitments in the program orientation meeting, in program materials, and on the program Web site. Also, faculty try to be careful in the language they use to identify field assignments. Specifically, faculty use the phrase "field experience" rather than "volunteering" when referring to this required component of the program.

Although students consider many of their field experiences to be eye-opening, mind-stretching experiences, sometimes the experiences backfire and reinforce students' previously held stereotypes. This is another significant problem that occasionally emerges among students. Faculty have found that the best way to address this problem is through careful supervision and to provide preservice teachers with opportunities to confront these beliefs in relevant coursework. As mentioned earlier, research supports opportunities like this that allow students to reflect on practice with guidance from faculty.

Placements

Placing students in optimal classroom settings is an ongoing challenge for teacher educators. As one might expect, situations have occurred where students were placed in settings that did not exemplify the kind of pedagogical practices that course instructors would like their students to observe and emulate. To help solve this problem, participating schools and faculty in the college worked together to model placements after practices and relationships characteristic of professional development schools (Darling-Hammond, 1994). When there is a need to reach out beyond the existing professional development schools, efforts are made, typically through staff development workshops, to ensure that participating teachers understand and are comfortable with the guiding principles and needs of the field experience. While our problems with "mismatch" are not solved, we continue to make progress.

Another problem has to do with the difficulty of finding enough classrooms in close proximity to the university campus for placements. For example, there are not enough ESOL classrooms in the local school district to accommodate preservice teachers taking the Language and Culture course (EDG 4930). Part of the problem is related to the fact that three different programs on the UF campus (e.g., Teaching English to Speakers of Other Languages certification program run by the Linguistics Department, the Early Childhood Education program, ESOL Endorsement Program) want to place their students in the limited number of ESOL classrooms available in the county. As a result, pre-professional teachers are divided up so that they work with the elementary school children half of the semester and with adult English learners the other half of the semester.

Communication and Professional Development

Despite well-intentioned efforts of faculty and school personnel to communicate, breakdowns do occur. One significant and ongoing problem is ensuring that all classroom teachers who serve as cooperating teachers are educated about the goals of the UESEP program and knowledgeable about core components of program coursework. This problem is exacerbated by a lack of resources available for cooperating teachers to engage in related professional development opportunities. However, creating circumstances that promote meaningful, ongoing dialogue between the university and schools is essential. At UF this kind of relationship has occurred in schools where partnerships have been nurtured, but these relationships are often difficult to create and maintain. In the next section, the perspective of a former school district administrator is provided to further highlight some of the issues associated with communication, collaboration, and professional development related to the UESEP program and its field experiences.

REFLECTIONS ON THE PROGRAM AND ITS FIELD EXPERIENCES FROM A DISTRICT PERSPECTIVE

Collaboration between school sites and the university is critical to the successful preparation of future teachers. Researchers and practitioners alike must move beyond Levin's (1990) early description of university and school communication as "an engagement in reality without required dialogue" (p. 63) and forge true partnerships built on trust, acceptance, and open communication. Clearly, the new design and planning process of the UESEP program represented a commitment to a collaborative relationship with the local school district.

Historically, the university and local school district participated in a positive working relationship, placing students in classrooms in traditionally designed field placements, often defined only by the number of hours spent weekly in the classroom. The newly structured field placements redefined the roles and responsibilities of both the cooperating teacher and the preservice teacher, merging coursework with meaningful field experiences. In an effort to offer a coherent field placement, multiple opportunities were provided for university and district collaboration. Key district and school personnel participated in planning meetings with university faculty, troubleshooting potential problems with issues such as scheduling, and incorporating specific teaching requirements into the already overburdened instructional day. This request for input one year prior to the implementation stage signified a true commitment to partnership on behalf of the university.

One unique feature of the UESEP field component is the assignment of preservice teachers in pairs or triads in single classroom settings, promoting reflection and a collaborative teaching model. Initially, some cooperating teachers reluctantly accepted pairs or triads into their classrooms, uncertain of the dynamics needed to support more than one preservice teacher in the classroom. However, informal interviews with cooperative teachers at the end of these first placements revealed a positive response. As one teacher reported, " Not only was it beneficial to have the support of two preservice teachers in my class, I saw dramatic growth in both participants as they strengthened the skills of one another" (see chapter 10 for more on learning in school/university partnerships). Principals and teachers alike expressed support for the program, while suggesting that the success of the placement was highly dependent upon the compatibility of the pairs or triads. This insight underscores the importance of coordinated placement decisions at the school and university level.

The theory to practice gap is a reality shared among most universities and school districts. The merging of both worlds is slowly occurring for this university and school district as formal and informal efforts break down unintentional barriers. School and district personnel serve as adjunct instructors for UESEP courses. Elementary school principals serve as representatives on the college coordinating committee that provides administrative leadership. Two professors-in-residence programs exist in the elementary schools. Grant opportunities support efforts to offer graduate credit hours for school teams interested in inclusive settings. Elementary principals participated in a yearlong administrative training in preventing early reading difficulties. All of these alliances contribute to an understanding and appreciation of each institution by the other.

The implementation of districtwide changes in field placements present challenges. The greatest challenge is providing meaningful opportunities for preservice teachers to interact with cooperating teachers. Time and scheduling restraints restrict student/teacher contact time to discuss fieldwork. These challenges are not new to field experience research, and the university and school district are seeking solutions to support meaningful communication and professional development for all.

CONCLUSION

Creating community is perhaps the most important ingredient for change (Davis & Sumara, 1997; Lave & Wenger, 1991; Lieberman, 1992; Pugach, 1999). By focusing future efforts on improving partnerships with schools and Florida communities, solutions to problems and significant changes will follow that further enhance the field experiences and ultimately the program. Teachers and college faculty must continue to value the idea that building bridges between research and practice is not sufficient. Conversely, uniting historically separate communities around common goals must be an essential aim. Although college faculty and school partners have worked diligently together to develop professional development schools, more of these kinds of partnerships must occur in the future. Progress toward this goal can occur incrementally by providing, for example, frequent opportunities for teachers and faculty to attend professional conferences with one another. Attending conferences together can stimulate productive dialogue by providing time in a context supportive of information sharing. Clearly, merging separate communities is a step in the right direction. Becoming merged communities focused on collaboration and learning can be achieved only if adequate resources are available and teachers and university faculty are rewarded for their efforts.

REFERENCES

Armaline, W., & Hoover, R. (1989). Field experiences as a vehicle for transformation: Ideology, education, and reflective process. *Journal of Teacher Education, 40*(2), 42–48.

Bondy, B., & Davis, S. (2001, April). *Lessons from ten years of a community-based field experience.* Paper presented at the meeting of the American Educational Research Association. Seattle, WA.

Darling-Hammond, L. (1994). *Professional development schools: Schools for developing a profession.* New York: Teachers College Press.

Davis, B., & Sumara, D. (1997). Cognition, complexity, and teacher education. *Harvard Educational Review, 67*(1), 105–125.

Ebby, C. B. (2000). Learning to teach mathematics differently: The interaction between coursework and fieldwork for preservice teachers. *Journal of Mathematics Teacher Education, 3*(1), 69–97.

Harper, C., Deluca, E., & Bish, D. (in preparation). *Getting a different perspective: English language learners and preservice teachers in a conversation partners program.*

Hutchinson, N. L., & Martin, A. K. (1999). Fostering inclusive beliefs and practices during preservice teacher education through communities of practice. *Teacher Education and Special Education, 22*(4), 234–250.

Lamme, L. (2000). Project Booktalk: Future teachers bring library books to day care homes. *Journal of Early Childhood Teacher Education, 21*, 85–92.

Lave, J., & Wenger, E. (1991). *Situated learning: Legitimate peripheral participation.* Cambridge, UK: Cambridge University Press.

Levin, R. (1990). Recurring themes and variations. In J. Goodlad, R. Soder, & K. Sirotnik (Eds*). Places where teachers are taught* (pp. 40–83). San Francisco: Jossey-Bass.

Lieberman, A. (1992). The meaning of scholarly activity and the building of community. *Educational Researcher, 21*(6), 5–12.

McIntyre, D. J., Byrd, D. M., & Foxx, S. M. (1996). Field and laboratory experiences. In J. Sikula, T. Buttery, & E. Guyton (Eds.), *Handbook of research on teacher education* (pp. 171–193). New York: Macmillan.

Nelson, T. (1999). Editor's introduction: Field-based teacher preparation—Experience and reflection on learning to implement and evaluate a field-based teacher education program. *Teacher Education Quarterly, 26*(2), 3–4.

O'Hair, M. J., & O'Hair, D. (1996). Connecting field experiences through communication. In D. J. McIntyre, & D. M. Byrd (Eds.), *Preparing tomorrow's teachers: The field experience, Teacher education yearbook IV,* (pp. 161–168). Thousand Oaks, CA: Corwin Press.

Pugach, M. C. (1999). Success, access, and the promise of communities of practice. *Teacher Education and Special Education, 22*(4), 269–271.

Wynn, M., & Kromrey, J. (2000). Paired peer placement with peer coaching to enhance prospective teachers' professional growth in early field experience. *Action in Teacher Education, 22*(2A), 73–83.

CHAPTER 6

Cross-Departmental
Teaching Teams

RODMAN B. WEBB, DORENE D. ROSS, AND CYNTHIA MCCALLUM

A s noted in chapter 3, in redesigning the Unified Elementary Special Education Proteach (UESEP) program, faculty were determined to create a coherent program with academic integrity. They were concerned, however, that the comprehensive nature of the program presented challenges to both coherence and integrity. They were concerned that integrating special education and general education coursework might weaken both areas. Would general education faculty have the special education knowledge necessary for successful integration of content? Would special education faculty have the content knowledge and general education knowledge they would need to teach redesigned courses? Another potential threat to coherence was that each course would be taught in multiple sections. How could the college ensure program coherence when many different people, including graduate students and adjuncts, would be responsible for teaching sections of the same course? These problems exist in many large teacher education programs but they become acute when course content cuts across traditional departmental boundaries.

To address these concerns, the planning committee (see chapter 4) formed course design teams. Typically the teams included faculty and graduate students from one or two departments, adjunct faculty, and in some cases public school faculty. In this chapter we describe the results of a study of the experiences and attitudes of course team members after the first year of implementation, and lessons learned that year.

CONTEXT AND PROCESS OF COURSE DEVELOPMENT

As described in chapters 3 and 4, faculty worked over a four-year period on various committees to create a unified program. A critical element of the design process was an emphasis on faculty collaboration. Kagan (1990) noted that successful change requires that participants have consensus about purposes and goals, and a culture that promotes collaborative problem solving and learning. For this reason Kagan argued that collaboration must become a norm in teacher education. Additionally, numerous teacher educators argue that reform in teacher education requires that faculty experiment more broadly with innovative pedagogy (Ducharme & Kluender, 1990; Holmes, 1995; Howey, 1989; NCTAF, 1996). Theories of adult learning indicate that teacher educators, like other adults, learn best when their learning opportunities are collaborative and involve others who focus on the same day-to-day work with students (Smylie, 1996). In fact, a consistent finding from research about effective staff development is that it involves significant levels of faculty collaboration and interaction (Sprinthall, Reiman, & Theis-Sprinthall, 1996). Additionally, Mersmeth (1994) noted that development of innovative pedagogy requires that faculty teach in environments that "encourage innovation and provide opportunities to share personal experience in the classroom" (p. 165). Cognizant of both the need and challenge of instructional innovation within higher education, reform reports from the '90s called for restructuring teacher education to encourage faculty to collaborate in planning, implementing, and evaluating their instruction (Goodlad, 1990; Holmes, 1995; NCTAF, 1996).

Collaboration was stressed in the development of the program and coursework (see chapter 3). As noted previously, the faculty created a program that requires integration of content and perspectives to create a coherent whole within and across courses. Thus, the program as designed requires that faculty from two departments collaborate in the design and delivery of many courses. A cross-departmental team of faculty, adjunct faculty, graduate students and in some cases public school teachers developed each course.

TEACHING TEAMS: DEFINITION AND POSSIBLE BENEFITS

It is important to note that we are talking about teaching teams and not about team teaching. In team teaching two or more faculty members plan and teach one group of students together (Cruz &

Aragoza, 1998; McDaniel & Colarulli, 1997). Unless one doubles class size, team teaching is costly and unrealistic within a large teacher education program. Instead, faculty, graduate students, and adjunct faculty have been organized into teaching teams. Each team is responsible for the instruction of approximately 210 students each year (five sections of each course one semester; two sections the other). On some of the teams, one faculty member from each of two departments teams in the coordination of the course; on other teams, one faculty member coordinates the course team. On all teams faculty work with doctoral students and/or adjunct faculty from one or two departments. All adjuncts and doctoral students are experienced teachers with recent classroom experience in elementary schools. Each team member teaches one section of the course.

Although the model involved teaching teams rather than team teaching, faculty hoped to reap similar benefits. The literature documents a number of potential benefits from team teaching. These include allowing instructors to draw on the individual strengths that each member brings to the course (McDaniel & Colarulli, 1997; Parson, 1994); encouraging team members to innovate and take risks (Parson, 1994; Robinson & Schaible, 1995); mutually reinforcing new styles of teaching; and helping to "check our ingrained tendency to slip back onto the banking mode of teaching with the student as receptacle" (Robinson & Schaible, 1995, p. 58). In addition to these benefits drawn from the literature, faculty also believed that teaching teams would help to ensure more consistency in course content across sections, an issue particularly important in a large program where part-time faculty or graduate teaching assistants teach several sections of each course.

METHODOLOGY

Several kinds of data were collected to document the experiences and attitudes of course instructors.

Program-Design Minutes and Field Notes

During the design process we kept official minutes and unofficial field notes. After meetings we circulated revised plans and sometimes open-ended questionnaires. Faculty wrote memos and made presentations at planning meetings. For this paper we analyzed these written documents to identify faculty perceptions about the potential benefits and disadvantages of teaching teams as part of the structure of the new program.

Teaching Team Feedback Meeting Field Notes

At the conclusion of the first year of instruction all course instructors were invited by Rod Webb and Dorene Ross, members of the program planning committee, to a collective meeting to describe the positive and negative aspects of their experiences during the first year of implementation. Webb led a focus-group discussion while Ross typed participants' comments into a laptop computer. Prior to the focus-group meeting, we had reviewed the faculty's early concerns list.

Although the focus-group discussion was freewheeling, Webb steered participants' attention to the three early concerns. The research team later analyzed focus-group data looking for old worries, new concerns, attitudes about collaboration, and assessment of the collaborative experience.

Team Member Survey

Drawing on data collected during the design process and at the team-teaching feedback meeting, we designed a 20-item questionnaire and distributed it to the 32 faculty and graduate students who taught program courses in the first year. Twelve faculty and nine graduate assistants returned the surveys.

Team Member Interviews

Using themes that appeared in the surveys, a semistructured interview was composed. Twelve faculty and 12 graduate assistants who had taught on teaching teams for at least two semesters were invited to participate in the interview study. Six faculty and three graduate assistants volunteered to participate in the interview study.

Below we report findings. We begin with faculty's early concerns and then report findings from the survey, focus-group discussion, and interviews.

EARLY CONCERNS OF FACULTY

When we first introduced the idea of collaborative course planning and teaching during the design process, many faculty members were apprehensive. At formal meetings and in private conversations professors expressed their worries, not as declarative sentences but rather as questions. Over time we sorted faculty concerns into three general categories: Instructional Autonomy, Instructional Improvement, and Cost-Benefit Calculations.

In early discussions, faculty asked, "Will collaborative teaching limit my instructional autonomy? Will others tell me what to teach, how to teach, and what to assign?" As discussions progressed, some worried that they might have to teach with colleagues whose philosophies, disciplines, and teaching styles differed from their own. McDaniel and Colarulli (1997) note that concern about autonomy is a major issue related to collaboration and team teaching:

> Real collaboration cannot help but create conflict; and it requires compromise, sharing of power and responsibility, exposure to ideas and teaching styles of colleagues, and loss of autonomy for faculty. Collaboration requires faculty to be responsible to each other for planning and teaching whereas previously they planned on their own time and taught in their own way. (p. 27)

An additional worry of faculty was that collaboration might not lead to instructional improvement as its advocates claimed. Individual instructors, they claimed, were best able to develop courses that were coherent and rigorous. Committees, on the other hand, would develop incoherent courses because all decisions would be the result of wrangling and compromise.

As a final concern, some critics contended that teaming, no matter how successful, would be too costly. Almost every author who writes about team teaching notes that it requires a major investment of time from participants (e.g., Bakken, Clark, & Thompson, 1998; Parson, 1994). UF faculty argued that time is an inelastic commodity. Time devoted to undergraduate teaching could not be expended on writing and research. Those latter activities, the critics contended, were essential to the life of a university and to faculty advancement. No one, they argued, was ever promoted on the basis of excellent teaching. New faculty reminded program designers that college administrators seldom mentioned teaching when discussing tenure requirements. Instead, they emphasized writing grants and publishing.

TEACHING TEAMS: LOOKING BACK AT THE FIRST YEAR

The survey results, interviews, and the field notes from the focus-group meeting revealed faculty perceptions about working in teaching teams. Faculty perceptions are organized around the early concerns expressed by faculty during the design process.

Instructional Autonomy

In the planning stages of the program, many worried that the collaboration would diminish professors' "instructional autonomy." When we asked our colleagues what they meant by "instructional autonomy," they explained that they were used to defining their own course goals, syllabi, assignments, and texts. Collaboration, they said, would make communal and public, decision making that hitherto had been individual and private.

Year-end data indicated that collaboration has dramatically changed course-related decision making. Most questionnaire respondents, focus-group participants, and interviewees said team members met regularly to discuss course content, syllabi, goals and objectives, field assignments, lesson plans, tests, and texts. What interested us, however, was that, by the end of the first year, collaboration was more praised than criticized. As we will see momentarily, faculty and graduate students no longer dreaded collaboration but, instead, listed its myriad benefits. When they had concerns, they did not direct them at collaboration, but rather at team members who had not fully participated in team activities. For example, one interviewee noted that only four of five members of their team participated in team-planning sessions. The interviewee noted: "It plagues me that we had this fifth person who (didn't participate)."

Instructional Improvements

Even in the program-planning process when resistance to collaboration was highest, few professors argued that collaboration would weaken their teaching, course content, or the teacher preparation program. Nevertheless, at the end of the implementation year we wanted to know if team members thought collaboration had improved or weakened their teaching and course content. Everyone we surveyed and interviewed reported positive collaboration outcomes. On the survey, 58% of responding professors said, "working with others enriched the content of courses" and 50% said that collaboration "stimulated instructional innovation." Seventy-five percent said collaboration improved course quality and the consistency of content across course sections. Although collaboration did at times create conflict or disequilibrium, faculty indicated that the conflict was productive. For example one interview participant expressed feeling "restrained, constricted, invaded, (and) overwhelmed" by the idea of collaboration; however, the interview ended with this faculty member's reflections on the experienced disequilibrium as being beneficial due to the process of working through conflict: "I think we are a stronger team because we have worked through so *many* things together. We have worked through things to rise to the top . . . but I learned a lot about myself, how to be patient . . . learned more about respecting other people and their philosophies and beliefs. It's been productive."

Of survey respondents 68% agreed that collaboration provided helpful structures that they modified when necessary. The same percentage said collaboration "was a great experience" for them, and 58% said teaming had been "a great experience for graduate students." Two-thirds agreed that the "course we delivered to students was improved" by collaboration. Most professors and graduate students agreed that the "content we cover in the course is about right." However, many of those responding to our survey worried that the new program perhaps was inflicting unreasonable workloads on students. Some worried, too, that students were complaining more than in the past and seemed less committed to learning.

In the focus group interview, we asked instructors to comment on the collaboration experience. These comments are typical of others we recorded:

- "I enjoyed working with my team and felt confident that our graduate students are capable instructors, although I did not observe their teaching. I would have liked to have spent more time communicating with my team members, but our schedules did not mesh well this semester. We met last week to debrief. We agreed to study the tutoring requirement and revise some of the course assignments. Otherwise, we agreed that we had a good first experience" (faculty member).
- "This is wonderful model" (faculty member).
- "We could not teach [this course] any other way. This has been a really good experience and continues to be" (graduate teaching assistant).
- "Team discussions help clarify content areas, objectives, and course goals. I enjoyed being a teaching assistant and developing the course Web site. Thank you for this opportunity" (graduate teaching assistant).

- "Because of the collaborative effort of five people, the students in the course received better instruction. Isn't that what it's all about?" (graduate teaching assistant)
- "I felt very fortunate to work with a colleague who is such an outstanding teacher. It was hard to keep up given the complicated course plans we made. I wonder how easy it is for more novice faculty and doctoral students to come in and teach like this. There are so many challenges in this new program that it is difficult to figure out how to reasonably meet them" (faculty member).

At the same time, there were some concerns about the collaboration process. In interviews some instructors, particularly graduate teaching assistants, felt that because of the team collaboration, the students perceived them as less "in control." A few believed they were evaluated more harshly because they used assignments or strategies in the course that they might not have chosen if teaching the course independently.

Collaboration Strategies

Although all professors thought collaboration had positive effects, not all teams collaborated in the same way. Collaboration strategies differed from team to team. Many met during the summer to plan their courses, but some did not. Faculty described their summer work in the year-end survey. These comments are typical:

- "The team leader drafted the syllabus, selected the texts, outlined assignments and field experience, then asked for feedback from the graduate assistants teaching sections of the course."
- "We met to plan the syllabus together. We established course objectives, assignments, and [field-experience] sites. We located and trained graduate students to teach sections of the course."
- "We met to develop course activities, lectures, and the syllabus. We basically developed most of these and refined our work during the semester."
- "We spent hours designing the course assignments, choosing a text, and setting up [field experiences]. We shared what we had done with graduate students. For the most part, all five sections used the same or similar texts, videos, assignments, and field experiences."
- "Two faculty members met several times to talk about the course framework, structure, and materials. One of us ordered

materials and drafted a syllabus and assignment descriptions. She provided syllabi and other course material to all instructors who then developed their own. A special education professor provided supplementary material for the course packet. We used any material we wanted from the course packet."

- "We met to develop the course framework. We drew heavily on the course design team's work. [One faculty member] ran three orientation sessions for three doctoral students and provided materials so doctoral students could begin their reading during the summer. We met during the week before classes to discuss the course. [The same faculty member] provided lesson plans for the first two weeks."

- "We met with school administrators to design field experiences. Taught three workshops for participating teachers. Piloted several teaching strategies in a graduate course. Designed materials, selected texts, etc."

- "We determined topics we would cover and strategies for addressing these topics. We agreed on readings for students and types of assignments they would complete. The faculty did most of this work (with graduate student suggestions)."

During the year some teams met regularly and discussed every aspect of course content and delivery. Other teams met less frequently and deferred to the leadership of one or two team members who shouldered much of the team's work. Two teams met only occasionally and reported less collaboration and more autonomy among team members. They also listed fewer benefits for teaming than professors on more collaborative teams.

One or two professors felt they carried a greater load than their fellow team members and worked to balance their sense of responsibility with their sense of fair play. "I'm struggling with my sense of responsibility," one interviewee explained. "That is, for whom and for what am I responsible? My own students? The program's reputation and quality?"

A few professors worried that they had not contributed as much as other faculty on their team. In an interview, one faculty member expressed guilt over not contributing as much as a colleague. She said, "I felt bad. The other person on our team got credit for coaching the doc students, so he took it upon himself to set up the weekly meetings with them and that time did not work well for me. I think I probably went to one, maybe two meetings all semester long. I felt bad about that. I don't think he minded. I apologized."

Some faculty acknowledged that they were not as committed to teaching and collaboration as others on their team and that they did not carry as much of the load as their colleague. They tended to think that their colleague's commitment to teaching was unusual and perhaps inappropriately high. They struggled to balance their sense of fair play with their commitments to grant work and research agendas. They worried that they might be criticized for not pulling their full team load but pointed out that they had volunteered to teach in the UESEP program when many of their colleagues had refused.

Most, but not all, graduate students reported that collaboration had helped them consider course goals, plan lessons, develop a syllabus and assignments, choose a text, and become better college teachers. One said, in the focus group interview, that she had been left pretty much alone and wished she had received more help. Another, in comments on the survey, worried that some graduate students might have too much autonomy: "I was completely on my own for all teaching aspects of this course. There was *no* collaboration, although the instructor with whom I had previously worked offered to help. Luckily, my students did not suffer because I had [a lot of] teaching experience. But I could have been better with collaboration."

Cost-Benefit Calculations

In the early going, many professors worried the new program would be so labor-intense that it would tax faculty resources and divert faculty efforts away from research and service activities. At the end of the first year we asked participating faculty about time and workload concerns. We asked faculty and teaching assistants how many hours a week they devoted to course preparation. Thirty percent of survey respondents indicated that they worked fewer than eight hours a week preparing for their course. Sixty percent devoted eight or more hours to these tasks.

All professors said that collaboration was more time-consuming than working alone. Two-thirds said planning and teaching a new course took more time than they expected and the rest said it took more time than developing a course on their own. Three professors said supervising graduate students took more time than they had expected. Four of 12 (33%) professors said the collaboration "took too much time and my writing and research suffered." Teaching assistants, on the other hand, said teaming had saved them time and that they learned from team discussions.

Half of the professors said the course preparation time had been "extensive" but noted that they were teaching a new course. They expected that when they were more familiar with the course it would take less time and they would be better able to balance the demands of teaching with those of research and writing. Forty-two percent of professors said they were conducting or planning research on the new program. Such studies included students' perceptions of the new program, student work and workloads, school/university partnerships, and students' perceptions of the impact of field experiences.

Three of nine graduate students said they were overwhelmed by course preparation work and the same number said that their studies suffered because of their teaching obligations. Six of nine said that teaming "was a great learning experience." The amount of faculty involvement seemed to influence graduate students' perceptions of the teaming experience. For example, in interviews one graduate student reported that the mentoring involved was invaluable, while another spoke of frustration over feeling like an "outsider" in the program. She noted that the supervising faculty member on her team was not teaching the course during that semester, placing the team at a disadvantage. She explained, "For the longest time I didn't realize there was a reflection theme going on here. How are you supposed to know that stuff? I don't know. Sometimes I don't feel like I'm as much in the know as I should be. I'm just kind of trying to keep my head above water here."

LESSONS LEARNED

Perhaps one swallow does not make a summer, but the arrival of the first swallow is usually a harbinger of warmer days to come. We say the same from our first course team evaluation. One set of positive data does not indicate that our goals have been met or that our work is complete, but positive findings suggest that we are making progress.

The data clearly show that faculty shifted their concerns during the implementation year. The general worries professors expressed in the planning stages of the program diminished or disappeared as faculty experienced collaboration. The skepticism that accompanied early debates was replaced by pragmatic, program-delivery conversations. Faculty who initially worried about instructional autonomy issues were now concerned with student workloads, course content, and the quality of their collaboration experience.

Additionally, there are indications that collaboration has diminished instructor isolation and opened valuable conversations about teaching and learning. The teaming process has proven to be a powerful professional development tool in the college. Collaboration has opened conversations about course content, teaching, learning, rigor, program continuity, and the possibility of continuous improvement. In an interview, one adjunct faculty member described the value of keeping these conversations going, and the value of the influence on one another that teaming fosters:

> I think I influence the people I work with. Some are irritated with me, but that's okay. I don't want to be a constant irritant, (so sometimes) I will keep my mouth shut. But I do believe in education we need to change. I can think of three people I have really influenced in their teaching. I have challenged others. I know that. But if we could come together as faculty and share professionally we could affect so much ... that atmosphere must be protected by leadership.

Indeed, we cannot imagine a more powerful, structurally integrated, inexpensive, professional development mechanism for higher education.

Our work with teaching teams has just begun. Although we are reluctant to suggest that collaborative course delivery is an innovation, it is nevertheless true that within higher education, collaborative course delivery is not standard practice. As we have worked through the first year of implementation, we have learned several lessons that may help others experimenting with similar strategies to improve teacher education pedagogy.

1. As is so often true in life (and certainly in any change effort), the anticipation is worse than the reality. Faculty anxiety about the move to teaching teams was very high during the planning process. It is important to note that one cannot plan away anxiety about change. Planning is important. It gives voice to faculty concerns and highlights issues that must be attended to in the change process; however, our experience suggests that anxiety continues until faculty have the opportunity to work their way through it. It was in the process of working through the details of implementation that faculty anxiety gave way to concerns about course quality and student learning.

2. A related lesson was that concerns about faculty autonomy became less significant as faculty began to engage in collaborative decision making. In the abstract, faculty expressed concern about threats to instructional autonomy. However, during implementation most reported that the collaborative dialogue about instructional content and strategies enhanced rather than constrained their instructional effectiveness.

3. Volunteerism is not as important as the skills, knowledge, and commitment that team members bring to the group. The literature suggests that team teaching works best when participants volunteer to participate (Bakken, Clark & Thompson, 1998; Cruz & Zaragoza, 1998). Although it certainly makes sense to use volunteers, in our context this was not possible. Because the entire program was restructured, everyone who teaches in the program is required to become a member of a teaching team. And membership on a team was determined by one's expertise and course teaching background. Faculty were justifiably concerned about whether this kind of "forced" collaboration could succeed. However, our first year of implementation suggests that this kind of collaboration can in fact work quite well. However, not all teams work equally well. Faculty experience suggests that teams work best when each team member contributes a fair share of knowledge, expertise, commitment, and time, and demonstrates a willingness to learn from others. A significant discrepancy in any of these areas throws a team into disequilibrium. Although team members stressed the need for different backgrounds and diverse ideas for a rich team, they also identified the necessity for respect among colleagues and the ability of team members to accept disequilibrium. When disagreement occurred on teams, the way these differences were handled affected team members' perceptions of the experience. Some teams simply agreed to disagree, others fought through the issues with emotions, while others simply reported no significant differences. Disagreement sometimes caused hurt feelings, even in successful teams. However, embracing disequilibrium as a mechanism for discussion and change seemed to create a successful team.

4. Similarly, not all teams looked alike. As a matter of fact idiosyncrasy seemed to be the only consistency across teams. Team structure, and even participation, depended on the perceived need for meeting. Some teams had full participation, while others had one absentee member who simply withdrew from "the team." However, nonparticipation was the exception. The individualization of each team was derived from contextual factors, such as location of offices, technology, and frequency of meetings. Successful communication

seemed to stem from friendships, flexibility, role definitions, and common expectations.
5. Faculty concerns suggested structural issues that the college has not yet dealt with. The faculty involved in this
first year of implementation clearly reported that teaching
as a part of a team within this teacher education program
is time-consuming work. They acknowledged the importance of this work but expressed concerns about the time
commitment involved. Every faculty member in a large
research university has to make decisions about the
appropriate balance between teaching and research.
Faculty teaching on teams expressed concerns about
equity and rewards. Will faculty who work on teaching
teams, especially those who take leadership roles, be
rewarded for this work? Will faculty who opt for teaching assignments where collaboration is not necessary
achieve greater success in research and grant productivity
(and therefore greater access to the "fast track" to success)? These questions have not been resolved, but faculty
working in this program do find benefits to collaboration
and several are working to invent ways to combine teaching and research productivity. Faculty are designing
research projects around their work in teacher education,
often projects that include graduate students. This
approach will work for some faculty. For others, whose
research agenda is not a clear match with teacher education, the tension between teaching and research may
become more intense over time.

CONCLUSION

At the end of this first year of implementation, faculty and graduate students on this first set of teams say that the effort was time-consuming, but they also have found it rewarding. Many faculty report
that their courses and their teaching improved. Graduate students seem
more confident in the content and pedagogy provided in their courses
and faculty are more confident that courses within the program, including courses taught by graduate assistants and part-time faculty, are
coherent and consistent with program purposes.

As we noted, we make no claim that collaborative course delivery
is an innovation. On the contrary, we would argue that collaboration is

fundamental to academic work and an essential part of academic freedom. If it appears to some that collaboration is a radical departure from current practice, that is only because we have strayed too far from our first and most essential obligation: namely to deliver coherent, integrated, sequential, and rigorous academic programs to our students.

REFERENCES

Bakken, L., Clark, F. L., & Thompson, J. (1998). Collaborative teaching: Many joys, some surprises, and a few worms. *College Teaching, 46*(4), 154–157.

Cruz, B. C., & Zaragoza, N. (1998). Team teaching in teacher education: Intra-college partnerships. *Teacher Education Quarterly, 25*(1), 53–62.

Ducharme, E., & Kluender, M. M. (1990). The RATE study: The faculty. *Journal of Teacher Education, 41*(4), 45–49.

Goodlad, J. (1990). *Teachers for our nation's schools.* San Francisco: Jossey-Bass.

Holmes Group. (1995). *Tomorrow's schools of education.* East Lansing, MI: Author.

Howey, K. (1989). Research about teacher education: Programs of teacher preparation. *Journal of Teacher Education, 40*(6), 23–26.

Kagan, D. M. (1990). Teachers "workplace" meets "professors of education": A chance encounter at 30,000 feet. *Journal of Teacher Education, 41*(5), 46–53.

McDaniel, E. A., & Colarulli, G. C. (1997). Collaborative teaching in the face of productivity concerns: The dispersed team model. *Innovative Higher Education, 22*(1), 19–36.

Mersmeth, K. K. (1994). The design of teacher education programs. In K. R. Howey, & N. L Zimpher (Eds.), *Informing faculty development for teacher educators* (pp. 139–174). Norwood, NJ: Ablex Publishing Corporation.

National Commission on Teaching and America's Future. (1996). *What matters most: Teaching for America's future.* New York: Author.

Parson, S. R. (1994). Program development, team instruction, and the impact on faculty members. *NASSP Bulletin, 78*(559), 62–64.

Robinson, B., & Schaible, R. M. (1995). Collaborative teaching: Reaping the benefits. *College Teaching, 43*(2), 57–59.

Smylie, M. A. (1996). From bureaucratic control to building human capital: The importance of teacher learning in educational reform. *Educational Researcher, 25*(9), 9–11.
Sprinthall, N. A., Reiman, A. J., & Theis-Sprinthall, L. (1966). Teacher professional development. In J. Sikula, T. Buttery, & E. Guyton (Eds.), *Handbook of Research on Teacher Education,* (2nd ed., pp. 666–703). New York: Macmillan.

CHAPTER 7

The Unified Elementary Program: Discussion and Critique

MARLEEN C. PUGACH

The prior four chapters describe the structure, history, and development of the Unified Elementary Special Education Proteach
(UESEP) program, provide detailed descriptions of the various field
experiences, and document the initial reactions of faculty who participated in the early stages of collaboration as they taught as members of
teaching teams. Together these four chapters portray a faculty working
together to transform the basic conception of what it means to prepare
a teacher well for contemporary schools. The program they developed
adheres to several of the qualities of coherent and effective teacher education practices as described by Howey (1996):

- conceptual framework and derivative themes,
- student cohorts,
- student portfolios, and
- a core curriculum.

Howey (1996) also called on teacher education to develop pedagogical
laboratories located on campus sites. The UESEP program works
instead with a variety of sites in the local public schools, including for-
mally identified professional development schools, as well as in other
local social service and educational agencies.

Chapters such as these are extremely helpful to teacher educators
who are involved in—and wish to move in the direction of—the radical
reconceptualization of teacher education precisely because they provide
a clear picture of what the new programs look like and how they function, but also how faculty and administrators in higher education actually go about the business of systemic reform in relationship to the

115

organizational structure of their particular institution of higher education. Further, this section of the book attests to the simple fact that the
reform of teacher education is possible. The fact that reform is possible,
however, belies the difficulties associated with getting there and the
complex issues that need to be addressed along the way.

My response to these four chapters is organized in three sections.
First, I will address themes that emerge across the chapters themselves,
with an eye toward the relationship between local and national themes
in teacher education reform. Following this, I pose and discuss several
questions these chapters raise in terms of the content and structure of
the UESEP program. The chapter concludes with a section on what can
be learned from the experience of the University of Florida program
reform and what this experience holds for other institutions of higher
education as they engage in local reform efforts, as well as what the UF
experience may mean for the collective project of teacher education
reform nationally.

LOCAL THEMES IN TEACHER EDUCATION REFORM

Three themes related to the process of reform arise in the discussion of the UESEP program. These themes are illustrative of the challenges that face all teacher education programs as they push ahead to
improve their programs. Although some of the themes echo concerns
that have been raised in the literature on teacher education reform, it is
instructive to see how they play out in a local context and how the faculty at the University of Florida responded to these challenges.

Theme 1: Reform is hard work that must be sustained over time to be successful

Collectively, these four chapters portray the huge effort that is
needed not only to reconceptualize programs, but also to implement
programs that are based on much greater levels of interaction and
responsibility for the quality of preservice teachers' experiences. In the
reconceptualization phase, faculty at the University of Florida continued their reform efforts even when their first pass at a redesign was not
well received among their colleagues. The notion of reform being hard
work, work at which faculty must persist over several years, is not
often enough discussed among teacher educators as they engage in their
efforts. The conventional notion that real reform takes between five
and seven years is no less true for reforming teacher education than it is

for reforming K–12 education, and it is illustrated well in the experience at the University of Florida, where it took nearly five years from initial inception to implementation.

Once the program approval phase was reached, the work had in reality only begun. The chapters described more hard work embodied in recursive efforts to improve the original design in at least four crucial areas, each requiring serious attention:

1. The relationship of courses to one another.
2. The content and structure of field experiences in relationship to the courses.
3. The development of school-university partnerships for the purpose of creating model sites for internships.
4. The transition to teaching in teams.

The authors in chapter 4 attributed some of their success in achieving reform to luck. It is not clear, however, that luck played as great a role as did the raw effort it took to engage in sustained planning and implementation over time. Further, rather than viewing barriers that were encountered along the way as obstructions to reform, each was approached as a problem to be solved (Fullan, 1993), and in several cases, to be worked on over time from a continuous improvement perspective. The requirement for universal ESOL (English Speakers of Other Languages) preparation is one good example. Although this mandate required a shift in program design, it was not allowed to derail the curriculum development process.

The authors did not specify precisely the contributions the codirectors of the reform process made to ensure that the effort continued and reached fruition. Given the length of time needed to create and revise the curriculum, cycle through the university governance hurdles, and embark on the implementation phase, consistent leadership over time was no doubt a critical factor in keeping the work front and center. The leadership displayed sensitivity and responsiveness to faculty concerns while continuing to push toward the goal. They also were able to sustain program development and implementation during changes in the college's central administration. Thus, although the entire effort was initiated by the dean in 1995, ownership was taken by faculty leaders who provided consistency in the face of subsequent administrative shifts.

Theme 2: Changing the culture of the organization

A second theme that reverberated across the chapters was the importance of changing the culture of the organization to support program development and implementation. Several instances were presented. For example, multiple stakeholders representing a wide range of faculty participated actively on the design teams, and their ideas were all given serious consideration in the design process. This process represented a level of collaboration that is not characteristic of most institutions of higher education, and inadvertently provided faculty with practice in the art of collaboration that is central to the faculty teams who deliver the program.

Second, attention was paid to how to support faculty collaboration, and a series of explicit strategies were put into place to address the need to develop a more collaborative culture. These srategies included a program of minigrants, as well as a specific set of guidelines for how collaboration was to be interpreted from the perspective of faculty load. Addressing the issue of how to foster collaboration was central to moving the work forward. (After a year of working in the program, it appears that faculty clearly value collaboration however, they still express concern about meeting the obligations of the academy when their work at the preservice level is so labor intensive.)

A third example of structural change is related to school-university partnerships. The authors refer to professional development schools as one important source of sites for internships. Such partnership development presents challenges to conventional notions of higher education and the role of faculty members. The authors did not provide much detail about the development of these partnerships, the range of faculty who are involved, and administrative or governance implications of these changes. However, it appears that several important relationships exist between the local schools, local agencies and organizations, and the College of Education to support the program. How much these various partnerships actually change the culture of the organization represents an important aspect of the theme of organizational change.

Theme 3: Resources to support reformed teacher education

This is perhaps a subtle theme that is threaded throughout the chapters, a null theme in fact, much like the concept of the null curriculum (Eisner, 1979)—but it is crucial to consider as the national project to reform teacher education moves forward. Like other faculties who are taking the charge to reform seriously, faculty at the University of Florida created a labor-intensive program that is heavily field-based and that demands more of its faculty and its students. Nowhere, however, did the authors state that significant new resources were available to them as they took on this monumental task. Instead, they appeared to make do with what they already had. For example, graduate students took on variations in their roles as field supervisors, and faculty loads were tinkered with to provide leadership for the interdisciplinary teams. Temporary new resources were available in the form of a $250,000 BellSouth grant, chiefly for program development and evaluation. However, no discussion of base budget increase to support the program redesign over time appears in the program descriptions and analyses.

It would seem reasonable to expect that the combination of the investment of faculty time, the relationship between the program development effort and the local PreK–12 schools, and the implications for how faculty work is rewarded might be accompanied by budgetary changes. The authors allude to the fact that some faculty expressed concern that the program redesign might inappropriately redirect resources to teacher education (from faculty research and graduate programs). Leaders of the reform effort wisely reflected the position that graduate education and teacher education are not mutually exclusive undertakings. Nevertheless, the intent of the redesign is clear in terms of the expectations for improving the preparation of beginning teachers. The human resource investment is well documented in these chapters. No evidence of a parallel level of fiscal investment, however, is apparent in the discussion. It seems crucial for program descriptions to include some attention to the economics of reform as a measure of the worth of faculty efforts in assuring that program redesign is accomplished.

SUBSTANTIVE QUESTIONS ACROSS THE CHAPTERS

These four chapters leave the reader with a good sense of the program structure, historical view of its development, and a realistic view of the problems and challenges the faculty faced in the earliest stages of implementation. Collectively the chapters certainly raise issues related to the themes identified above. In this section, however, I would like to raise three questions about the curriculum itself and its relationship to the major program goals and program themes that surface as a result of how the program is framed. The major program goals as stated in chapter 3 are:

- Preparing teachers who are capable of creating and maintaining supportive and productive classrooms for diverse learners.
- Preparing teachers who work collaboratively with school personnel, families, and members of the community to develop alternative ways of educating all children, including those who

have traditionally been labeled hard-to-teach and hard-to-manage and students who are linguistically diverse.
- Preparing teachers to work with students who are English Speakers of Other Languages.
- Preparing special education teachers to serve effectively as consulting teachers with their elementary teacher colleagues.

In addition, chapter 3 authors describe the two overarching themes of the program, which provide consistency and a conceptual framework to UESEP:

1. A commitment to democratic values, a democratic society, and the value of equity in education and society.
2. Knowledge of content and inclusive pedagogy, sufficiently developed to assure that teachers can make good decisions about the content and organization of the elementary curriculum.

How these goals and themes play out across the program is the focus of both of the questions in this section.

Question 1: How are the themes and goals connected over time?

Across the chapters, much is made of the importance of collaboration. The initial data offered in chapter 6 document the positive feelings faculty have about engaging in collaborative program development and delivery despite the labor-intensive nature of the commitment. The emphasis on collaboration is predicated on the need to achieve coherence and consistency across the program. The authors have provided a good picture of the difficulties of implementing collaboration as a general practice—for example, the time it takes to prepare for a new course as part of a team, the time that is taken away from research to engage in program delivery, the challenges of being responsible to others in considering what will and will not go into a particular course. We also have a good sense of how positive and powerful a force collaboration can be, even in the face of initial skepticism, in helping focus on the quality of one's teaching.

It is not clear, however, how the faculty makes decisions specifically about the content of the curriculum and how they are sharing the responsibility for addressing the goals and themes of the program. Are goals and themes apportioned to specific courses? Are they spiraled across the students' courses and experiences? What are the big issues that faculty members spend the greatest time and energy deliberating on, and how do they resolve their differences? In other words, what is the substance of the collaboration in which faculty are engaged?

Questions of substance are critical because it is within the deliberations over substance that consistency is or is not achieved within a teacher education program. How different instructors address the themes, and what students make of their instructors' points of view, are ripe areas for study as teacher educators make the transition from being responsible for individual courses to being responsible to a coherent program based on shared themes and goals. Obviously, in an era of performance-based assessment, the proof of consistency is in what graduates know and are able to do once they enter the classroom. In addition the culture of the school site remains a strong socialization factor in what new teachers do in their first years of teaching (Zeichner & Gore, 1990). The challenge of teacher education reform is to reduce the gap between what takes place during preservice education and in practice in the schools. As more programs design and practice thematically driven teacher education, data on how these themes play out in various programs will be a much needed addition to the literature on teacher education.

Question 2: How is diversity addressed?

These chapters convey well the programmatic commitment to preparing teachers to work with a diverse student population and the families of their students. Diversity is defined as being all-inclusive, covering diversity of language, socioeconomic levels, gender, race, ethnicity, and disability. Students have field experiences in multiple settings that emphasize various kinds of diversities. As faculty members plan for their courses, and more importantly, as they teach their courses, what are they communicating about diversity, and is the message consistent?

This is an important question because issues around the various diversities are not necessarily the same. (How are faculty helping students make distinctions between their responsibilities for being culturally responsive teachers, for example, and their different—but no less important—responsibilities for being responsive to the needs of students with disabilities, who may or may not also be students of color or students from low socio-economic groups [Pugach & Seidl, 1998]?) How do faculty present these distinctions? More importantly, what kinds of assumptions do faculty themselves make about the relationship among the various diversities and what the important distinctions are among them? Finally, how are assessments relative to diversity interpreted to ensure that appropriate distinctions are made between the sensitivity and skill required for working with students with disabilities and that required for working with students from multiple cultures and multiple language groups?

Efforts to prepare new teachers for working with diverse student populations is one of the strongest rationales for program redesign nationally, and no less so in the UESEP program. The theme of democratic education based on providing equitable education for all students is an appropriate umbrella for addressing the needs of various groups of students. It is in the nuances of program delivery, however, that the operational definitions of diversity and equity are worked out, and so, those nuances need to be brought to the surface and purposefully discussed and deliberated upon to build common understandings that can lead to program coherence.

Question 3: How is "inclusive pedagogy" defined?

Related to the question of defining diversity is how faculty in the program define *inclusive pedagogy*. The term inclusive education is chiefly associated with special education. If the program is using the term *inclusive pedagogy* to denote any approach a White teacher uses to meet the array of needs of students of multiple diversities, a huge potential pitfall exists in terms of how preservice students view the way they construct and implement their curriculum.

For example, it is possible that White teacher candidates may interpret *culturally relevant pedagogy* as *inclusive pedagogy*, potentially confusing the need for their own growth and development relative to cultural knowledge and cultural perspective-taking with making specific accommodations and modifications for students with disabilities. Clearly, these are not the same kinds of curriculum decisions and are based on very different views of what it means to work with diverse learners. Both sets of knowledge and experience are necessary for prospective teachers to be prepared to work with the full range of diverse students, but they do not both fall under the conventional definition of inclusive education. While it is clear that the UESEP program theme of inclusive pedagogy is not limited to working well with students with disabilities, how faculty use this terminology and how students perceive this terminology are critical issues to study.

These distinctions are particularly important in redesigned programs that purposefully integrate special and general teacher preparation, as is the case in the UESEP program. Several methods courses in this program specifically include in their titles the phrase *for the inclusive classroom*. Further, all students take courses in core teaching strategies and core management strategies, much of which is associated with highly explicit instructional and management approaches. That these approaches are emphasized in these courses is not in itself problematic; after all, in all classrooms there are students who need greater and lesser degrees of explicit, teacher-directed instruction and explicit, extrinsic forms of behavior management. What is potentially problematic is how preservice students relate the various pedagogies they learn, and how the faculty frames the "big picture" of instruction to enable students to use the repertoire of methods they acquire wisely. Do graduates simply believe they have acquired a bigger bag of pedagogical tricks, or do they have a way of making sense of the various methods they are learning? (The assessment process should be a tool to help faculty see if preservice teachers are making inappropriate assumptions about which methods are appropriate for which students. In addition, it is particularly important to determine if they are inappropriately making decisions about which students need more explicit instruction and extrinsic management strategies based on group membership rather than on individual need.)

Obviously, questions related to how themes are carried out across the program, how the concept of diversity is played out in every course and field experience, and how students view the concept of inclusive pedagogy are related to one another. As the program progresses, these issues all constitute areas for study that can inform not only UESEP, but other redesigned programs nationally, especially those that have actively pursued linkages between special and general teacher education.

THE UESEP EXPERIENCE: LESSONS LEARNED

The program descriptions offered in these chapters provide several important lessons for the national project of reforming teacher education.

Lesson 1: Resources matter.

Several sources of financial support were available to develop the new program. First and foremost, the institution received two federal grants to pilot unified programs in both early childhood and elementary education prior to the collegewide program redesign. Funded by the Department of Education's Office of Special Education Programs, these two preliminary efforts afforded some of the UF faculty the opportunity to participate directly in new relationships with one another. Also, the efforts provided graduate student support for prospective faculty members who might implement such collaborative programs themselves upon completing their doctoral programs. Faculty were able to build upon these experiences in crafting the final content and structure of the new program. Further, as a result of these grants, at least some faculty developed experience in what it meant to collaborate in the delivery of teacher education programs. In addition to these pilot programs, the $250,000 grant from BellSouth provided funds for development and evaluation. It also enabled faculty to secure minigrants as they made the transition from the traditional individual model of teaching to a collaborative model.

These external funding sources remind us that program development itself is costly work, in terms of both human and financial resources. While it is certainly the case that program development can take place on hard money alone, the sustained efforts needed to accomplish change of this magnitude are helped significantly when there is flexibility that external funds offer. However, temporary funds do not replace the need to recognize that achieving the highest quality programs of teacher education will require permanent funding sources far beyond those that are typically earmarked for teacher education. Various team-teaching configurations are costly, as are building solid, long-term partnerships with the public schools with institutionalized supports for supervising field experiences, reimbursed internships, and mentoring support for new teachers. Further, more complex systems of student assessment require resources to implement the assessments and track student progress. This is not business as usual in teacher education. Resources matter for program development, but they matter as well in terms of changing the regularities of program funding to enable high-quality teacher education to be implemented once the planning phases are completed.

Lesson 2: Professional development schools may only be a partial answer to the question of field experience sites.

In planning this program, faculty developed a wide-ranging set of field experiences in local school sites, in agency sites, and in long-distance school sites. One of the most important activities in relationship to field experience in this program development effort was creating new inclusive education sites where general elementary and special education elementary preservice students could spend protracted amounts of time. Some of the sites for field experiences were formal professional development schools, while many others were not.

The lesson this situation underscores is that a limited number of professional development schools will not be able to fill the needs of a large teacher education program that includes multiple field experiences for multiple purposes. The PDS sites appear to be important field experience sources for the UESEP program and providing support for them is a crucial issue for the program. However, whether or not the university and the local county schools can enter into a more extensive partnership that might lead to systemic change across the county schools is an important possibility to pursue. Entering into a long-term partnership for the express purpose of achieving systemic change is a much different undertaking than creating a solid relationship with a limited number of schools that nevertheless provide excellent models for a small number of students.

Lesson 3: Patience is still a virtue.

Any program reform effort that is to be sustained over time requires the kind of work that is exemplified in the development phase of the UESEP program. There are no quick fixes, especially in light of the institutionalized, organizational change that is required to redesign teacher education. Concomitant with the theme of reform being hard work that was raised across these four chapters, one of the essential lessons to be learned is that faculty and administrators who are engaged in this work need to recognize that change takes time.

This means that everyone involved in the process must recognize that it will take time to transform teacher education. Keeping the goal of high quality teacher education for the purpose of serving PreK–12 students at the forefront of faculty discourse about the program in which they are teaching is a crucial change for teacher education. Keeping your eyes on the prize, as it were, continues to be good advice, and provides the motivation to keep at the work of program reform and then program improvement once the initial reforms are in place.

CONCLUSION

Faculty in the College of Education at the University of Florida have undertaken a serious redesign of their elementary teacher education programs, adhering to much of the national discourse on what constitutes high-quality teacher education. By embarking on this work, they have demonstrated a deep commitment to preparing their graduates for teaching positions in today's complex and diverse classrooms. Faculty have worked together to create a program that sets new standards for what teachers should know and be able to do and have done so in the face of several potentially diversionary setbacks.

Now that the program is in place, two goals seem most critical. The first is a commitment to continuous improvement, and an acceptance that reform is only the starting point to ensuring that the quality of the program is sustained over time, in the face of changes in faculty and administration. The second is to use the data that accrue from the assessment process as the basis for informing the cycle of continuous improvement.

As more and more institutions of higher education engage in reform efforts similar to those at the University of Florida, these collective experiences will teach us much about the relationship among organizational change, collaboration, school-university partnerships, and improving how we prepare the nation's teachers.

REFERENCES

Eisner, E. W. (1979). *The educational imagination*. New York: Macmillan.
Fullan, M. (1994). *Change forces: Probing the depths of educational reform*. London: Falmer Press.
Howey, K. (1996). Designing coherent and effective teacher education programs. In J. Sikula, T. J. Buttery, & E. Guyton (Eds.), *Handbook of research on teacher education* (2nd ed., pp. 143–170). New York: Macmillan.
Pugach, M. C., & Seidl, B. L. (1998). Responsible linkages between diversity and disability: A challenge for special education. *Teacher Education and Special Education, 21*(4), 319–333.
Zeichner, K. M., & Gore, J. M. (1990). Teacher socialization. In W. H. Houston (Ed.), *Handbook of research on teacher education* (pp. 329–348). New York: Macmillan.

PART 3

Participant Perspectives

CHAPTER 8

Communication and Conflict
on Three Teaching Teams

MARY T. BROWNELL, JAMES MCLESKEY, PATRICIA ASHTON,
DAVID HOPPEY, AND RHONDA NOWACK

Because collaboration is at the core of the Unified Elementary Special Education Proteach (UESEP) program, we turn again in this chapter to the experience of faculty on teaching teams. Teaming presents challenges to most faculty members. When the members of a team come from different departments, those challenges can be magnified. Faculty from different disciplines (e.g., special education, curriculum and instruction, counseling) have various assumptions about their roles and responsibilities, and often come to a collaborative endeavor with differing beliefs about teaching, learning, and student discipline, among other things. This chapter examines the tensions that can arise when faculty members attempt to work across the borders of their discipline, and how these tensions affect the collaboration that occurs, and ultimately, the products of their work.

To provide a clear focus for this chapter, we examined the work of three teaching teams that worked across the borders of two departments—the School of Teaching and Learning (STL—called Curriculum and Instruction in many settings) and Special Education (SE). These teams were charged with developing courses that addressed emergent literacy, classroom management, and classroom instructional methods. We anticipated that faculty teams would have quite different perspectives regarding the content and delivery of these courses. This perspective was based, to a large extent, on our knowledge of the professional literature in general and special education. This literature suggests that faculty from general and special education tend to have strikingly different views of teaching, learning, and discipline (e.g., Heshusius, 1989; Skrtic, 1991; 1995). For example, special education instructional practice has been dominated for many decades by the perspective that "truth" in the social sciences can be determined through careful, systematic study. This truth then leads to scientifically based, validated interventions that may be used to help students with disabilities acquire certain skills in the most efficient manner possible.

In contrast to this perspective, faculty in general education tend to believe that a specific set of validated interventions does not exist. Instead, they believe that the teacher should use judgment in selecting practices that are appropriate for the students, the subject matter, and the objectives of the lesson. Thus, they subscribe to a more constructivist, child-centered view of learning (Grennon-Brooks & Brooks, 1999; Zemelman, Daniels, & Hyde, 1998). Hence, from the general educator's perspective, what children learn depends, to a large extent, on their prior knowledge, both informational and cultural, the social context in which they are taught (Irvine & Armento, 2001), and the degree to which the teacher can help them make connections between the known and the new. In contrast, special educators believe that students learn as a result of the use of effective, explicit instructional strategies that are faithfully delivered by the teacher.

Although differences between special and general educators' views of instruction and discipline historically have been dramatic, events since the mid-1980s (e.g., Biklen, 1985; Gartner & Lipsky, 1987; Reynolds, Wang, & Walberg, 1987; Will, 1986) have provided an opportunity for these professionals to come together and develop more integrated views of curriculum, instruction, and classroom management/discipline. The emphasis on the regular education initiative (Will, 1986) and later inclusion of students with disabilities in general education classrooms (Skrtic, 1991) began this movement. The 1997 reauthorization of the Individuals with Disabilities Education Act (IDEA), mandating that children with disabilities have access to the general education curriculum, has made this collaboration difficult to avoid. To achieve access to the general education curriculum for students with disabilities, special educators must consider how the general education curriculum is organized and delivered to students, while general educators must consider how they will provide the supports necessary within that curriculum to ensure that students with disabilities have appropriate access. The importance of aligning practices in general and special education is rapidly becoming evident in the number of dual, blended, and unified teacher education programs that have emerged in the last few years (Blanton, Griffin, Winn, & Pugach, 1997; Sherry & Spooner, 2000).

Webb, Ross, and McCallum (see chapter 6) described the development of cross- departmental teams and the overall perspectives of faculty about these teams. In this chapter we describe in detail how the collaborative process worked as three teams of educators developed courses that addressed classroom management and student discipline (Team 1), emergent literacy (Team 2), and instructional methods (Team 3) as part of the UESEP program. We further describe the tensions that emerged as this collaborative work proceeded. To gain insight into these issues, we interviewed the two primary faculty on each of these teams, one from STL and one from SE.

THE NATURE OF COLLABORATION ON THE THREE TEAMS

The initial expectations for collaboration in the unified program and how faculty actually collaborated provide a backdrop for understanding how different perspectives arose and the tensions that evolved surrounding those perspectives. In the UESEP program, high expectations existed for collaboration. Some of the most significant players involved in the creation of the program described these expectations as follows: "The program as designed requires that faculty from two or more departments collaborate in the design and delivery of every course. In addition, the program requires that faculty teaching courses within a common semester coordinate academic and field experience expectations. Thus, the redesigned program demands a great deal of collaboration" (Ross, Correa, & Webb, 1999, p. 4). The three teams of faculty we interviewed provided similar perspectives regarding how the collaborative planning process was intended to work (the ideal of collaborative teaming) as courses were developed, implemented, and monitored. This process is reflected in the following three aspects of collaboration, as described by the faculty who were involved in these endeavors.

Planning Content

Initially, each team was expected to discuss the course they were developing and come to an agreement regarding the general content of the course. As part of the development of the UESEP program, several courses previously taught by faculty from different departments were combined. Thus, discussions of course content were needed to educate faculty about previous content, discuss topics that were emphasized by colleagues as they addressed common content (e.g., effective instruction or classroom management), and so forth. Each team seemed to buy into this collaborative arrangement, especially as the course was being developed. The following quote is illustrative of what most faculty told us about this aspect of collaborative planning: "[My colleague] and I started talking about how we thought a classroom management course should be done, and what we thought the goals of the course should be."

Developing the Syllabus, Common Assignments, and Readings

After the planning team agreed on the general content/objectives for the course, all teams worked collaboratively to develop a syllabus that would be used across all sections of the course. This included common assignments and readings. One faculty member from Team 2 captured this aspect of collaboration when she said, "We wanted to develop the course using the same textbook across sections, [and the] same assignments across sections."

Developing, Implementing and Monitoring Class Sessions

Finally, to ensure continuity across sections of a course, to sustain these changes, as well as to prepare teaching assistants and other "novices" teaching a given course for the first time, it was assumed that course teams would meet frequently (weekly in most instances) as the course was being taught. However, not all faculty on the teams, particularly those in special education, embraced this component of collaboration. Only Team 3 met weekly to plan lessons, monitor how well the lessons worked, evaluate assignments, plan exams, and so forth. In the case of the other teams, the STL faculty members met weekly with the doctoral students, but the SE faculty members were absent from that collaboration.

TENSIONS THAT EMERGED IN THE COLLABORATIVE PROCESS

As with any collaborative endeavor, tensions of several sorts occurred as courses were developed and implemented. These tensions resulted from differences in the ways faculty from the two departments perceived their work, the course subject matter, and their professional identity in the academy. Many of these tensions were resolved on two of the teams when faculty implicitly agreed to limit the scope of their collaboration, and thus did not address some of the differences that existed. In contrast, a third team collaborated from the development of the course through the implementation and monitoring of course content. This team thus addressed a full range of issues concerning the collaborative process. Team differences are reflected in the following sections, which describe tensions that arose during the collaborative process, and how the respective teams addressed them.

Conflicting Views of Time and Work Priorities

Although extensive collaboration was expected of the teaching teams, some faculty, especially SE faculty, found it difficult to live up to this expectation. The tension that most influenced the collaborative process across teams related to priorities that participating faculty from the two departments placed on their professional responsibilities. Faculty on some teams placed a high priority on working closely with colleagues throughout the course development process, while others did not place such a high priority on these activities.

Many factors influenced the priorities for faculty involved in these collaborations, including issues such as faculty perspectives regarding their scholarly roles and the nature of the reward system for faculty. Interestingly, significant differences in priorities occurred among faculty across departments. For example, STL faculty had a longer history of working together collaboratively on course and program development than did faculty in SE, and much of their research related directly to the teacher education program. One STL faculty member, who highly valued collaboration, said, "It was my expectation that we would meet weekly and that we would design class sessions. I would have been disappointed if that isn't what we had done. That's what I had done on three prior course teams that I worked on."

In contrast, each of the participating SE faculty was responsible for at least one federally funded research grant , and each of these grants addressed topics that did not relate directly to teacher education or the UESEP program. Two of the STL collaborators, on the other hand, were managing funded projects directly related to UESEP. The SE faculty members' grant responsibilities resulted in different priorities for faculty, and typically led to less intense collaboration on the part of the course planning teams. In addressing this tension, one SE faculty member stated:

> They've defined our work as collaborative teams that get together on
> a regular basis to talk about experiences of teaching the course. They
> deliberate on content and the experiences with a variety of activities,
> and lesson plans and those kinds of things. That's the definition of

how it's going to work and I knew from the beginning it wasn't going to work for me ... for me to survive and do well in a number of areas, I can't pay as much attention to [collaboration] as people wanted me to do.

This perspective influenced how this faculty member's planning team proceeded with its work. For example, this particular faculty member met to develop a common syllabus and outline readings, content, and assignments, but did not meet thereafter with the team. He noted, "Looking back on why I met, there was an expectation I would. I artfully dodged those expectations after I found I could get by on my own."

The STL faculty member who worked on this team was not in full agreement with her colleague's perspective, but agreed that the team could work only if she recognized her collaborator's different priorities and how they would influence involvement in the collaborative process. She noted, " I did go into this experience with an idea of what collaboration should be like, and I think I mellowed a little bit and I think collaboration is important, but I don't think there's one way it has to work—I think it does make sense to look at the particular context."

These two faculty members thus worked out a definition of collaboration that was mutually agreeable, and more pragmatic, as they developed their course. More accurately, they made a deal to address the tension surrounding the development of this course. As one of the participants noted, "I've always viewed collaboration in an environment like this as something where deals are made."

A similar deal was struck by Team 1, for reasons similar to those described above. However, Team 3 was more involved in the three phases of the collaborative process, even though the two participants had quite different priorities. In part this collaboration occurred because the SE faculty member recognized that collaboration had some important benefits beyond those of developing some common understandings about the course content and assignments. She commented, "(Her collaborator) is a brilliant teacher who can engage her students better than I can. I wanted to learn from her.... She scaffolds her students better."

This SE faculty member also recognized that the time spent planning collaboratively meant that she did not need to do as much individual planning. Her STL colleague felt similarly, and recognized that working together allowed her to make the course better. She said,

This course, the kinds of things we were able to design into this course, the kinds of lectures, the kinds of cooperative quizzes, the way class sessions were constructed, we've got games in the course, I could never have put in enough time to make this course what it is. But the fact that we were both putting in the time [along with our other team members]. . . meant that we were able to design something that was superior to anything that either of us could have developed.

Juggling these different priorities created more and persistent stress for the SE faculty member, however. Although she thought it was important for students to engage in applied activities, she did not feel that she could put in the time to carry out those activities and evaluate them. She articulated these tensions when she said, "I felt like I could never keep up. I felt used up; all my creative brainpower was used up on research, and I didn't have any left over for my teaching." She indicated that if she taught the course again, she probably would not use as many assignments or would change them to make them more manageable; however, she was reluctant to take a strong stand on this issue, because she did not want to be perceived as a "poor team player." In contrast, her STL colleague thought that her SE collaborator expressed her stress more overtly, but in the end was willing to go along with the plan. She remarked,

I remember one time in particular she was incredibly distressed about how much time it was taking to grade a particular assignment, and I spent the whole weekend trying to figure out how we could modify it—what we could do to the course to make it better, to make it easier, less time-consuming, and when I came back to lay out those ideas, her response was, "No we don't want to change that!" She needed to emote, but it didn't mean she didn't want to do it.

Professional Autonomy vs. Program Coherence

The ease with which deals were struck to protect time and priorities was also due in part to faculty views on professional autonomy. For Teams 1 and 2, there was a conflict between the need for program coherence and professional autonomy, and these two teams chose to address this tension by collaborating in rather limited ways. This tension pervaded the interviews of Team 1. The STL member had been involved in intensive collaboration on other courses for more than five years. She began this collaborative process with high expectations for team planning and course consistency: "I expected that we would work together to get the whole thing sorted out, and I assumed we would have the same readings, textbook, and the same assignments. My expectation [of collaboration] was this is a 'We' thing . . . so we need to meet and talk."

In contrast, her colleague resisted her definition of the collaborative process. As explained in the above section on priorities, his resistance grew in part from his need to have time for research. His belief in the autonomy of the professorate further strengthened his resistance. He said, "What's valuable in [the] academy is the sense of a professor's autonomy. It goes with academic freedom and I think there're real problems when you're trying to control content."

Clearly, these two colleagues conceived of the purpose of collaboration differently. He conceived of collaboration as a means to gaining expertise where he lacked the knowledge to teach a class effectively. She, in contrast, had a broader view of collaboration. In addition to offering a way to gain knowledge from others, she valued collaboration as a way of creating program consistency as defined minimally by common content, assignments, and program materials. In fact, she held the view that program coherence takes precedence over the traditional academic expectation of professional autonomy:

> If we're going to call ourselves a program, that involves shared themes and goals, and there has to be some kind of collaborating so that we're sure that the students that are moving through the program have the same messages and experiences or else we're just... a collection of courses.

As the semester progressed, she developed a more contextual view of collaboration that incorporated his more limited view of the purposes of collaboration and enabled her to accept his resistance. In fact, by the third semester of the course, the SE faculty member had withdrawn from the course team and taught his class independently of the team.

In Team 2, the tension between professional autonomy and program coherence never surfaced as overt resistance in the interviews, as it did in Team 1. The STL and SE faculty members both held the view that collaboration involved jointly deciding on content, but believed that how instructors deliver the content is a matter of professional autonomy. The STL faculty member said, "You cannot have all of the uniformities you like. You've got to allow for individual variation across different sections. We tell our students that in the first place, the basics are the same but there will be some variations depending on the instructor." His team member readily accepted his position:

> We came to this agreement that we were going to be pretty autonomous in our classrooms.... We wanted to develop the courses using the same textbook across sections, same assignments across sections. We shared our exams, but we didn't use the same exams, and in the classroom with the students, we were pretty much autonomous. That was how it worked best for us.

Team 3 worked together effectively to develop common course activities and assignments. Although the special education member was concerned about the amount of work involved and expressed doubts about the validity of some constructivist methods covered in their course, she did not express concern that the expectation of program consistency infringed on her professional autonomy. However, in Teams 1 and 2 the faculty appealed to the norm of professional autonomy to avoid confrontation over two traditional conflicts between general education and special education faculty: the role of the teacher and the nature of knowledge.

Differing Views of the Classroom Teacher's Role

In two of the teams there was a tension related to perceptions about the role of the teacher. In STL, faculty tended to focus on designing classroom procedures and instruction to effectively reach all learners, often emphasizing prevention; whereas, the SE faculty members were more likely to emphasize interventions for individual students. As the STL member of Team 1 put it,

> I loved the way [the content] unfolded . . . we divide the course into the ideas of preventing behavior problems through establishing the community in certain ways and the other piece would be dealing with behavior problems when they arose. So, we had the prevention and the response pieces of the course and a lot of the prevention stuff is classroom management strategies.

From the SE member's perspective, his general education colleague's perspective was not comprehensive enough to fully prepare preservice teachers to cope with the behavior problems of individual students:

> Her orientation was much more homogenized . . . which has implications in terms of programming for a class. . . . I look at discipline from the standpoint of there's got to be contingencies for the entire classroom and you've got to talk about [the criteria you would use for] those kids you identified as at risk . . . and then you've got to think very seriously about that 1% in the classroom that are going to cause constant classroom disruption. From that aspect . . . the way that you think about discipline turns out to be different than it does if you're thinking about a more homogenous classroom. . . . That's where philosophical orientation broke down. . . . We've got to get into heavier kind of stuff because you're going to have these kids and they're going to be giving you chronic problems.

In Team 2, the special education–general education difference also surfaced as a conflict over the need to provide preservice teachers with strategies for dealing with the problems of individual students. The SE faculty member focused on the need to intervene with students with special needs:

> If things aren't going well ... we really need to be aggressive in terms of intervention ... and so I was wanting to make sure that we taught students about kids who are having problems and what they look like. What some of the typical profiles might be, and then how to intervene so that kids learn what they need to know so they can progress along with their peers. ... I really wanted the IEP and assessment ... in the course, and it wasn't in there initially.

Although her STL colleague did introduce the IEP, he did not adopt her perspective that preservice teachers should develop expertise in using behavioral assessment and remediation, and he was unaware that she continued to use these strategies in her classes.

In Teams 1 and 2, STL faculty members remained largely unaware that their special education counterparts believed that their approach to dealing with the needs of diverse students was limited because of the way they had negotiated their collaboration. In contrast, Team 3 seemed to work through these issues as part of the collaborative process. For example, they engaged in more intensive planning in the initial stages of course development. This included piloting the course, defining the instructional strategies that would be used in the course, and field-testing the instructional strategies with teachers in elementary classrooms. This intense collaboration continued when the course was implemented, as the faculty members continued to meet, plan sessions, and discuss how well specific class activities worked. Thus, the faculty members in Team 3 discussed their perspectives on the classroom teacher's role on many occasions and on many levels, and reached a common agreement regarding this issue. The STL faculty member summed up this resolution, as she noted, "I think there were differences between (my colleague) and me, but they're more in degree than in kind. I think we both see a continuum of kinds of instructional strategies that need to be used in classrooms with children."

Constructivism vs. Positivist Perspectives of Knowledge

Not surprisingly, tensions arose over views of knowledge that, as indicated in the introduction, are historically different for special and general education faculty. In Team 1 the tension between constructivist and positivist views emerged over whether the assessments in the course would be multiple-choice or essay. The SE member believed that multiple-choice tests were an effective means of assessment: "We had some philosophical differences [about tests] ... I know that through good test instructions and a well-crafted [multiple-choice] instrument you can differentiate in a valid and reliable way those that understand the concept and those that don't." His STL counterpart, however, preferred constructivist writing assignments that required students "to apply what they were learning" to a field setting. She accepted their divergent views on this matter by requiring a couple of these assignments of her students: "I had just decided that I'm not going to say [to him] you have to do it this way, and I wasn't willing to say okay I'll let that assignment go."

In Team 2, the constructivist-positivist tension arose over whether preservice teachers need to develop diagnostic-prescriptive skills. The SE team member described her view of the importance of these skills:

> A lot of times I think [elementary education] students ... never really know how to figure out where a kid is developmentally. That's a fairly hard skill to acquire and so I wanted them to at least play with that.... That you have to really figure out what you have in terms of learners.... What I had my students do was use [an] early reading assessment instrument ... with [a] child ... and [I] showed them then based on this information how we would develop some instructional goals for this student.

Her STL colleague, however, seemed unaware of the strength of her views, and believed that the team had decided in favor of a more constructivist approach: "We were struggling as to whether we should use a packet ... of tutoring programs, or we should use more of an open-ended type of tutoring program. And, eventually, I guess, we decided upon using [an open-ended approach]." He was unaware that his SE colleague continued to use the tutoring program, even after they had agreed not to do so.

The STL member of Team 3 was aware of the tension over constructivist and positivist views and had accepted the special education view that many novice learners need structure and support. Her SE counterpart acknowledged her own struggles to incorporate both views into her thinking when she questioned the value of some constructivist and behavioral approaches covered in their course. She believed that some constructivist methods lacked the empirical validation that she valued as a basis for sound practice, but at the same time, recognized the limitations of many special education practices.

> I am more enamored if it's a validated strategy.... I haven't seen
> [constructivist teaching] used very effectively and wonder what is
> realistic for these incredibly novice teachers, but then I think how
> important it is to include higher order-thinking and hands-on
> lessons. To be quite frank, instruction in special education is often
> boring.... I am not particularly enamored with Reading Mastery. It's
> too prescriptive.... I don't think we even know what special educa-
> tion kids can do because the instruction is often so remedial.

Despite this discomfort, the two members of Team 3 made compromises that enabled them to work together effectively, as the STL
team member put it:

> [My team partner] tends to be more directive than I, both in her
> thoughts about what teachers should be doing and I think in her
> approach to what she does in the classroom.... But I think what hap-
> pened as we taught the course is we both moderated.... I think [we]
> are both in the middle. I think I'm more to the constructivist end and
> [she] is more toward the directive end, but I think we're both in the
> middle. That's why I say it's a difference of degree but not kind.

BENEFITS FOR COLLABORATING FACULTY

In spite of the tensions that existed for faculty engaged in the collaborative process, each person accrued benefits that made the
endeavor, at least initially, worthwhile. Most of these benefits related
to the opportunities for faculty to learn from others who had expert
knowledge of a content area or an approach to instruction. For example, each of the faculty came into the collaboration with strong skills in
either "general" or "special" education," but needed to learn information from their colleague if they were to provide effective instruction in
their classes. One faculty member characterized the person she worked
with as an excellent source of ideas and information regarding the
course content. She explained, "Some of the materials, for example on
functional behavior assessment and positive behavioral supports or
aggressive kids or dealing with crisis with children ... this was all stuff
that was new to me, so I was hopeful that there would be collaboration
so that I would feel that I was doing a good job."

Other faculty, particularly those in SE, valued the knowledge their
STL colleagues had about teacher education, and felt that the collaboration allowed them to learn better pedagogy. As one SE faculty put it,
"[She has a] huge knowledge base of instructional materials to pull for
pre-service teachers, and has a large collection of interventions ... [she]
can engage her students better than I. I wanted to learn [to do this]."

Another SE colleague responded similarly. He said, "Quite frankly, she does a better job than I do (in getting students to participate in class). But I try to mimic it and approach class the way that she would go about doing that—it's much better for these students to discover stuff than me telling them."

Finally, the faculty viewed collaboration as a time saver, in that they could develop a much better course in much less time through collaboration than they could have developed in the same time working along:

> The first time you do anything it takes more time, it always does. But over time, when you're collaborating like that, it saves time. I could never have put in enough time to make this course what it is. But the fact that we were both putting in the time that we put in...meant that we were able to design something that was superior to anything that either of us could have developed.

LESSONS LEARNED AND IMPLICATIONS FOR TEACHER EDUCATORS UNIFYING THEIR PROGRAMS

Given how special education and general education practice has been characterized historically, we were surprised to find that collaboration on these teams went as smoothly as it did. Although, in this chapter, we focused on differences in the views and beliefs of faculty from the two departments, there were also similarities that most likely allowed these teams to agree on goals, readings, and assignments. We realized through our interviews that some commonalities between instructional views and beliefs, as well as a history of working together, enabled at least some level of collaboration and permitted the development of a unified program. Faculty on all three of the teams perceived themselves to have some type of shared vision for teaching and learning. The SE faculty member on Team 2 said it best when she described commonalities between her orientation toward literacy instruction and her colleague's perspective:

> I think one of the reasons why our team worked so well is because [my colleague] and I were very close to being on the same page so to speak. I mean, our philosophies are very, very similar in terms of literacy and how that happens, and that we think a balanced approach is the best way to go.

Additionally, most of the faculty interviewed believed that it was important to create perspectives of teaching and learning that balanced constructivist and positivist methods both for children in public schools and for preservice students in the college classroom. For instance, one

SE faculty member, when talking about his preservice students, said, "I don't believe that I open up their head and pour information in.... Putting them in a situation where they can construct their own meanings ... is the best way to go about instruction."

These similar perspectives are probably the result of a long history of collaboration between the two departments. For example, three of the faculty involved in the interviews developed a joint preparation program for elementary and special education preservice students that provided the impetus for the UESEP program (Bondy, Ross, Sindelar, & Griffin, 1995). In addition, with the exception of one STL faculty member, all of the faculty interviewed had worked together previously in collaborative endeavors, including course development, team teaching, research projects, grant management, and so forth. It is also important to note that faculty who worked together on course planning teams were carefully selected to ensure that they did not hold diametrically opposed views regarding the content they were to address. Previous relationships and careful selection of teams very likely reduced tensions that might have otherwise existed relative to course content. Additionally, teacher education is highly valued at the University of Florida, perhaps more so than at many comparable institutions. This value is reflected in several innovative teacher education programs that have been developed at UF, and the research that many of our faculty have done related to these programs (Bondy et al.,1995; Ross & Bondy, 1996; Ross, Correa, & Webb, 1999).

Teams also operated smoothly because, in at least two cases, faculty agreed to limit their collaboration to a degree. Professional autonomy on Teams 1 and 2 was the safety net that kept the teams from having to deal with the inevitable conflicts that would occur when they attempted to integrate their differing views of instruction, collaboration, and teaching. Professional autonomy allowed faculty to remain sufficiently isolated so they sometimes did not realize how different their perspectives were. Clearly, the tensions that emerged in the interviews would have become more prominent if Teams 1 and 2 had implemented collaboration as Team 3 had.

So, does maintaining a good degree of professional autonomy permit faculty from different disciplines and perspectives to work together, and if so, what does a high degree of autonomy mean for program cohesion? On the other hand, is a minimalist approach to collaboration the best we can expect in a large research university? The scholarship demands placed on teacher education faculty in research institutions are great and often present considerable hurdles for faculty engaged in teacher education reform (Ducharme & Ducharme, 1996b).

In our interviews, SE faculty were quite clear that they could not devote the time to collaboration and teaching that they felt was expected. From their perspective, doing so would negatively impact their ability to engage in scholarly activities, such as running grants, that are valued highly by the university, their department, and the field. It is important to note that securing grants is valued by many special education faculty in large, research institutions and an important part of the culture of their departments. Moreover, most special education grants do not focus on teacher education, so there is little opportunity for faculty to blend their grant research with their teacher education efforts. STL faculty interviewed, however, did not feel the same degree of conflict between grants and teaching because their teaching is better aligned with their research. As one STL faculty member put it,

> My other collaborative work has primarily been with [the STL member of Team 1].... And we have very, very tightly shared definitions of teaching and ways of thinking about teaching that fit into what we do. We don't have as much pressure or as much time committed to work on grants (as the Special Education department). Although there is a strong research agenda, we generally tie in our research agenda with what we're doing in our teaching, and so I think...many of the Special Education faculty feel more torn in terms of a conflicting agenda than I feel or the people whom I've been collaborating with feel.

What is unclear is how representative this STL colleague's views are of other faculty in her department and teacher education faculty at other major research institutions. Ducharme and Ducharme (1996b) seem to indicate otherwise. From their perspective, faculty in research institutions everywhere have significant difficulties attempting to balance the extensive time demands of any teacher reform effort and their own scholarship.

CONCLUSION

Faculty engaged in unifying their teacher education programs need to be aware that some common understandings must be in place for any type of collaboration to occur. Having faculty engage in collaborative projects prior to any attempt to unify a teacher education program may be fundamental for developing some of the shared understandings about curriculum and teaching they will need to work together. Finally, faculty will need to develop conceptions of collaboration that are realistic for their particular context. What is possible in an institution that focuses most of its efforts on teacher education may not be possible in a major research institution.

REFERENCES

Biklen, D. (1985). *Achieving the complete school.* New York: Teachers College Press.

Blanton, L. P., Griffin, C. C., Winn, J. A., & Pugach, M .C. (Eds.). (1997). *Teacher education in transition: Collaborative programs to prepare general and special educators.* Denver, CO: Love Publishing Co.

Bondy, B., Ross, D., Sindelar, P., & Griffin, C. (1995). Elementary and special educators learning to work together: Team building processes. *Teacher Education and Special Education. 18*(2), 91–102.

Ducharme, E.R., & Ducharme, M. K. (1996b). Needed research in teacher education. In J. Sikula, T. J. Buttery, & E. Guyton (Eds.), *Handbook of research on teacher education* (2nd ed., pp. 1030–1046). New York: Macmillan.

Gartner, A., & Lipsky, A. (1987). Beyond special education: Toward a quality system for all students. *Harvard Educational Review, 57*(4), 367–395.

Grennon-Brooks, J., & Brooks., M. G. (1999). *In search of understanding: The case for constructivist classrooms* (2nd ed.). Alexandria, VA: ASCD.

Heshusius, L. (1989). The Newtonian mechanistic paradigm, special education, and contours of alternatives: An overview. *Journal of Learning Disabilities, 22*(7), 403–415.

Irvine, J. J., & Armento, B. J. (2001). *Culturally responsive teaching: Lesson planning for the elementary and middle grades.* Boston: McGraw-Hill.

Reynolds, M. C., Wang, M. C., & Walberg, H. J. (1987). The necessary restructuring of special and regular education. *Exceptional Children, 53*, 391–398.

Ross, D. D., Correa, V., & Webb, R. (1999, February). *Teacher education reform through college-wide collaboration.* Paper presented at the meeting of the American Association of Colleges of Teacher Education, Washington, DC.

Ross, D. D., & Krogh, S. L. (1988). From paper to program: A story from elementary PROTEACH. *Peabody Journal of Education, 65*(2), 19–34.

Sherry, L., & Spooner, F. (2000). *Unified teacher preparation programs for general and special educators.* St. Petersburg, FL: Florida CSPD.

Skrtic, T. M. (Ed.). (1991). *Behind special education: A critical analysis of professional culture and school organization.* Denver, CO: Love Publishing Co.

Skrtic, T. M. (Ed.). (1995). *Disability and democracy. Reconstructing (special) education for postmodernity.* New York: Teachers College Press.

Will, M. (1986). Educating children with learning problems: A shared responsibility. *Exceptional Children, 52,* 411–415.

Zemelman, S., Daniels, H., & Hyde, A. (1998). *Best practice: New standards for teaching.* Portsmouth, NH: Heinemann Publishers.

CHAPTER 9

Learning in Partnerships: The Experience of Students, Teachers, and College Faculty

ELIZABETH BONDY, ALYSON ADAMS, AND VIRGINIA MALLINI

Although most of the faculty who teach in the Unified Elementary Special Education Proteach (UESEP) program would describe themselves as subscribing to a constructivist approach to teaching and learning, the meanings and complexities of constructivism and constructivist teacher education have yet to be examined and debated within the College of Education (COE). The program's purposes and conceptual framework hint at the faculty's constructivist tendencies. Commitments to diverse learners and families; collaboration among multiple stakeholders; development of alternative teaching methods; equity in education and society; and critical reflection on educational aims, teaching practices, and outcomes all suggest a constructivist view. Yet, it is fair to assume, particularly in a program that brings together faculty from different disciplines, that we do not share a common understanding of the purposes and practices of constructivist teacher education (Richardson, 1997; Tatto, 1998).

Richardson (1997) explained that while constructivism is not a "monolithic, agreed-upon concept," one point of agreement is that "individuals create their own understandings, based upon the interaction of what they already know and believe, and the phenomena or ideas with which they come into contact" (p. 3). In teacher education programs that define themselves as constructivist, faculty members use a variety of strategies to facilitate their students' understanding. Rainer, Guyton, and Wesche (2001) called these "key mediational experiences" (p.16). These experiences included program features and pedagogy that provided opportunities for social interaction, meaningful learning experiences, shared ownership, reflection, development of a personal theory of teaching and learning, and supportive environments. Goodman and Fish (1997) concluded that preservice teachers' knowledge of and perspectives about against-the-grain teaching (Cochran-Smith, 1991) were influenced by a complex interaction of their professional coursework, peer culture in the teacher education cohort, field experiences, and the knowledge and beliefs with which students entered the program. They and others (Fosnot, 1996; Mayer-Smith & Mitchell, 1997) advocated that teacher educators examine their own practices and the role they play in their students' perspectives and knowledge construction.

This chapter and chapter 11 illustrate the kinds of research being conducted in the UESEP program to gain insight into participants' experience of program features designed to facilitate construction of knowledge. The studies are in line with Wideen, Mayer-Smith, and Moon's (1998) recommendation for an ecological approach to the process of learning to teach in that they focus on multiple players and contexts. In this chapter the authors report on a study of participants (preservice teachers, practicing teachers, and college-based teacher educators) in the program's first classroom field experience.

The first classroom-based field experience was aligned with the learning goals of two courses students take concurrently. Developed by college and public school faculty, the coursework/fieldwork "package" was viewed as a partnership in that the two institutions linked together to help preservice teachers accomplish specified goals. The study of participants' experience revealed that what we perceived as a partnership was actually multiple partnerships, all of which contributed to participants' learning and perception of benefits from the experience. In fact, the partnerships appeared to scaffold a learning process in which participants created understanding. The chapter begins with background on the courses and field experience that were the focus of the study, provides an overview of the methods used to collect and analyze data, describes the study's findings, and highlights elements of the structure of coursework and field experience that appeared to facilitate learning in partnerships.

BACKGROUND

This study is grounded in the experiences of students during the second semester of their junior year when, within the context of a cohort group, they take four courses: Core Teaching Strategies, Core

Classroom Management Strategies, Emergent Literacy, and ESOL (English Speakers of Other Languages): Language and Culture. The companion field experience was developed to serve the Core Teaching Strategies and Core Classroom Management Strategies classes. Additional field experiences associated with the Emergent Literacy and ESOL classes are not discussed in this chapter (see chapter 5). The Core Teaching class focused on two main objectives: 1) developing knowledge of the theoretical foundation of instruction that ranges from teacher-directed to self-directed, and 2) developing practical knowledge for implementing direct instruction, cognitive strategy instruction, and inductive instruction. Main objectives for the Core Management class included: 1) developing knowledge of methods for establishing the classroom community, and 2) preventing problem behavior and analyzing and addressing problem behavior when it occurs. Teams of instructors from special education and general education taught both classes (see chapters 6 and 8 for more information about how teams operated).

To prepare teachers for the upcoming field experience, three COE faculty members recruited teachers from three elementary schools to participate in a series of workshops during the fall. Two of those schools were professional development schools closely associated with COE faculty. In the workshops, COE faculty focused on teaching the three instructional models the preservice teachers would learn in Core Teaching Strategies and then implement in the classroom. Instructors modeled the strategies, analyzed them with the teachers, developed rubrics with teachers for assessing the content and process of each strategy, and provided teachers with feedback on lessons they developed to illustrate the use of each strategy.

Students were organized in triads and assigned, for the most part, to the classrooms of teachers who had participated in the fall workshops. Triads attended their placements for one three-hour block per week for 10 weeks. For Core Teaching, the triad was required to develop, implement, and evaluate a lesson using each instructional strategy. For Core Management, triads completed 10 field assignments related to course topics such as organizing the classroom space, teaching rules and procedures, and examining teacher-student interaction patterns. The assignments required classroom observation, teacher interviews, and interaction with students.

METHODOLOGY

The study was designed to examine the experience of the cooperating teachers, teacher education students, and COE faculty who worked together in the Core Teaching and Core Management coursework and field component. The students were in the same cohort, had the same instructors for the two courses, and were placed at the same school for the field component. Initially, we wondered, "What do the various participants learn?" As we began to analyze data, we shifted our focus toward the contexts and processes of learning.

Data were gathered through retrospective interviews with nine students, nine cooperating teachers, and the two instructors. All 30 students in the cohort were invited to be interviewed. However, as interviewing was conducted during the summer, many students were not in town. All nine students who agreed to be interviewed were included in the study. Ten teachers had worked with triads, and nine of ten were interviewed. These nine students (all of them White, female, and of middle- and upper-middle class backgrounds, like the majority of our teacher education population) had worked with five of the nine teachers interviewed. The approximately 45-minute interviews were audiotaped and then transcribed. The three researchers coded the data and sorted data into categories that represented salient dimensions of participants' experience in partnerships.

LEARNING IN PARTNERSHIPS

Data analysis revealed that Proteach students, classroom teachers, and COE instructors perceived benefits from the partnerships in which they participated. In fact, partnerships provided the context in which participants learned new ideas and skills. They also provided the context for self-assessment and reflection. After a brief overview of the benefits participants perceived, we examine the kinds of partnerships available to participants and the processes by which participants learned in partnerships.

The Benefits of Partnerships

Proteach students described three kinds of benefits including knowledge of teaching and management strategies, understanding of self as teacher, and insights into the challenges of teaching. It is not surprising that students talked about teaching and management practices, since they were taking courses and completing field assignments in these areas. Nevertheless, we were struck by their detailed descriptions of what they learned, thoughtful analyses of classroom observations, and use of course concepts to describe their learning. Repeatedly, students linked coursework and fieldwork when they talked about teaching and management practices. The students uniformly perceived that they had learned a lot about the teaching models and management strategies addressed in their coursework, and they spoke intelligently about how, when, and why they would use them.

Understanding of self as teacher refers to Proteach students' insights into the students they hope to teach, what they still need to learn, and their preferred teaching styles. Students reported being grateful for the opportunity to work with a predominantly African American and low-income student body. Several noted a newfound interest in working at this kind of school. Students also reported that the experience helped them recognize things they still needed to learn and practice, such as developing engaging lessons for diverse learners and making on-the-spot adjustments to lessons when students did not respond as anticipated. Many students echoed the theme of the complexity of teaching a lesson and noted that they needed a lot more practice. They also reported insights into their preferences in such areas as classroom organization, teacher-student relationships, teacher language, and lesson formats.

The classroom teachers talked about four kinds of benefits including new knowledge, validation of existing knowledge, insights into the teacher education program, and the enjoyment of their relationships with Proteach students. New knowledge included the teaching models taught during the workshops and the management strategies and issues the Proteach students discussed with them in order to complete their field assignments. Teachers perceived that some of their existing knowledge was validated as they "put practice to theory" in the workshops. They were pleased to hear COE faculty provide support for practices they had used for years. Learning what was expected of them as cooperating teachers was another benefit teachers perceived as well as becoming informed about the newly unified teacher education program. Finally, some teachers talked about their enjoyment of relationships with the triads of Proteach students placed in their classrooms. Teachers were grateful for the opportunity to talk about teaching in an informal, comfortable setting.

The two COE instructors noted that they gained knowledge, experimented with unfamiliar teacher education pedagogy, and were challenged to ground theory in the world of practice. For example, one instructor learned about functional behavior assessment and crisis management. The other experimented with teaching strategies she had never before used in her many years of college teaching. Both reported on the benefits for students and for themselves of linking theory to practice. With their students shuttling back and forth, physically and conceptually, between university coursework and public school classrooms, instructors were confronted with the sometimes messy connections between theory and practice and helped their students draw on each to inform the other.

The Kinds of Partnerships

In describing the benefits of partnerships, students frequently alluded to the conditions that fostered their learning. We came to see those conditions as representing multiple partnerships: COE/school partnerships, the within-triad partnership, the core course partnership, and the cross-departmental teaching team partnership.

COE/elementary school partnerships. We had assumed that the partnership between the COE and the elementary school would promote participant learning. We were correct, but we found that there were actually several partnerships in place: coursework/fieldwork, teacher/triad, COE faculty and teacher workshops, and COE faculty and teacher co-instructors.

Coursework/fieldwork. In this partnership, the COE and elementary school were connected through the careful development of assignments that linked course content directly to the field placement. An instructor explained the rationale for designing the two courses in this way:

> I think we all underestimate how difficult teaching is, and how difficult it is to try to implement a pure teaching model. It's much easier to model it in a university than to try it on-site with kids. . . . We wanted not to teach the models in isolation. We wanted them to have the opportunity to work in classrooms, to observe, attempting to implement even though they are just getting started. Otherwise, it's a theoretical exercise, as opposed to something that's really capable of happening.

Students were aware of the close connection between coursework and fieldwork and noted that it enriched their learning. One explained,

> The field-based assignments were great for class discussions, and the lessons we had to create really helped me to understand the purpose and function of the types of lessons—direct instruction, cognitive strategy instruction, etc. So far, those two classes and the field experiences have been my most meaningful.

Another student said,

> We had to answer weekly questions on what we did that week, and the questions pertained to our reading. So we had to look for some-

thing in our actual classroom. So, we didn't just read about things, we got to actually go out and see them. You know, like does the teacher go around the whole classroom? Does she pick a variety of students to answer questions? That type of thing. That worked out really well.

Students recognized how the instructors facilitated their learning by structuring discussions about the field placements and related assignments during both courses. Said one, "It was really great to have that experience linked to a time when we can discuss what went on and what we were learning." Another student said,

> In Core Teaching, we were talking so much theory in that class that it could've been such a boring class. I mean, that's all we talked about was theory, models. But it was nice to talk about how our lessons went, what to do for our next lessons, get ideas for what to do. She would show us examples.... The assignments themselves were linked—we would teach and then write about how it went.

This student continued talking about the instructor's importance as facilitator of this partnership:

> We might have linked the class and the field experience on our own ... but having the instructor talking to us about what went on in our classes gave us an opportunity to get a discussion going, so it wasn't just us thinking on our own. There is a difference between a bunch of students who think they know everything criticizing their teacher and talking about how she is doing everything wrong compared to talking about it to our instructor.

Teachers also benefited from the coursework/fieldwork partnership. One teacher described how students' assignments improved her practice:

> It actually helped me out as a teacher. For one assignment, they had to watch me walk around the room, and it made me realize I don't do that enough. It helped them reach their objectives, and it helped me realize where I needed to improve.

Similarly, another teacher commented :

> I know they were taking their classroom management course at the same time. I think the class definitely made a difference. On the days that they came in to observe specific things that I was doing, that was very beneficial because I had never experienced something like that. It was really interesting to hear them talk about some of the things they were learning ... that class was beneficial for all of us!

Teacher/triad partnership. The relationship between the teacher and the triad fostered a learning environment that extended and enriched the information presented in coursework. One student explained,

> She gave me a lot of practical information. She was very encouraging about assignments and teaching experiences.... She also conducted a morning meeting so that we could see how one actually worked. For the most part, she gave my partners and me some "real world" experience that we could not have gotten elsewhere.

Teachers mention this relationship as being one of the most beneficial aspects of the experience. They frequently told us about relationships with students that were personal and often extended beyond school business. For example, a teacher said,

> I feel like I made some new acquaintances. My Wednesday group presented me with a huge plant and wedding gift, and I felt that we had established a relationship. We could sit and talk about teaching from a very informal standpoint.... There were times that... involved laughter, there were times when someone even cried because one of my student's sister and father were killed. So, a lot of emotion went into the few hours that they spent in my room.

Teachers spoke about this partnership as having more than just personal benefit, however. Many of them also used this partnership to further their own professional development, making it an active learning experience for themselves as well as the students. One teacher said:

> I don't like to participate in anything if it's not a learning experience for me, so I asked [the pre-interns] to sort of, not necessarily assess me, but give me feedback in terms of strengths and weaknesses, because I want to learn from them. They have something to offer me and I have something to offer them... it makes me a better teacher and it acknowledges that just because you are inexperienced that doesn't mean you don't have something to offer.... Let's get better at what we're doing here. The idea is not to be judgmental, but to improve our teaching skills. So I knew I had to get myself in a mindset where I felt confident about what I was doing, and I was willing to listen as well.

Teachers' learning was obvious to students as well. One student commented on her teacher's efforts to improve: "Seeing someone who has been teaching for so long still trying to improve. I mean, she was working on that the whole time we were there, and even asked for input. It was great to see some true reflective teaching."

COE faculty and teacher workshops. COE faculty developed workshops to prepare teachers for the upcoming field experience, familiarize them with the substance of the two courses for which students would have field assignments, and involve them in refining plans for the next semester. Teachers' reactions were uniformly positive. Most teachers noted, as this one did, that the workshops either gave them new knowledge or validated existing knowledge about teaching:

> The workshops were very beneficial...I had no idea before about rubrics, and it was very useful. It showed me how to develop one and how to use it. The cognitive strategy approach was different for me, and the workshops helped me understand it and be able to use it effectively.

Some teachers focused on the workshops as preparation: "I thought we were well trained, and we had the information we needed to start." Likewise, another commented, "The professors did a good job of preparing us for [the pre-interns]."

Some teachers saw the workshops as an opportunity to be involved in teacher education. One teacher spoke at length about this:

> Unless we share a degree of what goes on in this program, we can't fix it. I went to the training with an open mind and a belief that this was as much for the classroom teacher as for the university. I prepared myself to help and become a real part of this program, assuming that I would also have a voice.

Another teacher recognized this as being different from her previous experience supervising interns: "You know with the interns I've had over the years that I've been supervising, we never got called in to the seminars, we never got to give feedback."

Many teachers appreciated being treated as professionals and having an impact on course design by developing the student evaluation rubrics for the lessons in the Core Teaching course. Said one, "I felt honored as a professional to be involved with the training. I felt like the university worked hard to accommodate us and be sensitive to our needs, to treat us as professionals."

COE faculty and teacher co-instructors. The Core Classroom Management course was cotaught on-site by the professor-in-residence and a classroom teacher, both of whom were involved in our study. The COE instructor explained the rationale behind coteaching: "We tried to balance what students see as 'book knowledge' with her experience in the first-grade classroom."

Both instructors alluded to ways in which they benefited from the coteaching partnership. The COE instructor said, "I was able to do more self-assessment because I was getting Donna's [first-grade teacher's] feedback on how things were going." The coteaching prompted Donna to look at her classroom teaching in new ways. For her, classroom management had always been a matter of doing what seemed right; she had never before read or studied about it. The students found the class to be highly credible due to the blending of theory and practice the instructors provided.

Within-Triad Partnership. Students' learning was affected by the partnership with their peers in the triads. They worked closely with their peers to develop, implement, and evaluate lessons for Core Teaching and complete assignments for Core Management.

Some students spoke at length about the benefits of having peers engage in feedback and reflection with them. One commented,

> I think the three people going at once might seem like too many at one time, but it was really good for feedback for each other.... Writing our lesson plans, keeping in mind how the kids would answer, how they should be set up to be most conducive to paying attention, and then having our peers watch. The reflection really played in.

Although some teachers were unsure how to work with the unfamiliar triad structure, they were generally enthusiastic about the opportunities it provided the Proteach students. A teacher explained,

> I didn't have the opportunity to give them feedback on their academic lessons, but they were able to give each other feedback on their academic lessons.... I would never want to go back to just one (pre-intern).... I thought it was a real strength of the program, because it's non-threatening for them to be able to observe each other and give each other feedback rather than just always a supervisor observing. It's very different to be observed in a classroom where both students are familiar with the children and the procedures, rather than go visit somebody and watch them because your procedures are very different. You have a lot of knowledge when that's your classroom and you bring that knowledge with you to your observation and its really very different. I think feedback has to be more meaningful from this type of experience.

One teacher also recognized how this partnership helped promote collaboration skills:

> [In my teacher education program] I liked to work alone and it took me a while to be able to work with other people, as a team. I really liked how they worked together as three because they could bounce ideas off one another. When you get a job, sometimes you do that...so I think it's better to be on a team in the beginning. ...And also it's good for their confidence to be together in the beginning.

Core Course Partnership. Many students perceived a link between the courses Core Teaching and Core Management and seemed to benefit from this partnership as well. Students often commented that the content of each course complemented the other and spoke highly of this connection. A student explained,

> I mean, they worked together. Not only learning how to do the lesson, but how to handle the students during the lesson. We learned a lot of different techniques and what's important, like calling on students and stuff. It made the lesson go a lot smoother. They connected that way.

Even when students found this connection overwhelming, they continued to see the value in linking the two courses, as one student reflected,

> Everything overlapped for those two classes so much, which is sometimes a good thing, but it was really confusing sometimes to try to figure out what you were doing for what. I don't know...they are so enmeshed. Like when we were doing our direct instruction lesson, also watching for behavior problems.

Another student responded,

> I think they were well connected. I think it worked really well. We had little things to do each week—and a lot of times I was confused as to what was due for each class because they were so well connected—which I don't know if that was a good or bad thing. But I thought it went really well because you can't really do instruction without management.

Cross-Departmental Teaching Team Partnership. Related to the Core Course partnership was the partnership that evolved within the teaching teams made up of faculty and doctoral students from general and special education. Collaborative course planning and ongoing course team meetings resulted in opportunities for learning in partnership. In particular, instructors described learning new content and instructional strategies. One instructor reported,

> I learned new things through working with my special education colleagues to plan and teach the class. For example, I was not familiar with functional behavior assessment and positive behavior supports....I might not have ever learned about that if I had not been teaching this class in collaboration with special education people. Another example would be related to ADD. I did some work looking into ADD and actually ended up ordering a videotape for our library. Also, all the crisis management stuff, dealing with really violent behavior in kids. It was all new to me.

The instructors also found that their teacher education pedagogy was enriched through interaction with instructors with different teaching styles. One of the instructors said,

> My teaching improved because of my collaboration with my special education colleague....I think I learned to be more specific. I used more lecture in that class than I have generally used, and despite the fact that I used more lecture, it was still a highly interactive class. But I think I placed more emphasis on trying to really clarify their understanding....My colleague tends to have a more explicit style of teaching, and I think that was good for me. That combination of styles meant that we used a wide diversity of strategies in the class, and that was really productive for the students.

Another aspect of this teaching team partnership was the mentoring that occurred between instructors and doctoral students on the team. The instructors commented about how this aspect of the partnership forced them to be more meticulous than usual in their planning. Because they wanted to help the inexperienced doctoral students succeed, they planned and discussed course concepts, lessons, and assignments in detail. In doing so, they gained new insights into the material they taught.

DISCUSSION: A PROCESS OF LEARNING IN PARTNERSHIPS

Within multiple partnerships, students, teachers, and instructors appeared to consider and reconsider ideas through a process of collaborative reflection. They encountered material, practiced or applied it, received feedback, and made judgments about its value. They then either moved back to the practice phase in which they applied the material in context or moved on to another new idea. Participants engaged in numerous learning cycles simultaneously throughout the semester as they interacted in multiple partnerships.

The learning cycle is similar to the reflection cycle described by Ross, Bondy, and Kyle (1993). Whereas the reflection cycle is sparked by the recognition of a dilemma that prompts a teacher to consider plans for addressing the dilemma, the learning cycle is sparked by the recognition of a new concept, skill, or teaching practice. All participants encountered unfamiliar material; this occurred in the university or elementary classroom, a teaching team meeting, a triad study session, or a teacher workshop. Having encountered the new material, the participant "tried it out" either because he or she was required to, in the case of a student doing a field-based assignment, or compelled to, in the case of a COE instructor teaching new material or trying a new teaching strategy, or a teacher helping students complete their field assignments. There was then the opportunity for feedback, frequently in multiple forms. For example, the student who implemented a direct instruction lesson received feedback from the children, the members of the triad, the cooperating teacher, the COE instructor who reviewed the lesson plan, and classmates who discussed the lesson as part of a class activity. The COE instructor who attempted a new teaching strategy received feedback from her students, her co-instructor, and the members of her teaching team. Participants then formulated their judgments of the new material by considering the various kinds of feedback. Sometimes the next step was to practice or apply the material again; sometimes participants moved on to new material, thereby jump-starting the active learning process.

With few exceptions, all three groups of participants showed evidence of collaborative reflection in partnerships. Perhaps it is not surprising to find this occurring among students and instructors in a teacher education program that emphasizes reflection. However, most of the cooperating teachers described their learning in a similar way; that is, they interacted with ideas and people in multiple partnerships. Although cooperating teachers' learning has been described as a reciprocal process (Lemlech & Hertzog, 1999) of imparting and receiving knowledge, we found that the multiple partnerships helped teachers engage in a more elaborated learning process highlighted by collaborative reflection and self-assessment.

IMPLICATIONS: LEARNING PARTNERSHIPS AS KEY MEDIATIONAL EXPERIENCES

Partnerships in the first classroom-based field experience provided at least several of the key mediational experiences that Rainer, et al. (2001) described as supporting learning in constructivist teacher education programs. In particular, partnerships provided for social interaction, meaningful learning experiences, shared ownership, reflection, and supportive environments. Furthermore, partnerships appeared to be structured in such a way as to mediate the learning of all three groups of participants. One teacher spoke for many of the participants when she said, "It was a totally positive experience for all of us, anytime you get better at what you're doing.... I think we need to be willing to assess ourselves at all times. . . . This kind of experience allows you to do this."

What features of the experience played a role in promoting partnerships and scaffolding the active learning process? Although many of them are related to one another, we have organized them into course-based structures and school-based structures. Course-based structures included cross-course collaboration, collaborative course planning and team meetings, the use of co-instructors, linking field assignments to course readings, and basing class activities on course concepts and related field experiences. School-based structures included voluntary participation, the long-standing school-COE relationship, the quarter-time assignment of the professor-in-residence to the school, holding class sessions at the school, and the student triad structure.

Course-based structures helped establish some of the key partnerships. The two courses were developed in tandem; in fact, at one point they had been conceptualized as a single course. When the substance and structure of two courses are linked, students have double the opportunity to process their learning. Collaborative planning within cross-departmental teaching teams helped instructors to approach actively the new and familiar material they were teaching. Similarly, the co-instructor arrangement helped the teacher and COE instructor to approach theory and practice thoughtfully and examine their own practice in light of feedback from the other. The field assignments, carefully linked to course readings, were often cited by students as powerful supports to learning. Further, making field assignments the subject of structured class activities effectively scaffolded the feedback and judgment phases of the learning process.

Several school-based structures warrant consideration. Because school and teacher participation in the field experience was voluntary, teachers tended to be enthusiastic about their efforts. Their participation was fostered by the longstanding partnership between the school and the COE. One of two official professional development schools in the district, the school had a trusting relationship with the COE, especially with the professor-in-residence who had worked there for two years and was familiar with most of the staff. Consequently, when she invited them to participate in the workshops, they confidently agreed. The professor-in-residence was also the instructor who co-taught the management class at the school with a first-grade teacher. The well-developed connections between the school and the COE helped teachers to participate whole-heartedly and facilitated problem solving when issues arose during the semester. The school-COE partnership, the fact that the class met at the school, and the presence of the first-grade teacher co-instructor helped develop the preservice teachers' sense of belonging and commitment to the school. They quickly grew familiar with the people and the facility and developed a sense of the school as "our school." This kind of commitment appeared to promote a seriousness of purpose and effort among Proteach students. Because their instructors knew all of their cooperating teachers, classrooms, and many of the children with whom they worked, they were able to participate with them in detailed examination of their experiences. The triad arrangement provided additional opportunities for collaborative reflection as did the partnership with classroom teachers who had been carefully prepared for their participation. Teachers appeared to feel like partners with the Proteach students because they were familiar with the content students were learning and the roles they were to play in facilitating student learning.

CONCLUSION

In this study we sought to describe general trends across participants. In doing so we have neglected participants who did not engage in collaborative reflection, such as the two teachers who viewed their role as teaching the Proteach students what they needed to know. As a result, they saw themselves as teachers, not learners. We wonder what kinds of adjustments might help participants such as these engage in a process of active knowledge construction? Despite this and other lingering questions, we are confident that we have identified program structures that promote the kind of learning we want to see in our students, ourselves, and the school personnel with whom we collaborate.

REFERENCES

Cochran-Smith, M. (1991). Learning to teach against the grain. *Harvard Educational Review, 61*(3), 279–310.

Fosnot, C. (1996). *Constructivism: Theory, perspectives and practice.* New York: Teachers College Press.

Goodman, J., & Fish, D. R. (1997). Against-the-grain teacher education: A study of coursework, field experience, and perspectives. *Journal of Teacher Education, 48*(2), 96–107.

Lemlech, J. K., & Hertzog, H. H. (1999, April). *Reciprocal teaching and learning: What do master teachers and student teachers learn from each other?* Paper presented at the meeting of the

American Educational Research Association, Quebec, Canada. (ERIC Document Reproduction Service No. ED 429975).

Mayer-Smith, J., & Mitchell, I. (1997). Teaching about constructivism: Using approaches informed by constructivism. In V. Richardson (Ed.), *Constructivist teacher education* (pp.129-153). London: Falmer Press.

Rainer, J., Guyton, E., & Wesche, M. (2001, April). *The effects of constructivist teacher education: A review of the literature*. Paper presented at the meeting of the American Education Research Association, Seattle, WA.

Richardson, V. (1997). *Constructivist teacher education: Building a world of new understandings*. London: Falmer Press.

Ross, D. D., Bondy, E., & Kyle, D. W. (1993). *Reflective teaching for student empowerment*. New York: Macmillan.

Tatto, M. (1998). The influence of teacher education on teachers' beliefs about purposes of education, roles and practice. *Journal of Teacher Education, 49*(1), 66–76.

Wideen, M., Mayer-Smith, J., & Moon, B. (1998). A critical analysis of the research on learning to teach: Making the case of an ecological perspective on inquiry. *Review of Educational Research, 68*(2), 130–178.

CHAPTER 10

Joining the Conversation About Families and Teaching: Counselor Educators' Perspectives on Teacher Preparation

ELLEN S. AMATEA AND JOANNA JENNIE

In this chapter we describe our experience as counselor educators working with other educators to develop and teach a course entitled Family and Community Involvement in Education. The course is designed to enhance teachers' skills in initiating and sustaining positive working relationships with students' families and with other school staff. First, we discuss how counselor educators' involvement in teacher preparation arose from our acquisition of a series of conceptual "lenses," which have shaped the way we think about our work in schools. We then describe traditional expectations about family-school interactions that inadvertently erect and maintain barriers to building collaborative relationships, and the practices introduced in our course to counteract those barriers. Finally, we highlight shifts in our thinking and teaching that have occurred, and note how these shifts have now come full circle to influence our practice as counselor educators and as teacher educators. We hope to encourage other teacher educators and counselor educators to invest in similar training for teachers and counselors to develop collaborative relationships with the families of their students—and with each other.

OUR CONCEPTUAL FRAMEWORK FOR WORKING WITH FAMILIES

Like many counselors who work with children and families, we have experienced a series of transformations in our understanding of

163

and inquiry into the social worlds of children, transformations that have had significant political and ethical implications for our clinical practice and training. In the 1970s our focus shifted from the individual child in isolation to a more inclusive view of the child's behavior contextualized within various systems in which he or she lives. With this move "from psyche to system" (Neill & Kniskern, 1992, p. 121), we began to pay more attention to the child's situation in life and the impact of the child's network of relationships on his or her behavior.

In the 1980s our thinking shifted further, from perceiving ourselves as objective outsiders observing the child's system of relationships to acknowledging our position inside the child's system as participant-observers (Keeney, 1983). This second shift challenged us to contextualize ourselves and to account for the impact of our observations of and interventions with our clients and the systems with which they are involved. In the 1990s our thinking shifted again as we widened our lens to examine the potential of our belief systems and our cultural discourses to construct different possible universes of meaning for our own behavior, the behavior of our clients, and the relationship systems of which we are a part.

The perspectives emerging from these shifts in consciousness have impacted how we think about change, especially our ideas about who is our client, the coconstruction and reconstruction of our clients' realities, and how we position ourselves vis-à-vis those realities. Expanding this choice of lenses has led to a reconsideration of the roles of school counselors and implications for their practice in schools. We now focus not only on individual students experiencing problems in school or in the context of their family-school relationships, but also on how counselors and teachers, in conjunction with other school staff, might change the larger cultural discourse of blame and judgment that often organizes their relations with students and their families to one of collaboration and co-ownership.

We believe that counselors can help their colleagues to purposefully block the blaming that undermines many family-school problem-solving routines by (a) helping them learn how to focus on identifying a problem, (b) determining who might be available to help solve the problem, and then (c) searching together for solutions rather than fixating on assigning blame (i.e., trying to determine who caused the problem and why).

In addition, counselors can collaborate with their colleagues to expand opportunities for interaction with caregivers (i.e., adults who have primary responsibility for the care of children) that are driven more by a desire to build positive alliances with them than solely by the need to respond to problems. By evaluating and redesigning traditional routines of school life such as Back-to-School Night and parent-teacher conferences, school staff can more purposefully construct active, co-decision–making roles with students and their caregivers (Weiss & Edwards, 1992). For example, what do caregivers want their children to learn in school? What are they worried about? What do they know about their children's strengths and needs that may not be evident in the classroom or from the results of standardized tests? Engagement in this manner allows staff to interact with caregivers in positive, non-problematic ways. The progression in our thinking and framework provided the context for our entry into teacher education and the invitation to participate in the Proteach course-design process led us to consider how these new lenses might fit for future teachers.

BUILDING POSITIVE ALLIANCES: RETHINKING FAMILY-TEACHER RELATIONSHIPS

How do our new lenses shape our thinking about teachers' relationships with their students' families? Educators have long recognized the importance of families in influencing students' academic achievement. However, it was not until the late 1980s and 1990s that more systematic attention was given to how educators might work with families to enhance student learning and achievement. This new interest in families was generated by the results of research on the families of preschool and school-age children (Clark, 1983; Dornbush, Ritter, Leiderman, Roberts, & Fraleigh, 1987; Kellaghan, Sloane, Alvarez, & Bloom, 1993; Snow, Barnes, Chandler, Goodman, & Hemphill, 1991). This research demonstrated that families appear to be the crucial ingredient in determining whether a child succeeds in gaining an education.

As a result of these findings, a variety of innovative practices to involve families in the teaching and learning process were developed by early childhood educators working with low-income families (Bronfenbrenner, 1974; Davison, 1998; Scott-Jones, 1987), by educators working with language-minority children (Delgado-Gaitan, 1991; Delpit, 1995), and by educators attempting to restructure and reorganize schools (Comer, Haynes, Joyner, & Ben-Avie, 1996; Senge, Cambron-McCabe, Lucas, Smith, Dutton, & Kleiner, 2000).

Coupled with this growing interest in the family's role in children's academic success were increased pressures placed on schools by the larger political-legal context to include families in educational decision making. For example, the U. S. Congress passed a law requiring that "by the year 2000, every school will promote partnerships that will increase parent involvement and participation in promoting the social, emotional, and academic growth of children" (Goals 2000: Educate America Act, P. L. 103–227, 1994). Furthermore, to comply with Title I mandates under the Improving America's Schools Act, administrators are required to specify in district plans how they will consult with caregivers. Thus, federal legislation has defined an active role for caregivers in educational decision making for their children and for the community at large. This role, according to Tony Wagner, president of the Institute of Responsive Education, is to ensure that caregivers "are not the passive, token 'yes' folks" (Hoff, 1994, p. 1). Implicit in this legislation is recognition of the interdependence of home and school in socializing children (Coleman, 1987), and of the importance of consistency and harmony between these two contexts. In addition, with the use of legislatively mandated high-stakes testing, school grading, and school vouchers as strategies to improve school performance, families now are expected to judge the quality of their children's schools and make decisions about where their children attend school.

As a result of these changed expectations, educators have begun to rethink their involvement with students and their families. Rather than interacting with families merely on an as-needed basis, educators are consciously examining the beliefs undergirding their family-school relations and are proposing a co-expert or partnership paradigm to replace the "authority-client" model that has traditionally characterized family-school relationships (Epstein, 1995; Swap, 1993; Weiss & Edwards, 1992). In the traditional model, the teacher's role is that of "sole expert" who assesses students' needs, identifies concerns or problems that merit attention, decides what type of instruction or solution is necessary, and determines how students and their families should be involved. In this sole-expert model, educators are expected to assume unilateral or dominant roles in educational decision making with a philosophy of "doing to" or "doing for" students and families. In contrast, in a collaborative or partnership model educators "work with" students and their families together to identify resources for taking action to solve children's problems and to celebrate their learning (see appendix D).

Consequently, by the late 1990s the term "family involvement" came into widespread use to reflect the expanding recognition that families are important stakeholders who need and deserve to be engaged in conversations about their children's learning. In addition, school staffs began to analyze their current practices with families and to create more opportunities to invite students' families to participate in the teaching and learning process.

MOVING FROM RHETORIC TO ACTION: A DESCRIPTION OF WHY AND HOW WE INCLUDE COUNSELING IN TEACHER EDUCATION

How widespread are these changes? Researchers have unequivocally demonstrated that when caregivers are involved in their children's education, children have higher educational achievement, better attendance records, and more positive attitudes toward education (Henderson & Berla, 1994). Yet most teachers do not routinely develop or sustain a cooperative process of planning and problem solving with the families of their students (Epstein, 1995). Even with the development of a variety of new models and strategies for enhancing family involvement, many school staffs and caregivers report feeling that they continue to work at cross-purposes with one another (Binns, Steinberg, & Amorosi, 1997). On the one hand, teachers, counselors, and administrators report feeling frustrated in their efforts to involve caregivers in resolving children's problems or significantly changing their educational experience. On the other hand, loving caregivers often report that they feel unable to demonstrate their investment in their children in ways that are recognized and validated by the school. Thus, caregivers often feel disconnected from the school and hopeless about influencing their children's education. As a result, both caregivers and educators often experience pessimism and demoralization (Harry, 1992; Norman & Smith, 1997).

Despite the importance and potentially positive impact of family involvement, teachers and families often find it challenging to work together productively. In the course we address the barriers that hamper efforts to improve these types of relationships (Swap, 1993; Weiss & Edwards, 1992). One barrier commonly noted by teachers and parents is a lack of ongoing, routine, two-way communication between schools and families for sharing information, developing educational plans, and solving problems. Activities in which this type of communication could take place are not typically part of the school calendar. This lack of routine communication sometimes leads to a high degree of alienation between families and schools (Harry, 1992; Procidano & Fisher, 1992).

Our course addresses this concern by presenting the traditional models of family-school relations (e.g., protective and school-to-home transmission models) and contrasting these with the collaborative or partnership models (Swap, 1993; Weiss & Edwards, 1992). Through self-reflection and interviews with their families of origin, our students analyze the paradigms in place during their education and that of their caregivers. They then analyze the paradigms implicit in their vision of themselves as teachers. We examine traditional school-to-home communication strategies and their consequences, and then consider how these might be altered to create a more collaborative relationship structure.

A second barrier to creating more collaborative relations between home and school is that school staff often lack skills to elicit and constructively use input from students and their caregivers. Because most school professionals are trained in separate specialties by academicians who operate with substantial autonomy and academic freedom, most educators have little experience with resolving differences of opinion or working for collective action. Consequently, school staff know how to talk at families, not with them. In addition, most of the interactions that do occur are triggered exclusively by problems. As a result, families generally expect their interactions with school staff to be adversarial (i.e., they expect to be blamed for their children's difficulties), and teachers often feel the same way.

To overcome this barrier we practice active listening skills and strategies for blocking blaming. In addition, we introduce a structured model for resolving problems in which caregivers and students are invited to jointly engage with the staff. After viewing videotaped examples of the process, our students practice this family-school problem-solving meeting format in role-plays. Through these routines we demonstrate how teachers can create and strengthen the network of caring adults who can address and solve children's problems.

Limited role conceptions constitute a third barrier. Rather than viewing caregivers as active codecision-makers or partners, most school staff view caregivers either as having deficits that educators should address, or as capable only of being passive supporters or audience members. Many parent-involvement efforts described in the literature (e.g., Harry, 1992; Procidano & Fisher, 1992) inadvertently reinforce a deficit view of caregivers. Problem-oriented programs intended to prevent reading difficulties, pregnancy, substance abuse, dropping out, or truancy are illustrative of this thrust. Regrettably, focusing initially on deficits alienates families and schools from one another, rather than connecting them.

We introduce students to practices that allow all caregivers to be integrally involved in the education of their own children—not just caregivers of children who are having difficulties. Our goal is to help families, their children, and school staffs build on their strengths and collaborate around a shared vision of how students can grow and succeed rather than fail or risk failing. We do this by showing our students how to redesign traditional family-school routines such as

Back-to-School Night and parent-teacher conferences as collaborative endeavors, which include the child and emphasize how the child can develop and succeed. We give particular attention to the practice of student involvement in evaluation and conferencing in its many forms (Austin, 1994). Such approaches focus not on how teachers can "fix" families or "save" their children, but on what families and schools can create together.

The perception of cultural, socioeconomic, and racial differences between school staff and families can create another barrier in communication and decision making. Although the research evidence is overwhelming that almost all caregivers value schooling and achievement and want to be involved in their children's learning, research also reveals that many families feel unwelcome in schools and/or unsure as to how to interact with their children's teachers or to contribute to their education (Harry, 1992; Procidano & Fisher, 1992; Swap, 1993). Increased family diversity and a sense of being different from school personnel may exacerbate caregivers' discomfort (Finders & Lewis, 1994).

Although there is no question that changing economic and social conditions have led to less family participation during the school day, caregivers are, nevertheless, concerned about their children and do want them to succeed. Therefore, rather than unnecessarily restrict the roles caregivers play in their child's schooling to those that occur at school (e.g., classroom volunteerism, instructional support, or audience), family-school events need to underscore the role of caregivers as codecision-makers and illustrate the belief that everyone—caregivers, teachers, and students alike—has a job to do to ensure the student's educational success, whether caregivers can come to school or not.

We examine the sociopolitical contexts of race, class, and power and how these impact family-school relationships. Our students are encouraged to consider how the unconscious position of privilege might impact future relationships with children and families (McIntosh, 1989), how to recognize and transform stereotypes about diverse families, and how to demonstrate their respect for caregivers' contributions to their children's learning.

TRANSFORMATIONAL PRAXIS

Among the many challenges we have encountered in developing and teaching this course is the extent to which we "practice what we preach." Given the constraints not only of traditional administrative practices in postsecondary education but also students' expectations about what constitutes an undergraduate course experience, we have been intrigued and challenged by the possibilities of creating a model of collaboration that mirrors collaborative practices in schools. We have utilized student feedback and ongoing instructional collaboration to make several significant shifts not only in course content but also in our planning and teaching process.

What is "Family Involvement"?

First, our very definition of and language about "family involvement" has changed. Our students often begin the semester with dichotomous assumptions about families being either too involved or intrusive ("telling me how to do my job") or not involved at all or avoidant ("they don't care about their child's education"). We challenge students to reframe those assumptions, as well as the idea that families must reproduce the activities of the school in order for "real" learning to occur outside of school. We explore the contributions that families make in the course of daily life that are rich opportunities for learning but don't necessarily duplicate what happens in classrooms. We are becoming more mindful of the significance of caregivers' ongoing attempts to respond to their children's schools in spite of years of negative experiences with those schools.

Beyond "Open House"—Infusing Family Collaboration Throughout the Curriculum

A significant shift occurred for Ellen when she realized that she had focused only on teaching about noninstructional interactions (e.g., family-school problem-solving meetings, back-to-school nights, and student-involved conferencing). While these are all effective strategies for building collaborative relationships, they may easily be perceived as extra or add-on work, of lesser priority to overwhelmed and over-worked teachers than "real" instruction.

We decided to showcase instructional strategies developed by talented teacher-researchers who gave caregivers a real voice in their children's education. McCaleb (1994) and Shockley, Michalove, and Allen (1995) provided vivid examples of how teachers can create interactive modes of instruction in which caregivers have an active role (e.g., students conducting interviews with caregivers, families writing stories and creating family storybooks together, caregivers and students developing reading and writing journals that go from home to school and back again). We incorporated these real-world examples of collaborating with caregivers and making decisions with them (rather than for them) about their children's learning into our course experience. As the course evolves, we have continued to build on the philosophy that children's learning is the central task of schooling (Ladson-Billings, 2001), and all family-school activities should be organized around that premise.

From "Show and Tell" to Learning by Doing

The course begins by introducing students to theoretical models of family-school relationships and practical applications of those models. Very quickly it became clear that no matter how much we described or had students read about collaborative practices, the most powerful student learning occurred during experiential activities with such skills as blocking and bypassing blame, conducting family-school problem-solving meetings, preparing children and caregivers for student-involved conferencing, and participating in meetings for Individualized Educational Plans (IEPs). One instructor organizes her class into family teams in which each family represents at least one aspect of family diversity that teachers are likely to encounter in their future classrooms (e.g., children with special needs, families headed by grandparents, foster care families, immigrant families, families headed by gay or lesbian caregivers).

One Step at a Time: Reducing Anxiety About Encounters With Diversity

In addition to coursework, first-semester Proteach students also participate in a field experience as a mentor and tutor of a low-income child. Through our collaboration with the faculty responsible for the mentoring program, our students interview the caregivers of their mentees as a home-visitation experience, a practice that is increasingly endorsed in many parts of the country. Not surprisingly, many students who previously had little direct experience with diversity were overwhelmed by this project, and fearful about traveling in neighborhoods that they perceived as unsafe. They also reported that caregivers were hostile, unresponsive, and/or indifferent to requests for interviews.

After the first semester, Ellen suggested subdividing this dreaded interview assignment into smaller steps so that it would not be so scary and intimidating—or so unlike what teachers might really do with the time they have available in their regular school day. We now guide students through the relationship-building process in "baby steps," linking the contact much more closely to the tasks of the individual teaching or tutoring of the student. Students in their teaching/mentoring role now seek to discover what they can learn from the child's caregiver that can enhance the child's learning and what the caregiver would like to learn from them about their child's progress.

Practicing What We Teach: Creating Collaborative Classrooms

If our collaborative model encourages the development of positive relationships with caregivers before problems occur, how do we develop similar relationships with our undergraduate students? If we suggest that they, as teachers, should inquire about caregivers' goals and concerns regarding their children's education, what contradictory messages do we send if we do not ask the same of them? If we endorse "shared decision making" and "co-ownership" among caregivers, teachers, and other school professionals, how do we demonstrate and practice these lofty concepts within a traditional college of education? These are just a few of the questions that Joanna has begun to experiment with by making contact with students before the semester begins, by seeking their input regarding their learning needs and interests before publishing the syllabus, and by engaging in a very purposeful exchange of e-mail and written messages. Students' reactions to these experiences parallels published reports of family-school collaboration (e.g., Swap, 1993; Weiss & Edwards, 1992). The goal is for students to experience these activities as less problematic and time-consuming than they thought and thus become more willing to engage with the families of their future students in similar ways.

Becoming Partners: Developing a Collaborative Teaching Team

The traditional norms governing the organization and management of schools and postsecondary institutions emphasize hierarchy, individualism, and bureaucratic specialization rather than dialogue, relationship, and reciprocity. These norms often devalue collaborative planning by school staff with each other as well as with students and their families (e.g., allocating no time for regular, frequent, and compensated meetings between key participants). Instead, teachers and professors tend to work in isolation from one another and their workday is often tightly scheduled with little or no flexibility for collaboration, resulting in few opportunities for interaction with other members of their own department, much less faculty members from other departments, or from educators or families from the public schools. We decided to change these norms.

Five professionals participated in our original course-design team: a faculty member and two doctoral students from the Department of Counselor Education and a faculty member and one doctoral student from the Department of Special Education. Over the past two years, both faculty members have moved from direct teaching to consultative and supervisory responsibilities for the course, and new doctoral-level student instructors join our team as others graduate. Despite, or perhaps even because of, these ongoing changes in instructional staff, we have successfully developed and maintained a sense of joint ownership and collaboration among team members.

Several events highlight our progress in becoming partners in this instructional effort. First, because we were developing a unique course experience for teachers that emphasizes the role of families as co-owners and codecision makers, we had to develop many of the teaching materials from the ground up. Because this task was too big for just one person or one department working alone, we truly needed each other's expertise and energy to accomplish our curriculum development goals. Consequently, we felt a sense of shared need and shared ownership for creating and teaching the course. Second, because each member of the design team was deeply committed to the vision of families having a voice in their children's education, we each brought a level of energy and passion to this work effort that created a joint sense of mission and stimulated our creativity.

We developed a clear task focus as we identified our goals as a team and determined how we would monitor our progress toward our goals. We chose to make the development of a curriculum guide a priority, along with the coordinated resolution of any student problems we might face. To accomplish these goals, we met weekly, establishing a regular, ongoing, structured, and systematic means for creating and developing the instructional experience. We each contributed to the development of the curriculum based on our individual interests and expertise. One team member, for example, developed a module about student-involved conferencing; another focused on family-school problem-solving meetings; and still another developed lessons on the family's role in the identification, assessment, and planning for children with special learning needs. We each brought not only a unique set of strengths and competencies to the team but also different perspectives on the situations we faced.

We set up a timetable for the development (and later revision) of various lessons in the course and used that timetable to schedule the presentation of lessons and activities to the team at the weekly meeting. We engaged in a lot of information sharing and joint decision making about our goals, expectations about our students' level of conceptual development, policies regarding the evaluation of student work and style of participation, and teaching practices. Commenting on this, one of our doctoral students stated, "The time committed to weekly meetings gave me space to be reflective about my work, to seek new ideas and feedback from other team members, and to continually improve the quality of my teaching " (A. Allen, personal communication, July 2001).

We also used our weekly team meetings to deal with problems that emerged as we taught the course. As mentioned previously, one problem concerned students' negative reactions to the caregiver interview assignment. Although we encouraged students to conduct the interview in the family's home or neighborhood, many students resisted and complained that caregivers were unfriendly and uncooperative and their neighborhoods too dangerous to enter. As these reactions emerged, we brought this problem to the team for discussion. We worked on not being overly reactive (i.e., jumping to conclusions about the students' intentions and perceptions), and instead attempted to understand their perspectives. We also consulted with the faculty member responsible for the mentoring program for guidance in restructuring the assignment to make it less anxiety producing. As a result, we were able to develop a clearer support structure for students struggling with this assignment (and for each other) as we sought a balance between challenging and supporting them.

A key feature in the development of our team was not only our clear sense of purpose and development of routines for setting goals, planning and implementing projects, exchanging information, and clarifying responsibilities, but also our strong commitment to co-equality. We sought to give each member an equal opportunity in decision making. Consequently, rather than the course curriculum becoming a rigid, prescriptive guide, team members are encouraged to adapt it to fit their own unique style and expertise and that of their students. Moreover, as crises develop, we pool our resources and expertise to respond to individual and group crises collectively and to revise our team agenda accordingly. For example, to introduce students to the hidden influence of social power on family-school relationship building, we encouraged our team members to use a simulation game that depicts the impact of inequities in social power. To introduce our teammates to the value of the simulation, we demonstrated the simulation in each of their classes. Team collaboration occurred again when two team members with well-developed local networks set up a panel presentation for students in all five sections of the course at which caregivers of special-needs children talked about their experiences with and preferences for working with educators.

In summary, becoming partners has required us not only to make a commitment to spend time together and to share the workload, but also to learn how to organize and structure our time and develop a process for working together. We also had to develop ground rules for dealing with different perspectives and priorities. At this time our work together continues to evolve and we are excited by the level of innovation and creativity that we discover in ourselves and encourage in our team members as a result of this shared experience.

RETHINKING SCHOOL COUNSELOR PREPARATION

Focusing on the world of teachers and families has led us to view the role of the school counselor with very different eyes. We now find ourselves asking questions about the ways in which counselors routinely position themselves with teachers, children, and families, questions we never thought to ask before now.

How do we position ourselves with children and families? Do we inadvertently reinforce the view of families as deficient and dysfunctional by the ways in which we work with them? Do we really believe that families are coexperts on their children's learning or are we organized to "save" children from their families? Do we routinely include children and families in making decisions and identifying, addressing, and solving problems? Do we promote a commitment to cultural diversity by examining whether we (as well as teachers) deliver services to families and teachers in ways that respect their values and traditions?

How do we position ourselves with teachers? Do we really view our roles with teachers as interdependent and mutually beneficial? Do we develop our goals, practices, and routines by sharing ownership—or do we "do our own thing" and try to persuade teachers to agree with what we have already decided is best for everyone concerned? Do we really bring teachers in on common concerns? Although every problem does not need to be resolved through collective problem solving, far too often counselors operate like "lone healers" who work separately from teachers and from students' families.

These types of questions invite us to look with very different eyes at our own counselor preparation program to assess how effectively we prepare counselors with the skills and attitudes needed to work effectively in schools with children, families, and teachers. Thus, this experience of working within a teacher education program has strongly impacted our ideas about the training we provide to counselors as well as that provided to teachers.

REFERENCES

Austin, T. (1994). *Changing the view: Student-led parent conferences.* Portsmouth, NH: Heinemann.

Binns, K., Steinberg, A., & Amorosi, S. (1997). *The Metropolitan Life survey of the American teacher 1998: Building family-school partnerships: Views of parents, teachers and students.* New York: Louis Harris & Associates.

Bronfenbrenner, U. (1974). *Is early intervention effective? A report on longitudinal evaluations of preschool programs* (Vol. 2). Washington, DC: U.S. Department of Health, Education and Welfare.

Clark, J. M. (1983). *Family life and school achievement.* Chicago: University of Chicago Press.

Coleman, J. (1987). Families and schools. *Educational Researcher, 16*(6), 32–38.

Comer, J. P., Haynes, N. M., Joyner, E. T., & Ben-Avie, M. (1996). *Rallying the whole village: The Comer process of reforming education.* New York: Teachers College Press.

Davison, M. L. (1998). *Yearbook: The status of Pre-K-12 education in Minnesota.* Minneapolis: University of Minnesota Office of Educational Accountability, College of Education and Human Development.

Delgado-Gaitan, C. (1991). Involving parents in schools: A process of empowerment. *American Journal of Education, 100*(1), 20–46.

Delpit, L. (1995). *Other people's children: Cultural conflict in the class-room.* New York: New Press.

Dornbush, S. M., Ritter, P. L., Leiderman, D. F., Roberts, D. F., & Fraleigh, M. J. (1987). The relation of parenting style to adolescent school performance. *Child Development, 58,* 1244–1257.

Epstein, J. (1995). School/family/community partnerships: Caring for the children we share. *Phi Delta Kappan, 76,* 701–712.

Finders, M., & Lewis, C. (1994). Why some parents don't come to school. *Educational Leadership, 51,* 50–54.

Goals 2000: Educate America Act, P. L. 103–227. (1994). *The national educational goals report.* Washington, DC: U.S. Government Printing Office.

Harry, B. (1992). *Cultural diversity, families, and the special education system: Communication and empowerment.* New York: Teachers College Press.

Henderson, A. T., & Berla, N. (1994) *A new generation of evidence: The family is critical to student achievement.* Washington, DC: National Committee for Citizens in Education.

Hoff, D. (1994). New laws give schools chance to fight. *Education Daily, 27*(230), 1.

Keeney, B. (1983). *Aesthetics of change.* New York: Guilford.

Kellaghan, T., Sloane, K., Alvarez, B., & Bloom, B. (1993). *The home environment and school learning: Promoting parental involvement in the education of children.* San Francisco: Jossey-Bass.

Ladson-Billings, G. (2001). *Crossing over to Canaan: The journey of new teachers in diverse classrooms.* San Francisco: Jossey-Bass.

McCaleb, S. P. (1994). *Building communities of learners.* New York: St. Martin's Press.

McIntosh, P. (1989). White privilege: Unpacking the invisible knapsack. *Peace and Freedom, 6,* 10–12.

Neill, J. R., & Kniskern, D. P. (1992). *From psyche to system: The evolving therapy of Carl Whitaker.* New York: Guilford.

Norman, J. M., & Smith, E. P. (1997). Families and schools, islands unto themselves: Opportunities to construct bridges. *Family Futures, 1,* 5–7.

Procidano, M. E., & Fisher, C. V. (1992). *Contemporary families: A handbook for school professionals.* New York: Teachers College Press.

Scott-Jones, D. (1987). Mother-as-teacher in the families of high- and low-achieving low-income black first-graders. *Journal of Negro Education, 56,* 21–34.

Senge, P., Cambron-McCabe, N., Lucas, T., Smith, B., Dutton, J., & Kleiner, A. (2000). *Schools that learn: A fifth discipline fieldbook for educators, parents, and everyone who cares about education.* New York: Doubleday.

Shockley, B., Michalove, B., & Allen, J. (1995). *Engaging families: Connecting home and school literacy communities.* Portsmouth, NH: Heinemann.

Snow, C. E., Barnes, W. S., Chandler, J., Goodman, I. F., & Hemphill, L. (1991). *Unfulfilled expectations: Home and school influences on literacy.* Cambridge, MA: Harvard University Press.

Swap, S. W. (1993). *Developing home-school partnerships: From concept to practice.* New York: Teachers College Press.
Weiss, H., & Edwards, M. (1992). The family-school collaboration project: Systemic interventions for school improvement. In S. Christenson, & J. Conoley (Eds.), *Home-school collaboration: Enhancing children's academic and social competence* (pp. 215–243). Silver Springs, MD: National Association of School Psychologists.

CHAPTER 11

Learning from Students' Perspectives on Courses and Field Experiences

ELIZABETH BONDY, LYNNE STAFFORD, AND ANGELA MOTT

Loughran and Russell (1997) began the description of their approach
to constructivist teacher education with an important reminder:
"Preservice student teachers enter their teacher education programs
with differing perceptions of what they think their [program] should do
for them in 'teaching them to teach'" (p. 164). In order to prepare them
to begin their teaching careers, the authors assert that teacher educators
must "meet them on their own terms." Their commitment to understanding how their students view the world of teaching and learning is
elaborated in the set of principles that guide the teacher education program with which Loughran is associated. For example, the principles
include "Prospective teachers have needs which must be considered in
planning and implementing a program and these change through their
preservice development," and, "Student teachers should see the preservice program as an educational experience of worth" (pp. 165–166).
Guided by these and other principles, instructors have developed a program that has been successful in promoting students' knowledge of and
reflection on pedagogy because of the continuous focus on "seeking,
recognizing and responding to [students'] particular needs and concerns
for professional growth" (p. 180).

The authors of this chapter report on a study that was motivated
by similar concerns about meeting students on their terms. Faculty,
graduate students, and public school colleagues had worked feverishly
to design a teacher education program based on commitments to democratic values and the development of knowledge about subject matter
and pedagogy. They attempted to build coherence across the semesters

of the program as well as during individual semesters. They tried to align carefully developed field experiences with coursework. Although these features have been shown to hold promise for influencing preservice teachers' views in desired directions (Tatto, 1998), the large size of the program and the diversity of instructors were potential threats to its effectiveness. The faculty implemented the program knowing that mid-course adjustments would be necessary. They viewed insight into students' perspectives as essential to program improvement.

METHODOLOGY

The purpose of the study was to understand the perspectives of the first class of Unified Elementary Special Education Proteach (UESEP) students on their coursework and field experiences in the program. The study was conducted following their completion of the junior year (first two professional semesters) of the program.

Data were gathered through retrospective interviews with 39 students. All 150 students from the first class were invited via e-mail to participate in the study. Because the e-mail contact was made during the summer session, some students were out of town or occupied with summer jobs. Interviews were conducted with all of the students who responded affirmatively to the e-mail invitation. This included 37 female and two male students, 38 of whom were European American and one of whom was African American. Most of the students were of traditional college age, between 20 and 22, while two were in their late 20's.

The interview protocol was developed collaboratively by the authors of this chapter (a faculty member, doctoral student, and UESEP student) and the instructor for a graduate level qualitative research course. Interviews were conducted by 19 students in the qualitative research course and the second (Lynne Stafford) and third (Angela Mott) authors of this chapter. Interviews were audio tape recorded and lasted approximately 45 minutes. Interviews were transcribed in preparation for data analysis.

Data were analyzed by the three authors of this chapter. First, one researcher analyzed five interview transcripts to identify salient categories. Then, the other two researchers each analyzed five transcripts to determine the utility of those categories. Following some adjustment of the main categories, the researchers analyzed all of the interviews for data related to the codes. Although many stories could be told based on the student interviews, the researchers agreed that the most informative story for instructors in the UESEP program and elsewhere was the story of students' views of their experiences in the program.

BACKGROUND

As described in chapter 3, UESEP students are organized into cohorts that take most core courses together. Students in this study had completed their first and second semesters in the program (see chapter 3). The first semester courses focused on diversity, equity, collaboration, and reflection. Faculty viewed the semester as establishing the themes of the unified program and building a foundation for the remainder of the program. The two community-based field experiences provided students direct contact with children, families, and communities that for most of them were unfamiliar. In Bright Futures, students were paired with children who lived in one of six local public housing neighborhoods. They met twice per week with their students and engaged in mentoring and tutoring activities. For Project Book Talk, students went in pairs to home daycare sites in low-income neighborhoods to read and do book-related activities with prekindergarten children. All of the courses used readings, assignments, and in-class activities that were relevant to the two field experiences.

In the second semester, the courses tended to be more methods-oriented and field experiences were, with one exception, school-based (see chapter 3). All UESEP coursework was aligned with field experience. For their ESOL (English Speakers of Other Languages) course, students worked in an ESOL classroom for half of the semester and spent the other half in weekly conversation with university students learning to speak English. For the Core Teaching and Management courses, students worked in an elementary classroom for one three-hour period per week. The Emergent Literacy course required that students work with a partner to provide reading tutoring for an individual child in a school's after-school program. In all of the field experiences, students completed observations and assignments that were aligned with the content of the relevant courses (see chapter 5 for more on field experiences).

"REAL LIFE STUFF" AND OTHER FEATURES OF "GOOD" COURSES AND FIELD EXPERIENCES

Several students used the phrase "real life stuff" to refer to program content that matched their view of what teachers need to know and be able to do. In general, students were enthusiastic about course-work and fieldwork that they viewed as providing insight into and/or strategies useful in the real world of teaching. Their interviews also revealed characteristics of courses and field experiences that fostered "real life stuff." Here we present students' views by describing features related to courses and field experiences.

Common Features

There were certain features that "good" courses and field experi-ences had in common. These features included opportunities to learn what teachers do, insights into and understanding about teaching, and alignment between coursework and fieldwork. The common thread in these features was the emphasis on "real world things," or as one stu-dent said, "You know that's stuff you're really going to need."

Opportunities to learn what teachers do. The students valued expe-riences that closely resembled what they believed they would be doing as classroom teachers. They believed they knew what they should be doing in the program as is indicated by the student who remarked, "That is what we are supposed to be doing now, before we step into our internship."

In coursework, then, students valued opportunities to learn and practice teaching strategies that they believed teachers would use. Across the board, students valued what they called "practical" classes, or classes that were in their words "more what we're going to do in the classroom." For instance, one student remarked, "The ones that I think are the best are the ones that are really practical. Teaching strategies and classroom management are two classes that were just practical. You learned what to think about when you're trying to manage 30 kids."

Similarly, another commented,

> A lot of the stuff we did ... was very useful, very practical. For exam-ple, the grant proposal ... was so beneficial. I can really see myself using that the first year. ... I teach in order to get books. ... I showed that to my mom, who's also a teacher, and she said, "Wow! I wish I learned stuff like that when I was in college."

Good field experiences also provided opportunities to learn what teachers do. In general, students valued the classroom-based field expe-rience more than the community-based experiences because they viewed them as more like real teaching, as one student explained:

> [The classroom experience] was more useful than Bright Futures or Book Talk. As a teacher, how much time will I get to work individu-

ally with a student? The [classroom-based experience] was more like a classroom will be. I had a young teacher with new ideas, and she was able to communicate with us because she was young. It was good to see how classroom management worked. I was in a fourth grade, and I was there for all the testing, to see how that goes. So it was good; it wasn't fake like a project you do for a class grade.

Another student elaborated on this perspective:

The one where I was actually in a classroom this past semester was most beneficial to me because I was actually working with a whole class rather than just a single student.... We got to ... make lesson plans and ... teach the class.

These students and their peers agreed that a good field experience was one in which they could observe events and try activities in real classrooms. Although other field experiences may have been viewed as having some value, they were not as well received as those that matched the students' view of what they would do as teachers.

Providing new insights and understandings about teaching. Practical experiences were not only those that taught specific strategies. Students favored classes and field experiences that gave them new insights into how to teach. For example, one student commented on the value of his Child Development class:

I think probably the class that really stands out in my mind ... was my first semester child development class. It was so relevant to what we were learning. When I look at students, I draw on knowledge of what I learned in that class. What stage of socialization are they at? At that age, what should they be able to do? What should they not be able to do? That's where we learned about the zone of proximal development and scaffolding.

Another student commented on her Family and Community Involvement Class, "You really weren't learning to ... write a lesson plan or any of that in there, but I think we were learning other things about understanding the children and their families to better help us work with them."

Similarly, students valued field experiences that gave them new insights into the work of teaching. They described field experiences that helped them learn about themselves and the students they will teach. About her ESOL field experience, one student commented,

That was helpful because, even though I'm from [a small Florida town], we don't have diversity. I wasn't used to that growing up. I can see more how to talk with [ESOL students] and use pictures and stuff like that, and to work with them individually.

Similarly, another student said, "I've been moved out of my comfort zone to work with students that need more of my attention, that require a lot more, and that's been the most positive to me."

Alignment of fieldwork and coursework. The students indicated that a feature of good coursework and fieldwork was their careful alignment with one another. In other words, students liked courses that were closely linked to fieldwork, and vice versa. In response to her field placement experience, one student stated, "It was great because we could apply what we learned from our Core Teaching Strategies class." Another student said, "Because of the fact that we got the experience of actually working with an entire classroom, we learned what you should do to teach a direct instruction lesson, what you should not do, and the difference between the two." A student commented enthusiastically on aligned fieldwork and coursework when she said,

> Every field component is tied directly to what we're learning in the classroom.... It has been a positive experience to actually take what we've been learning about assessment, teaching styles, methods of classroom management, and work with students directly and be able to apply it and find out what works best for us and what doesn't.

When students perceived that courses and field experiences were closely linked, they were confident that, as one said, "it will totally benefit us in the long run." Coordinated courses and field experiences contributed to students' views that what they were learning would help them to teach. As one said, "I'm not going to be totally surprised when I go into the classroom."

Course Specific

For Proteach students, having a good instructor was the most prominent characteristic of a good course. If the instructor was knowledgeable, ran an interactive class, and made personal connections with students, the students tended to perceive the class as being useful or helpful.

Knowledgeable instructors were seen as "up-to-date in the current trends in education." Students described them as "advanced" and "educated" people who were able to keep students "up-to-date." In addition, students saw knowledgeable teachers as having considerable classroom experience to share with their students. One explained, "She would tell us personal stories, and your heart would go out for what she did, and that influences you and impacts the way you teach."

Students valued instructors who facilitated classroom interaction because they believed they learned best under those conditions. One explained, "They let us do group work, which is good interaction. I think discussion is good because it helps me remember the material better. I think the more I can manipulate the material, the better I can remember it." Not surprisingly, students also valued the opportunities to try out new strategies with one another rather than simply listen to them being described, as the following quote illustrates:

> We learned about morning meeting, and instead of her standing up there and saying, "These are the parts of the morning meeting, and this is what you do in each part," we had to break up into groups and actually conduct a morning meeting so we could have a better understanding of things...and in one class the teacher demonstrates the lessons, and then we...do one which makes us feel how it is to be the student in the class and then how it is to be the teacher out in the field.

Instructors who made personal connections with students were perceived as good teachers. One student addressed the significance of this caring attitude of instructors when she said,

> They seem real interested in what you have to say and seem concerned about what kind of grades you make and how you are coming along on your paper. They'd always check in to see if you had a question. They're always there.

Another agreed that certain teachers "were always readily available to talk to you." Students used the word "nice" to describe teachers they liked. These teachers were approachable, interested in students, accommodating, and understanding.

Field Experience Specific

Students were generally positive about their field experiences and agreed with the student who said, "Getting to work with school-aged children early on is great!" Nevertheless, some field experiences were viewed more favorably than others. Students believed that good field experiences provided an opportunity to have an impact on children's learning and to reinforce or confirm their decision to become a teacher.

Opportunity to have impact on children's learning. The Proteach students were particularly pleased about field experiences in which they could see evidence that they had made a difference in the lives of the children. One said, "The girl I was tutoring was just not getting any-where with her reading, and then one day everything clicked, and she really improved!" Another said, "I like the mentoring thing, the Bright Futures thing. I thought it was a good idea. Like, I really saw her progress from day one. You know, I felt like I made a difference in the girl's life." The importance of this feature was highlighted by the students who were unable to detect that they had had any impact on the children. One explained, "I just sat there with this little girl a couple of afternoons a week." Similarly, another disenchanted student lamented, "Maybe it helped the little kids to read to them—maybe, I don't know. I didn't see the long-term effects."

Reinforces/confirms their decision to become teachers. Students found some field experiences to be profoundly moving. In particular, students became animated when they described a field experience as confirming their choice of professions. One student explained, "That was the first time I left that school or class or anything thinking, 'This is what I really want to do.' That was the moment that I was like, 'Wow, I really want to be a teacher!'" Other students viewed some field experiences as making all the lectures and coursework worth the effort they required. A student commented, "I really think that it's good to go out into the schools, because it really makes you realize that even though the class work is hard . . . it's really worth it."

MISSING THE POINT: STUDENTS' CONCERNS ABOUT COURSES AND FIELD EXPERIENCES

Many teaching teams met frequently during the summer before the new program was implemented and weekly throughout the semester to design and refine their courses. Despite the faculty's intensive and pro-longed efforts to develop important and engaging courses and field experiences for the UESEP program, some students were critical. It became clear that in some cases, instructors' and students' views of courses and field experiences were out of alignment. Following a review of students' concerns, we consider elements of the context that help explain their views.

Irrelevance

Students saw elements of some courses and field experiences as "irrelevant" to teachers' work. When describing courses, for example, they referred to irrelevant information, in-class activities, and assignments. Their comments included, "Some of those topics were ridiculous!" and "Nobody cares about that!" Such comments indicated that students did not understand the purpose of certain activities and assignments or their relevance to teaching.

Similarly, when describing field experiences, students sometimes failed to recognize a connection between the field experiences and their futures in the classroom. This view was particularly apparent regarding the community-based field experiences. This student's remarks were typical:

> I didn't feel like I was learning a lot that I could use for my teaching. I want to teach third grade.... I don't know—an hour a week to go to these people's house and read to a baby? I don't know.

Another said, " I felt like the University of Florida was just getting a good name for sending us out to volunteer in the community. It didn't prepare me to be a teacher at all." These and similar comments made it clear that too often students were failing to learn what the faculty viewed as essential lessons available to them in coursework and field experience. That is, they seemed to be missing the point.

Quality of Instruction

Students complained about the quality of the instruction used in some of their classes. They identified what they viewed as poor instructional strategies, such as an overemphasis on presentation of facts and a focus on memorization of content for tests. One student elaborated,

> It was strictly memorizing. And if you could memorize it, you got an A on the test. I got an A on the test, but I don't remember any of it. Because everybody just made up mnemonics or whatever or just drilled and practiced and just got it into short-term memory and out the next day.

Another student commented on a class where handouts and lectures prevailed:

> They come into the classroom and they hand us dittos, and they might ask for participation and things, but I really come out of the class thinking, "Wow I—or my scholarship—paid that much money for a class that you know I could have learned that myself?"

Quality of Information

Students voiced concern about the quality of the information they encountered in some classes. They saw some of the material as common sense and/or repetitive. For instance, a student remarked, "You could have taught me that in five hours. I did not need a whole semester; they should have focused on something more." Another said, "It was the same information repeated twice over from classes I had in community college." In addition, students expressed concerns about what they deemed an overemphasis on theory without clear links to practice. On this subject a student said, "They spent a lot of time...talking about the theories...but not much was said about how to teach...which should have been the focus, in my opinion." Another student astutely noted, "It was a foundations course and maybe everybody was expecting a lot more hands-on."

Inconvenient

Some students pointed out that certain field experiences were inconvenient for them. By "inconvenient," students typically meant that it took them too long to drive to the location. They were particularly distressed when they drove to the setting only to find that their assigned child was not there on that day. One student explained, "They were so far away! I mean, I spent a good 45 minutes driving each way. And sometimes, I'd get there...and my girl wouldn't show up." Another student echoed this concern when she said,"We'd drive all the way out there to hear someone say, 'Sorry, there's soccer practice or a field trip. Go home.' That seemed to happen a lot."

Inadequate Opportunity to Learn About Teaching

Although the convenience of field experiences influenced some students' views of their worth, the opportunity to observe teachers work directly with students or to interact with students also affected their assessment of the experience. Students viewed certain opportunities as more valuable than others, as the following interview excerpt indicates:

> We'd have an hour and a half in the classroom when the kids would do one or two activities to get ready for the morning. The timing was difficult...and we had to always be there when they were in music or PE, so we didn't get any good stuff...like seeing the teacher lead a discussion, or read a story, give them an activity to do, introduce a subject they hadn't talked about before, or do a science project, or something. We didn't see any of this.

This student's comments suggest that certain kinds of classroom observations are more worthwhile than others. The student also assumes that observing in music and physical education classes is not worth-while. This student, and others, appeared to have an image of what they would need to know how to do as teachers, and they wanted field experiences that matched their expectations. These students were quick to criticize field experiences that failed to provide what they viewed as the "good stuff."

INTERPRETING STUDENTS' CONCERNS

A number of contextual factors help explain students' concerns about their first-year coursework and fieldwork:

Getting started: The students we interviewed were the first group to enter the UESEP program. Because we were not able to experiment with a pilot cohort, nearly everything the faculty did was new and untested. It was not surprising to find that even with careful planning, students sometimes did not perceive courses and field experiences as faculty had intended. To their credit, the faculty anticipated that problems would surface, planned for formative evaluation, and recognized that there was the potential need for substantial revision.

Instructor zeal: In their enthusiasm to develop an innovative, coherent, and effective program, the faculty designed comprehensive courses that were often linked to field experiences. Some students were overwhelmed by the demands of their first two semesters. In fact, most faculty revised course and field expectations based on student feedback and consultation with colleagues within and across teaching teams.

Program size: The number of students admitted to the program (150 in the first semester) presented challenges to program effectiveness. For example, every course had five sections taught by instructors from as many as three different departments. It was challenging to maintain coordination within a course team; it was more than challenging to maintain coordination and coherence across courses.

Instructor background: Three aspects of instructor background are relevant. One, some experienced instructors were teaching undergraduates and/or preservice teachers for the first time in their careers. They soon recognized that some of the assumptions on which they based course planning and instructional strategies required revisiting. Two, some instructors were novice teacher educators who never had taught young adults. Three, some instructors were recruited late onto course teams; consequently, they had not been involved in the conceptualization and design of the course. Teaching was particularly challenging to the novice instructors and instructors who were assigned late to teaching teams because of the expectation for coherence within teaching teams. These instructors worked to be good "team players" by attempting to implement the courses as their teammates were doing. However, since they did not always have the same breadth and depth of understanding of their courses as their teammates, they sometimes felt unsure of themselves and lacked confidence in answering students' questions about material and assignments. Students, who already felt stretched to the limit, were particularly irritated when their questions were met with, "Let me check with [another instructor] about that." Graduate teaching assistants and adjunct faculty were particularly challenged by these conditions of their teaching assignment.

ADDRESSING STUDENTS' VIEWS

Student feedback can be hard to take. When faculty have worked diligently over several years to create a new and powerful program for students, criticism can be that much harder to swallow. To the faculty's credit, however, many took steps to understand students' perspectives and revise their courses to improve effectiveness.

Most instructors did not wait for data from this study to begin examining students' responses to their courses and field experiences. Instructors gathered data in several ways in addition to having students complete the university's course evaluation form. One instructor conducted individual interviews with student volunteers early in the semester following the course. Another conducted a focus-group interview of volunteer students, also in the semester following the course. Instructors created a variety of written feedback forms. For example, one instructor had students rate each assignment in the class on a scale of one to five, with one representing "keep it" and five representing "get rid of it." Students were asked to provide explanations for their ratings. Another instructor had students specifically address redundancy of coverage across courses and between previously taken courses and her course. Others had students identify strengths and weaknesses of the course and make recommendations for improvement. These attempts to elicit students' views indicate the instructors' eagerness to improve their courses and the UESEP program.

RECOMMENDATIONS FOR TEACHER EDUCATORS

Insight into students' perspectives on courses and field experiences can help teacher educators improve program effectiveness. Their views suggest some general principles that could help teacher educators meet students on their own terms.

Directly Assess and Address Students' Expectations and Prior Knowledge

When a program experience does not provide what students expect, it may be perceived as a disappointment. For example, students may expect to learn teaching strategies in a course that was intended to provide foundational knowledge. When instructors understand students' expectations, they are in a better position to help them understand the purpose of the course, its relationship to other courses and experiences in the program, and its relevance to classroom teaching. Instructors can gain insight into students' expectations by having them discuss and record insights with a partner or in a small group. This can also be done individually as an in-class free-write or one-minute response activity.

Similarly, when instructors understand students' prior knowledge, they can shape curriculum and instruction to accommodate students. Instructors can accomplish this by providing checklists of topics that students can rate to indicate they know a lot about the topic, have heard of the topic, or have never heard of it. Although there always will be variation across students, there are also frequently themes that emerge from this kind of assessment. These themes provide valuable guidance for instructors.

Use Implicit and Explicit Instructional Strategies

The data indicate that although there were trends across students' views of their coursework and field experience, there were also differences in the way students viewed particular elements of the UESEP program. Different assessments of the program were related in part to differences in the ways students approached their learning. Some students approach their teacher education program with an inquiring mind and an openness to learning. They approach learning to teach as a puzzle to be solved and work to fit together the pieces of the puzzle. These are the students about whom faculty say, "I wish I had a whole class of students like her!"

The challenge for teacher educators is how to work with students who approach their program from a narrower perspective. These are the students who seem to skim the surface of their coursework and field experiences, rejecting that which doesn't match their definition of what is important. They retain bits of information from a variety of experiences, but they do not integrate the bits into a coherent whole. The data on students' views suggest that instructors must find ways to help more students recognize the purpose, relevance, and value of their experiences in the program. Faculty must not assume that students are "getting it"; as these data show, many students are missing the point. Explicit explanation of purpose, relevance, and value may help students assimilate material that they otherwise might reject. Explicit discussion of connections between program elements may help students integrate knowledge. Further, opportunities to apply new ideas in real or simulated teaching contexts with accompanying opportunities to examine field-based experiences in the college classroom may help students value course content and field experience that they otherwise might view as irrelevant.

Use a Variety of Approaches to Assess Students' Conceptions and Misconceptions

UESEP instructors generally agree that they cannot afford to wait for the student feedback that comes from the required university course evaluation form. They are experimenting with a variety of ways to gain insight into students' views of program experiences. While some instructors have instituted a mid-semester anonymous feedback activity, others elicit feedback on a weekly basis. Some describe themselves as constantly revising their practice based on student feedback. These instructors observe students for signs of resistance or discomfort and seek alternative strategies to try to re-engage them with the course. Individual, small group, and whole class formats may be used to get oral and written data on students' views. Simply asking students, "What kinds of changes would help you learn better in this course?" can help instructors understand students' perspectives and provide direction for mid-course adjustments.

Consider Realities of Students' Lives When Designing Programs

The interview data provided instructors with insight into the demands of students' lives. The majority of students hold jobs that require 20 or more hours per week. A growing number of students have children, and many commute more than two hours per day to attend the university. Given that time and money are scarce commodities for many students, some of their concerns about courses and field experiences are hardly surprising. When designing courses and field experiences, teacher educators must seek to balance the accomplishment of program goals with the demands of students' lives outside of the university. One way in which this can be accomplished is by coordinating readings, assignments, and field experiences across courses (see chapters 5, 9 and 10). Doing so requires a willingness to collaborate and compromise with colleagues.

CONCLUSION

If teacher educators hope to help students learn to teach according to a constructivist approach, surely they must work with students in constructivist ways. This commitment requires that we engage with their views or meet them on their own terms. Peterman (1997) and others have described the challenges of constructivist teaching in higher education. Although demanding of our time, patience, and ingenuity, this approach to teaching requires no more than we expect our students to do with the children in their future classrooms. When we attend to our students' views we are in a better position to build bridges between them and the knowledge, skills, and dispositions we want them to learn.

REFERENCES

Loughran, J., & Russell, T. (1997). Meeting student teachers on their own terms: Experience precedes understanding. In V. Richardson (Ed.), *Constructivist teacher education: Building a world of new understandings* (pp. 164–181). London: Falmer Press.

Peterman, F. (1997). The lived curriculum of constructivist teacher education. In V. Richardson (Ed.), *Constructivist teacher education: Building a world of new understandings* (pp. 154–163). London: Falmer Press.

Tatto, M. (1998). The influence of teacher education on teachers' beliefs about purposes of education, roles and practice. *Journal of Teacher Education, 49*(1), 66–76.

CHAPTER 12

Views from the Inside:
An Outsider's Perspective

RENEE TIPTON CLIFT

It isn't easy to maintain a balance among the actions that promote program improvement and those that protect a fledgling program from rapid extinction. Activities such as rigorous self-evaluation, reflective analysis of one's own practice and that of one's colleagues, or sharing data that are both positive and negative, are not likely to occur without an agreement among faculty and administrators to create and sustain a nondefensive environment in which participants work collaboratively toward continuous improvement. Time, resources, ideological differences, competing goals, and the absence of historical, organizational, or cultural norms for surfacing issues and problems often implicitly and explicitly discourage open discussions of processes and outcomes of practice (Argyris, Putnam, & McClain-Smith, 1987; Clift, Veal, Holland, Johnson, & McCarthy, 1995). Furthermore, the creation of a positive, enthusiastic image for a new program is often necessary in order to maintain institutional, financial, and personal commitment to the program.

As a set, the chapters in Part 3 strive for an appropriate balance between advocacy for and critical reflection on Unified Elementary and Special Education Proteach (UESEP). It is very, very unusual for faculty from across departments to come together to plan, implement, and critically evaluate themselves, one another, and the program. It is even more unusual that they would share their data and their thoughts publicly. The authors provide us with a critical insiders' perspective that foregrounds the diversity among perspectives that one can find at many, if not most, large teacher-education programs at research-intensive institutions. As a faculty member working in a university much like the University of Florida, I will provide an outsider's view in the role of critical friend.

I was an undergraduate in the secondary program at the University of Florida in the late '60's and early '70's. During this time, the elementary program offered students the option of working individually to learn a given skill or body of knowledge through a series of tasks and activities. At the end of the unit, or activity, the student would demonstrate competency on the content and objectives of the activity and begin another one. Not only was Florida one of the leaders in the competency-based teacher education movement, it was also a major site for the process-product research on effective teaching behaviors, under the direction of Robert Soar and colleagues (Brophy & Good, 1986). Those of us who were in secondary education (like our peers in the elementary program) were steeped in the humanistic tradition of teacher education (Combs, 1974). We were taught to create our units and plans with little or no reliance on a textbook; we were encouraged to think of ways to encourage self-actualization (Maslow, 1968).

In the mid-'80's I reconnected with Florida when the university developed Proteach, a program based on research on effective teaching that also encouraged the development of reflective practice (Ross, 1990). At the time, faculty members from many teacher-education programs were meeting at conferences to discuss how we might encourage and assess reflective activity. Clearly, the University of Florida College of Education has been and still is a place where innovations in teacher education were valued and where research on teaching and teacher education is the norm.

SEEKING ANSWERS THROUGH MANY QUESTIONS

The innovations chronicled in Part 3 of the volume describe the challenges of learning to work in teams, across departments, and across university boundaries. The data are not always flattering and the authors' stories are not always tales of overwhelming success. Instead, what we read in these chapters is a data-based account of the early stages of program change. The participants are actively using ongoing data collection and analysis as they refine their new program. In the first part of this chapter, I briefly summarize the data, analysis, and interpretations of the University of Florida team and the questions that they raised for me. In the second part I discuss some of the advantages and problems inherent in conducting research on one's own teacher education program.

Collaborative Teaching

In their chapter, Mary Brownell, James McLeskey, Patricia Ashton, David Hoppey, and Rhonda Nowak address the numerous tensions inherent in collaborative planning and teaching. Three teaching teams working across two departments sought to enable prospective elementary teachers to think about emergent literacy, classroom management, and teaching methods. In so doing they found it necessary to incorporate the more constructivist perspectives of the School of Teaching and Learning faculty with more behaviorist perspectives of the Special Education faculty. Interview data were collected from the two primary faculty members on each team (one from each department). The interviews documented that the nature of collaborative planning and instruction varied with the team, as did the tensions that arose throughout. Planning involved ways to combine courses taught in the separate departments and developing a syllabus to be used across multiple sections of the course (often taught by doctoral students). Teaching meant more than instruction in that it also involved meeting with one another and the doctoral students to monitor course implementation.

The nature of collaboration. The phrase, "collaboration was expected," can be found throughout the chapter, but in reality collaboration was a priority for some faculty, but not for others. One team, assigned to teach a course on instructional methods, met weekly with the doctoral student instructors to debrief and plan for future instruction. On the other teams the special education faculty were not present for weekly meetings with the doctoral students. The authors suggest that one reason for this might be that the special education faculty did not have a long history of working collaboratively on instructional tasks and, in part because of responsibilities for grant administration, experienced an overload of responsibilities. Collaboration became something to negotiate within teams. For the teams that did not meet regularly, collaborative planning was perceived as overly stressful, but sometimes useful in that one could learn from one's colleagues. For the team that did meet regularly, collaborative planning was perceived not only to serve as an occasion for ongoing professional development, but also as a time-saver in that they could partition responsibilities.

The negotiation of autonomy. One team, assigned to teach about management and discipline, was unable to successfully negotiate the boundaries between independent, autonomous instruction and negotiated curriculum. A second team, teaching about emergent literacy, was better able to negotiate curriculum, but varied when it came to instruction. Some of the negotiation involved differing views of the classroom teacher's role on managing behavior (prevention vs. intervention) and focus (whole class vs. addressing individual behaviors). Some of the negotiation involved differing views of knowledge (assessing convergence on concept attainment vs. divergent expressions of concepts as applied in practice) and the need to acquire skills (diagnosis-prescription vs. open-ended tutoring). What is interesting is that in two of the teams, the negotiation was never resolved—individual instructors acted as they were accustomed to act, regardless of the accord that was negotiated—and their counterparts were unaware that they did so. The team that met regularly used the conflicting views as an occasion to think through the limitations and contributions of their own and their partner's conceptions.

Why collaborate? Why not? Based on their interviews, the authors identify several benefits of collaboration. First, partners learned from one another about curriculum, pedagogy, and instructional resources. Second, collaboration enabled faculty to develop common goals and to identify areas across the teacher-education program in which differing beliefs are expressed and promoted. But they question the institutional culture's ability to promote collaboration—especially when there has been no such history. They also question individuals' abilities to safely engage in collaboration when it is perceived to work against the norms and activities that are necessary for promotion, tenure, and salary increases.

Collaborative Decision Making and Problem Solving

Ellen Amatea and Joanna Jennie examine collaboration from a slightly different perspective. They are interested in enabling teachers to build collaborative relationships between schools and families from a counseling perspective. For the authors this means disengaging from any attempt to assign blame for problems and to focus instead on identifying the problems and working together toward resolution.

Students in a course titled, "Family and Community Involvement in Education," addressed barriers that may prevent them from becoming more collaborative such as their own backgrounds and experiences, skills such as active listening and strategies for blocking blaming; role conceptions in which parents are seen as resources (as opposed to deficits); and misperceptions based on cultural, racial, and socioeconomic differences between teachers, children, and families. Teaching collaboratively was an issue in a previous chapter; teaching people to act collaboratively is an issue for these authors. Learning from their students in a form of action research has been essential for course improvement.

Transforming university teaching to follow practices recommended for classroom teachers. The authors realized that talking without demonstrating often leads students to reject the talk. They began by providing real examples of teachers who included caregivers in instruction—and included the caregivers in decisions about the instruction itself. They created simulations of family teams and worked through situations teachers were likely to face from diverse perspectives. They placed students in the community in order that they might interview families—many of whom were very different from the prospective teachers. And they openly collaborated with one another to demonstrate the need for ongoing analysis and improvement. For the authors, all of this meant transforming their position of faculty instructor into a role of guide, in which professors get to know their students before class, discussing their needs ahead of time, and working with them to create a meaningful curriculum. During team planning meetings they reported that teaching activities are shared through demonstrations, resources and community contacts are shared, and questions are raised and discussed. Learning and teaching have become more reciprocal among faculty members and among faculty and students. Chapters 9 and 11 also address teacher education students' learning, but through more formal means such as retrospective interviews and surveys.

Early Field Experiences

Elizabeth Bondy, Allyson Adams, and Virginia Mallini studied participants' perceptions of the students' first classroom field experience. Nine prospective teachers, nine classroom-based teachers, and two university-based teachers were interviewed during the summer, after the semester had ended. Perceived benefits were identified within and across the participants' groups.

Benefits from the redesigned courses. The students reported on links between coursework and fieldwork, and they were able to discuss how they would use strategies from the program in their own teaching. They also reported that they learned about themselves, especially things that they realized they did not know about the nature of students and about the activities and routines involved in teaching. The classroom teachers reported learning new instructional strategies, but they also felt that the program validated and appreciated their teaching expertise. They were especially pleased when students and faculty reported about learning new things from them. In addition to learning about teaching from the teachers, university teachers commented positively on the challenges to connect ideas to practice when courses become more and more field based.

Benefits of the partnership. The authors noted that the idea of partnership is not one-dimensional and that multiple partnerships come into being with the creation of the new courses. Students and classroom teachers and university teachers worked together to plan and assess implementation of assignments and instruction. Not only did this serve as an opportunity for professional development, it increased the notion that all participants—students and teachers—are teacher educators. The partnerships enabled ongoing reflection and created a structure for learning about how to teach and to improve through communal analysis of experiences.

Program Participants

Elizabeth Bondy, Lynne Stafford, and Angela Mott studied the perspectives of the first class of UESEP students by interviewing 39 volunteers (of the 150 in the first class) during the summer of 2000 following the first year of the program. Categories of response were surfaced and negotiated, leading to the identification of opportunities and benefits of the program, as well as constraints and problems.

Opportunities and benefits

The students agreed on the following features that led to good experiences: opportunities to learn what teachers do; increased understanding about teaching; and alignment or congruence between coursework and fieldwork. Having a good instructor was a key factor in program satisfaction. A good instructor was perceived as current, experienced, and available. Facilitating interaction among students and between students and teachers and making personal connections with students were also important. A good field experience enabled the prospective teachers to interact with students and to ascertain some influence on their learning.

Concerns

When the purpose of activities or assignments was not clear, the students dismissed them as irrelevant. This was equally true for course and field experiences. Assessments that stressed memorization and instruction that relied primarily on lectures or handouts were perceived as not helpful and a waste of time. Repetitive information—either within the program or between the program and preprogram instruction—was not appreciated, particularly when it was not practice-based. Finally, structural concerns, such as the time and distance required to participate in field experiences and make it back to class on time, were mentioned. This was particularly a concern if the field experience was perceived as passive with few or no opportunities for interacting with students.

And so the chapters in Part 3 have provided us with pieces of an unidentified puzzle picture. If we were to have all of the pieces (which we do not), would we have a picture of a unified teacher education program? Would we have a montage of people and ideas related to one another, but far from unified? Would we have a picture of teacher education? Of higher education? Is it possible that there would be no picture at all, but only some combination of form, color, and texture that changes with the light, the temperature, and the rotation of the puzzle?

QUESTIONS ABOUT QUESTIONS AND ANSWERS

There is no question that different professionals—within and outside of the field of education—have competing views of the nature and purpose of teacher education. Linda Darling-Hammond (2000a) and the National Commission on Teaching and America's Future (1996, September) position preservice teacher education as a crucial first step toward career-long education and continued improvement. In contrast, the recent report issued by the United States Secretary of Education, (U.S. Office of Education, 2002) dismisses mandatory preservice teacher education and calls for the deregulation of entry into the profession. Marilyn Cochran-Smith (Cochran-Smith, 2001; Cochran-Smith & Fries 2001) provides a very detailed and comprehensive discussion of both of these positions and the very different visions they espouse. In the first article Cochran-Smith (2001) categorizes questions about the outcomes of teacher education into three categories: long-term impact; test scores; and professional performance. She argues that the competing visions of what constitute desirable outcomes of teacher education rest on competing assumptions of what is valuable, what goals are desirable, and where priorities lie. "These assumptions shape the ways terms are defined, the ways data are selected and analyzed, and the interpretive frameworks within which conclusions are formulated" (pp. 529–530).

In the second article, Cochran-Smith and Fries (2001) argue that policy makers and analysts appeal to three interrelated warrants (evidentiary, accountability, and political) for promoting some policies and denigrating others—and for claiming that their approach has the advantage of occupying the "high ground of common sense" (p. 13).

> When the advocates of two very different agendas each stake out the high ground, it is doubly difficult to remember also that the warrants each side uses to make its case are tied to their positions within institutional structures and connected in complicated ways to larger viewpoints on society and social relationships within society, viewpoints that go well beyond schools and schooling. (p. 13)

As a set, these two articles provide us with a macro view of the issues; the chapters in Part 3 provide one very interesting micro view. In order to continue working on the puzzle, both views are crucial.

What Can We Learn About Teacher Education From UESEP?

The UESEP accounts remind us that teaching and, therefore, teacher education are very personal and sometimes emotional endeavors. While we can use neutral terms such as negotiation and compromise, collaboration is not a neutral process. When ideas, preferences, and beliefs about curriculum and instruction conflict (as they inevitably will), the resulting curriculum will favor certain proponents; the others will lose the argument and, possibly, professional status. A commitment to teach together or to develop a common curriculum is a commitment to work through the disagreements in ways that will minimize damage to one's collaborators. Together, the chapters in Part 3 suggest that a history of working together is helpful; ongoing feedback from students is helpful; but an institution that seeks to encourage collaborative activities would be well advised to create structures and supports that can assist participants through periods of conflict. One important lesson we can learn from UESEP is that it is possible to build an analysis of conflicting views into the curriculum so that they can be contested and debated. It is also possible to teach professors, teachers, parents, and students strategies for problem identification and analysis to enable all participants to work productively even when they disagree.

We can also learn that collaboration across specializations, roles, and teaching assignments results in important learning opportunities for everyone. Not only can one learn about content, students, or instructional strategies, but the negotiation and the surfacing of diverse views is a crucial factor in continuing to learn professionally and personally. Every chapter in Part 3 reported incidents of such learning. Every chapter contained anecdotes and examples of changes in practice as a result of working together. And when collaboration includes students there is an increased opportunity to learn how to vary instruction and assignments to best meet their needs.

Finally, we can learn about the importance of dynamic interaction among department, college, and university administrative leaders, faculty leaders, and student leaders. Collaboration is not only personal, it is also political. As roles and expectations are modified, administrative policies make such modifications safe for individuals—or not. When budgets are tight as priorities are set, administrators need the support from the collaborators in order to keep the program going—or not. Ongoing research and program evaluation can help provide evidence that supports continuing, modifying, or abandoning the program.

What Can We Learn About Teacher Education Research from UESEP?

The first and most important lesson we can learn from UESEP is that commitment to documentation is important and possible. So often programs are developed, implemented, partially abandoned, and then abandoned. Or they are modified and institutionalized. The chapters in Part 3 provide us with considerable insight into some of the factors that move a program in one direction or another. Assuming that the research is ongoing, the authors will have a complete story in five or six years' time. If more of us were to follow their example, we might begin to enable policy makers with information on how to encourage and sustain desirable changes in teacher education.

The second lesson we can learn is that we researchers often rely on retrospective data. We over rely on volunteer students' retrospective perceptions as opposed to a direct examination of their constructions of teaching and learning as they develop over time. While ongoing assessment of student learning and development occurs within courses, we need better ways of studying development across courses and field settings, and on into actual teaching practice. While such research is often advocated, we have few examples of how it might actually be conducted and what resources and methods it would take to do so.

A final lesson is that an inside view, while crucial, is limited by the hierarchical relations inherent in studying our own students and by the power relations inherent in studying our colleagues and ourselves. Just as most qualitative researchers learn to gather data from different vantage points, we need to learn how to judiciously select and utilize differing data gatherers and to triangulate among gatherers as well as data points.

What Can We Learn About Ourselves as University-Based Researchers, Teacher Educators, and Citizens?

UESEP tells us that we can advocate all of the changes we want to advocate for PreK–12 teachers, but when it comes right down to it, we find it hard to change ourselves. We have varying commitments to changing our roles, our relations with others, and ourselves. And, when we do decide to change entire programs, roles, and relationships, we often jump into the process with bits and pieces of the macro and micro views of the whole, but we seldom carefully sketch, design, gather resources, experiment, and slowly create, assess, and modify our new programs. Our university course approval and budget processes make it difficult to do so; our state approval processes make it almost impossible.

CONCLUSION

More than anything the chapters in Part 3 tell us that teacher educator/researchers continue striving for desirable changes and to create programs of high quality that produce capable and committed beginning teachers. Criticisms of teacher education and teacher educators in the United States are as prevalent today as they have been ever since there were formal curricula for prospective teachers (Borrowman, 1956). It would be understandable if overregulated teacher educators and underfunded teacher education researchers did not produce volumes such as this—politically it might be wiser to focus on the good and to hide the problematic. But that would not help us learn more about how what we do impacts our colleagues, our students, their students, and the community. And attempting to document and understand teacher-education process and outcomes, along with the values that underlie both the research and the programs, is what it means to be a researcher or a reflective teacher within or outside of teacher education.

REFERENCES

Argyris, C., Putnam, R., & McClain-Smith, D. (1987). *Action science.* San Francisco, CA: Jossey-Bass.

Borrowman, M. (1956). *The liberal and technical in teacher education: A historical survey of American thought.* New York: Columbia University, Teachers College, Bureau of Publications.

Brophy, J., & Good, T. L. (1986). Teacher behavior and student achievement. In M. C. Wittrock (Ed.), *Handbook of research on teaching* (3rd ed., pp. 328–375). New York: Macmillan.

Clift, R. T., Veal, M. L., Holland, P., Johnson, M., & McCarthy, J. (1995). *Collaborative leadership and shared decision making: Teachers, principals, and university professors.* New York: Teachers College Press.

Cochran-Smith, M., (2001). The outcomes question in teacher education. *Teaching and Teacher Education, 17*(5), 527–546.

Cochran-Smith, M. & Fries, K. (2001). Sticks, stones, and ideology: The discourse of reform in teacher education. *Educational Researcher, 30*(8), 3–15.

Combs, A.W., Blume, R. A., Newman, A. J., & Wass, H. L. (1974). *The professional education of teachers* (2nd ed.). Boston: Allyn & Bacon.

Darling-Hammond, L. (2000). Teacher quality and student achievement: A review of state policy evidence. *Educational Analysis Policy Archives, 8*(1), 1–49.

Maslow, A. H. (1968). *Toward a psychology of being* (2nd ed.). New York: Van Nostrand Reinhold.

National Commission on Teaching & America's Future. (1996). *What matters most: Teaching for America's future.* New York: Author.

Ross, D. D. (1990). Programmatic structures for the preparation of reflective teachers. In R. T. Clift, W. R. Houston, & M. C. Pugach (Eds.), *Encouraging reflective practice in education: An analysis of issues and programs* (pp. 97–118). New York: Teachers College Press.

U. S. Department of Education, Office of Postsecondary Education, Office of Policy Planning and Innovation. (2002). *Meeting the highly qualified teachers challenge: The secretary's annual report on teacher quality.* Washington, DC. Available from http://www.ed.gov/offices/OPE/News/teacherprep/index.html.

PART 4

Student and Program Evaluation

CHAPTER 13

Performance Assessment: Overview of Challenges and Directions

CATHERYN WEITMAN

Entering the performance-based world in higher education is cumbersome yet manageable. Faculty in the state of Florida must expand their focus to include documenting the skills, abilities, and actions students possess at the conclusion of the program, a requirement for state and national program approval and accreditation. This adjustment is demanding of faculty because it requires that individual philosophical beliefs become the subject of discussion and perhaps debate. Issues such as academic freedom come to the surface. Faculty who have grown accustomed to being responsible for their own course content and for student performance in an individual course must think more broadly about student learning and how to provide evidence of that learning. In this chapter I introduce performance assessment by examining its definition, discussing some challenges to its implementation, and providing directions for those who are already or soon to be engaged in this work. In doing so, I provide an introduction to chapters 14 and 15 that follow on performance assessment in the Unified Elementary Special Education Proteach (UESEP) program at the University of Florida.

DEFINITION AND GOALS

The National Council for Accreditation of Teacher Education (NCATE, 2002) defines performance assessment as "a comprehensive assessment through which candidates demonstrate their proficiencies, professional, and pedagogical knowledge, skills, and dispositions, including their abilities to have a positive effect on student learning." (p. 55). Two key concepts emerging from this definition are comprehensive assessment and demonstration of proficiencies. The Center on Learning, Assessment, and School Structure (CLASS, 1997) suggests that a comprehensive system of assessment is one that is longitudinal, "assessing the same performances over numerous times, using a fixed scoring continuum, to track progress (or lack of it) toward a standard" (p. 36). Performance assessment, then, is a longitudinal process that assesses and tracks proficiency levels against intended targets or standards (i.e., knowledge, skills, abilities, and dispositions) over time against a fixed rubric. In Florida, those standards are represented by a set of 12 "Accomplished Practices" for educators.

According to Wiggins (1998), assessment ought to be educative. This is certainly the case with performance assessment. Educative assessment practices ought to inform; that is, they ought to provide rich and useful feedback to the faculty for enhancing students' ability to meet the desired standard, target, or outcome. How close or far away from the desired target or outcome was the student? What was the feedback conveying about the proficiency level of the student toward meeting the desired standard, target, or outcome? The second function of Wiggins's educative assessment schema focuses on educating. When evaluating progress toward a desired target or outcome, the feedback should teach something about instructional or curricular validity. For example, the assessment should provide insight into questions like, "What instructional occurrences allowed the student to be successful? Unsuccessful? Did the students have enough opportunities to master the desired outcomes?" The last function of Wiggins's educative assessment schema is that of auditing the processes of teaching and learning. Only through an inventory of progress toward the desired outcome and the processes used to get there, can one improve. In essence, the audit provides the data to inform and educate.

CHALLENGES TO IMPLEMENTATION

Changes in Faculty Thinking

One of the main challenges to implementing performance-based assessment lies within the heads of university faculty who are accustomed to thinking about their roles in particular ways. For example, faculty members typically become experts and scholars in their specific areas. They focus on their course content and how to communicate it effectively to students. Performance-assessment shifts attention from course content to students' abilities to demonstrate what they have learned. Often, this shift has been demanded of faculty without much warning or assistance. Understandably, faculty can feel confused and resentful. Similarly, faculty who have focused on their individual areas of expertise may resist focusing more broadly on student learning in the program as a whole. If they are accustomed to fashioning individual course objectives, they may resist recasting those objectives in the language of the standards on which the assessment is to be based. In addition, faculty who are committed to active research agendas may resist the time demands of revamping what they perceive as perfectly strong course syllabi.

The Language of Performance Assessment

Faculty role definition is not the only challenge to the implementation of performance-based assessment. The language of this kind of system can also pose a challenge. For example, faculty who are not accustomed to rubrics and portfolios must now become familiar with these concepts. Rubrics answer the question, "What does mastery (and varying degrees of mastery) for an achievement target...look like?" (CLASS, 1997, p. 39). One typically develops rubrics by beginning with the middle category, such as "acceptable," then adding criteria to achieve a "target" rating and removing criteria to establish the "unacceptable" level. Although many faculty are familiar with a definition of portfolio, CLASS (1997) explains that a portfolio "serves two distinct purposes: providing a documentation of the student's work, and serving as the basis for evaluation of work-in-progress or work over time" (p. 38). Portfolios can be all-inclusive, a chronology of progress that documents competency, or selective, collated with a specific outcome in mind (Huba & Freed, 2000); faculty must decide whether they want to use portfolios and, if so, which kind they want to use.

Distinguishing Between Course Assignments, Performance Tasks, and Classroom Projects

The distinctions between "performance tasks" and classroom projects (or activities) also raises new issues for faculty. Wiggins and McTighe (1998) contend that instructional activities and performance assessment tasks are different. One feature of performance tasks is that they are enduring, unlike instructional activities. That is, performance tasks are constructed to hone critical, authentic, and multifaceted abilities and knowledge required beyond PreK–12 schooling. Another feature is that performance tasks require integrated critical thinking skills that conform to desired outcomes, unlike instructional activities, which often feature segmented or isolated skills. The performance tasks yield a product, which concentrates on outcome expectations, not the ability to follow to completion specific directions (Chicago Public School, 2002).

CLASS (1997) explains, "A performance task thus demands that we bring to bear a repertoire of knowledge and skill to solve a problem or (to work) through a series of judgments and actions. Most tasks are goal-directed: they are 'done' when we have successfully fashioned a performance or product to specifications" (p. 16). These specifications must be directly connected to the critical elements distinguishing proficiency levels found in the assessment rubrics. Based on the assumption that performance tasks ought to ultimately improve instruction and learning, Schalock (2002) asserts that performance tasks are "developmental in nature to reflect growth in proficiency...through(out) the program,...designed around *actual classroom settings*, and require that knowledge and skill acquisition be *integrated and applied*" (p. 67). While a classroom activity or project may have the attributes that characterize performance assessment, it also may not. Thus, redefining teacher education courses so that they focus on performance assessment requires that faculty re-examine all course experiences and activities and redesign those used for assessment purposes.

In redesigning courses, it is important to attend to the difference between course-based assignments and performance tasks, and here the literature on performance assessment provides confusing guidance to teacher educators. You will note that Halsall and Vernetson (see chapter 14) draw on definitions provided by Campbell, Melenyzer, Nettles, and Wyman (2000). Yet, even within this one source, there is a difference between the definitions provided in the text and those in the glossary. Campbell et al. (2000) note that traditional instructional course-based assignments are narrow in scope, not valued by students, and lack integration of course concepts and links to authentic practice. They distinguish traditional instructional course-based assignments from performance tasks by noting that performance tasks are "broader in scope, are more authentic, are 'more likely to elicit a student's full repertoire of skills,' and reflect a range of goals," outcomes, and/or standards (p. 27). Yet in their glossary, Campbell et al. (2000) provide a much narrower definition of performance tasks. There they suggested that performance tasks are discrete instructional assignments, addressing "a limited number of course objectives or outcomes and, most often only one program standard" (p. 150). They provide examples of teachers' everyday responsibilities that are disjointed skills and abilities. Thus, Campbell et al. (2000) seem to exemplify the misconception that Wiggins and McTighe (1998) present regarding instructional activities and pedagogical performance tasks. Conceivably, the process of working through a performance-based assessment is progressive. In other words, we start with instructional assignments because that is what we have and are familiar with; as we grow, however, in our experience and knowledge, we change to more comprehensive performance tasks.

One wonders whether Halsall's and Vernetson's (see chapter 14) usage of the term "performance task" stems from a belief in course-based performance tasks, or programmatic ones—another significant distinction in the literature on performance assessment. You will see that the performance tasks utilized in the University of Florida UESEP model are conflicting as well. The faculty members appear to employ the Campbell et al. (2000) model at the course-design level; yet they also use the discrete course-based tasks as supportive documentation of a programmatic performance project, the electronic portfolio, which looks holistically at the competencies of students throughout the program. It is important to note that several of these "course-based" assessments bridge multiple courses, are conducted in authentic field settings, and address complex performances, yet one is still left with a question about whether a set of discrete tasks can be used to assess progress and proficiency toward meeting program standards. This dilemma is one that haunts many institutions. Perhaps the issue can be resolved by determining if performance-based assessment is focused on course-related tasks (i.e., activities) or on complex projects reflecting competencies gained in courses? Possibly, courses provide the formative level of performance assessment for programmatic performance projects, like the Teacher Work Sample Model, which are dependent upon prior and previous experiences gained in course content.

Since many institutions begin with course-based tasks, a look at key steps in their design might be helpful. Danielson (2002) outlines four steps in designing assessment tasks: 1) establish consensus on the desired outcomes—the knowledge, skills, abilities, and dispositions—that students should possess when they finish the course and/or program; 2) agree on what is expected—how will faculty know that students truly understand the desired outcome; 3) develop rubrics for public use (shared with students), which reflect different proficiency levels; and 4) establish what constitutes an acceptable mastery level of the submitted student product or performance. These four steps mesh well with McTighe and Wiggins's (1999) framework for designing performance tasks. Wiggins and McTighe (1998) would add that faculty need to determine if diverse demonstrations of the outcome are considered necessary and how much redundancy or practice is needed to demonstrate acceptable mastery levels.

The issue of documenting performance and the development of performance-based assessment systems opens a Pandora's Box. The more development, the more questions; the more we think we know about performance assessment systems, the more we do not. Much of the research on assessing student learning is conducted on, with, and for PreK–12 assessment systems. What seems apparent is that the concepts, design elements, definitions, and methodology are applicable to post-secondary settings as well. Yet, the mission of post-secondary education is more expansive than the mission of K-12 systems, creating a clear dilemma for post-secondary faculty.

As faculty grapple with performance-based assessment, they must construct meanings of new concepts and perhaps adjust definitions of their roles in the institution. They enter an unfamiliar world and often one that was not of their choosing. It is not surprising that they may drag their feet. The institution must take steps to help faculty examine the meaning of and rationale for change as well as the more mechanical matters of how the change could be accomplished and the impact of such change on the institution as well as on individual faculty members.

DIRECTIONS FOR IMPLEMENTATION

Steps in developing and implementing performance-based assessment include 1) determining what is to be assessed; 2) identifying how that which is to be evaluated will be judged; 3) developing opportunities for students to demonstrate the desired standard; 4) providing feedback loops to both students and faculty; and 5) gathering and utilizing assessment results to improve teaching and learning.

Huba and Freed (2000, pp. 68–85) outlined critical considerations for examining the adequacy of a performance-based assessment system. Their work encourages faculty to develop an assessment system that is systemic, conceptually sound, and focused on continuous improvement. In determining whether the plan is systemic, faculty should consider whether the assessment system is ongoing rather than episodic, has broad-based support from all members of the educational community (e.g., faculty, administrators, state officials), and is linked to the mission of the institution.

In determining whether the plan is conceptually sound, faculty should consider whether the assessment system is focused on questions, explicit purposes, and values that faculty care about. In addition, the system should be grounded in a clear conceptual framework that can guide decisions about teaching, curriculum, learning, and assessment. Finally, the work of Huba and Freed suggests that an assessment system should lead to continuous improvement. The system should be data-based, clearly focused on performance, and lead to improvements related to the core purposes of the educational program. They stress that a sustainable system must be cost-effective, based on data gathered from multiple measures, and must support efforts to increase diversity within an educational program. Additionally, they note that any system grounded in continuous improvement should itself be continuously evaluated so a plan for regular evaluation of the assessment system must be developed.

When faculty address these considerations as they develop an assessment system, it ensures they will develop a sense of ownership for the system and assume responsibility for assessment and for the learning experiences leading to outcomes. Thus these issues can serve as a useful framework for reading the chapters on performance assessment that follow.

INQUIRY IN PERFORMANCE-BASED ASSESSMENT

As programs within teacher education units engage in performance-based assessment, the opportunity for research flourishes. At this time, there are important questions to be answered in the areas of performance documentation, portfolios, external evidence (vs. internal), and accountability.

If there is truly a difference between course-based instructional assignments and performance tasks as McTighe and Wiggins (1999) assert, how can one clearly determine if and when assignments are used appropriately for assessing performance? Are traditional assignments ever appropriate for assessing a learner's performance? When are traditional assignments unusable for performance tasks? Can individually designed course-based tasks be used to assess programmatic outcomes? We need a better understanding of the kinds of tasks that provide the best insight into our students' learning. Therefore, systematic investigation of those tasks is necessary.

There also are a number of questions about the use of portfolios in performance-based assessment. These questions are related to the kinds of portfolios students might assemble, the selection of evidence for the portfolio, and the assessment of material once it is in the portfolio. For example, are there alternative processes that could capture the overall development of students' performance as effectively as a portfolio? Is there a difference in the quality of performance between self-selected portfolio entries vs. faculty required entries? How much documentation is enough? Popham asserted that 2.7 demonstrations are needed (*Debra P. v. Turlington*, 1979), but failed to say how those demonstrations should evolve; should they be formative, summative, or an accumulation of both? Furthermore, how can performance in portfolios be assessed consistently? What is the role of portfolio reviewers as opposed to faculty members who might assign and grade course-based entries into a portfolio? In short, how effective are portfolios and anthologies, or is their popularity a matter of familiarity rather than effectiveness? Is the sum of the individual course-based tasks collated into a cumulative document indicative of program performance? Perhaps the portfolio process duplicates previous efforts to assess performance, such as the data gathered from course-based tasks. If this is the case, are cumulative capstone portfolios, or anthologies, useful?

Guskey (2003) and Marzano (2003) both found that internal assessments are more beneficial for improving student learning than external measures. Nevertheless, in order to reach the *Acceptable* proficiency level of the indicator *Data Collection, Analysis, and Evaluation* for Standard 2 (see NCATE, 2002, Standard 2, p. 22), institutions must collect data "using multiple assessments from internal and external sources." How should faculty devise feedback instruments that provide forthright and significant feedback?

The NCATE standards now require teacher preparation programs to document candidates' competence, collect and analyze data, and make program and candidate improvements based on data. The accountability system documents preservice teachers' knowledge, abilities, skills, dispositions, and the impact they potentially have on PreK–12 learners. Are program performance-based accountability systems useful for graduation decisions? If so, should these systems differ from accountability systems used for certification decisions? Is the focus on accountability different depending on its purpose (i.e., program improvement vs. certification)? Questions about kinds of accountability and the systems appropriate for each remain to be explored.

CONCLUSION

The University of Florida's UESEP faculty set out to establish a performance-based system that embedded multiple approaches to determining the capabilities of their elementary special education teacher education candidates. In chapters 14 and 15, the authors provide insight into the ways in which the faculty have struggled with performance assessment, their first stab at a performance system, and the questions still to be answered to make the process "educative" for the preservice teachers.

REFERENCES

Campbell, D. M., Melenyzer, B. J., Nettles, D. H., & Wyman, R .M., Jr. (2000). *Portfolio and performance assessment in teacher education*. Boston: Allyn & Bacon.

Chicago Public Schools (2002). *Selecting tasks for performance assessments*. Instructional Intranet [Online]. Available: http:// intranet.cps.k12.il.us/Assessments/Ideas_and_Rubrics/Assessments_Tasks/Select/ [2002, April].

Danielson, C. (2002). *Enhancing student achievement; A framework for school improvement*. Alexandria, VA: Association for Supervision and Curriculum Development.

Debra P. v Turlington, 475 F.Supp. 244 (M.D. FL 1979). United States District Court, M.D. Florida, Tampa Division. No. 78-892 Civ. T-C, July 12, 1979, As amended August 7 and 8, 1979.

Guskey, T. R. (2003). How classroom assessments improve learning. *Educational Leadership 60,* 5, 6–11.

Huba, M. E., & Freed, J. E. (2000*). Learner-centered assessment on college campuses: Shifting the focus from teaching to learning*. Boston: Allyn & Bacon.

Marzano, R. J. (2003). *What works in schools: Translating research into action*. Alexandria, VA: Association for Supervision and Curriculum Development.

McTighe, J., & Wiggins, G. (1999). *The understanding by design handbook*. Alexandria, VA: Association for Supervision and Curriculum Development.

National Council for Accreditation of Teacher Education (2002, edition). *Professional standards for the accreditation of schools, colleges, and departments of education.* Washington, DC: Author.

Schalock, M. D. (2002). Assessing teacher work samples. In Girod, G. R. (Ed.), *Connecting teaching and learning: A handbook for teacher educators on the teacher work sample methodology* (pp. 65–89). Washington, DC: American Association of Colleges for Teacher Education.

Wiggins, G. (1998). *Educative Assessment. Designing assessments to inform and improve student performance.* San Francisco: Jossey-Bass.

Wiggins G., & McTighe, J. (1998). *Understanding by design.* Alexandria, VA: Association for Supervision and Curriculum Development.

CHAPTER 14

Performance Assessment

SHAREN HALSALL AND THERESA B. VERNETSON

Like many teacher education programs, the approach to assessment at the University of Florida (UF) has been fairly traditional. All students were required to pass basic skills tests on program entry. Individual instructors evaluated student performance in coursework. Program administrators monitored students' Grade Point Averages, and students who failed to meet minimum standards were put on probation or dropped from the program. University supervisors and classroom teachers evaluated student performance in classrooms using a common set of criteria. Students experiencing difficulties were placed on Performance Improvement Plans. In most cases, student performance improved; in a few, the students dropped out or were dropped from the program. Graduates took and 100% passed required certification tests, and employer feedback was uniformly positive.

Despite the strong performance of UF graduates on all available indicators of competence, in restructuring the program UF faculty began talking about performance assessment for a variety of reasons. The revision of the program coincided with an increase in professional dialogue among teacher educators about the shortcomings of traditional assessment and the importance of ongoing performance assessment. Although all Florida teachers are required to take pencil and paper tests to demonstrate their competence and UF graduates do well on the tests, these tests are widely criticized. Their predictive validity has been found to be weak (Grover, 1991; Haertel, 1991; Haney, Madaus, & Kreitzer, 1987), and they have been found to be culturally biased resulting in depressed scores for minorities (Porter, Young, & Odden, 2001). In addition, such tests oversimplify the complex variables that teachers must consider in making teaching decisions

(Darling-Hammond, Wise, & Klein, 1995; Tellez, 1996) and separate content and pedagogical knowledge, which in classrooms must be integrated (Porter et al., 2001).

Faculty had similar concerns about employer feedback. The state requires that all teacher education institutions collect employer feedback data, and UF graduates do exceptionally well on such assessments. However, principals tend to give teachers uniformly high ratings suggesting that employer feedback may provide little authentic validation of the performance of graduates (Dywer & Stufflebeam, 1996; Peterson, 1995). Although the faculty had more confidence in their internal assessments of students, they also felt that there had not been enough dialogue about standards or assessment and that the quality of assessment varied considerably across instructors and field supervisors.

Simultaneously, the professional conversation in the state and nation had begun to focus more clearly on the importance of performance assessment. The purpose of performance assessment, of course, is to allow teacher preparation students an opportunity to reflect on their work, to synthesize course learning, but above all to assess performance that reflects the real-life work of teaching (Campbell, Melenyzer, Nettles, & Wyman, 2000). Although Alverno College has used performance assessment for 20 years (Diez, Rickards, & Lake, 1994), the discourse in teacher education did not turn to performance assessment until the early '90s. At that time, a number of professional activities began to converge around performance assessment. These included: the development of the Interstate New Teacher Assessment and Support Consortium standards and a portfolio system for assessing the seven areas of standards (INTASC, 1995), the work of the Educational Testing Service (ETS) in developing the PRAXIS observation system that included performance assessment (Dywer, 1994), the development of portfolio and assessment center exercises as part of the National Board Certification process (NPBTS, 1996; 2002), and the addition of outcome-based standards to the National Council for Accreditation of Teacher Education (NCATE, 1998) accreditation process.

In 1993 consistent with the national attention on performance assessment, the Florida legislature directed the Education Standards Commission (ESC) to identify competencies for teachers related to the goals of the state's education accountability act. Following multiple reviews of their work by practitioners, teacher educators, and others, the ESC adopted a set of 12 Florida Educator Accomplished Practices (FEAPs), professional standards that are similar to the standards in many other states, specifically the INTASC standards. The 12 Practices, defined at three levels to represent the developing expertise of teachers, fall within the following broad areas: Assessment, Communication, Continuous Improvement, Critical Thinking, Diversity, Ethics, Human Development and Learning, Knowledge of Subject Matter, Learning Environments, Planning, Role of the Teacher, Technology. Each state-approved teacher preparation program is required to document through ongoing performance assessments that students who complete the program have demonstrated achievement of the 12 FEAPs.

The convergence of a major restructuring effort with faculty concern about the quality of current assessment efforts and national and state attention to performance assessment created the context for the revision of the assessment system. Grounded in the work of a number of faculty who had been experimenting with alternative assessment strategies such as portfolio assessment, performance tasks, and assessment rubrics, a more comprehensive and performance-based approach to assessment began to emerge.

Performance assessments have been described as "performance projects" and "performance tasks" (Campbell et al., 2000, pp. 34–35). Projects cover the totality of course objectives and provide the opportunity for teacher preparation students to demonstrate the "desired outcomes of the course" (Campbell et al., 2000, p. 34). Performance tasks by contrast usually "reflect a limited number of course objectives, standards, or outcomes" (Campbell et al., 2000, p. 35). Frequently a performance task is focused entirely on one aspect/objective of a particular standard. Total course objectives are not addressed, but particular aspects, which reflect specific standards, become the focus. Although some courses include performance projects, faculty were encouraged to design their performance tasks to target a small number of standards (FEAPs) that would be assessed. The performance assessment system for the Unified Elementary Special Education Proteach (UESEP) program consists of three components: 1) Electronic portfolio documentation of course performance tasks designed by faculty members to demonstrate one or more of the FEAPs, (see discussion in chapter 15); 2) pre-internship performance assessments; and 3) a final student teaching (graduate internship) performance assessment. A description of these components follows.

COURSE-BASED PERFORMANCE TASKS

During the baccalaureate phase of the UESEP program, students participate in various field experiences including an intensive 14-week pre-internship during the last semester of the senior year. The full-time graduate internship experience is during the fifth (master's) year. The early field experiences are paired with courses and sequenced developmentally as UESEP students assume increasing responsibility for teaching and student learning. Many, but not all, course-based performance tasks are grounded in these early field experiences in which students document their performance relative to the FEAPs. For example, during the first semester of the junior year, each student is paired with a child who lives in a local public housing neighborhood (Bright Futures project). During the semester, each student teacher meets with the child to work on school related activities. The student teacher submits performance tasks for review by the course instructor. One example of a performance task related to the Bright Futures project is a child observation task completed for EDF 3115, Child Development for Inclusive Education. The purpose of this task is to demonstrate the ability to apply developmental theory. UESEP students observe their child for 10 hours and keep a log of their observations and notes on each tutoring session. Students write an analysis paper, which describes how developmental theory applies to learning in three domains: Cognitive, Emotional and Social development. A sample of how this analysis is formulated for cognitive development follows in figure A.

Figure A: Cognitive Development

(a) Describe an incident in which you used disequilibrium to stimulate a student's cognitive development.

(b) Describe the nature of the student's problem and then describe how you created disequilibrium to foster the student's thinking about the problem.

(c) Evaluate the strengths and weaknesses of Piaget's approach to motivating cognitive development in this instance by referring to specific student responses to support your conclusions and indicate changes in your responses that would have improved the outcome for the student.

During the first two years of the program, students are required to document their performance related to the FEAPs in their electronic portfolio. Chapter 15 includes a matrix that shows which Practices are demonstrated in each course. In addition, that chapter provides a comprehensive description of how course-based mastery of the FEAPs is documented. The electronic portfolio is built upon the course-based performance tasks. The development of performance tasks required that many faculty restructure their course assignments so that the performance tasks were clear. In addition, faculty were encouraged to develop grading rubrics to provide clear descriptions of and feedback about expectations. Many faculty were already using grading rubrics, but for others this strategy was new. To assist faculty, we held a summer workshop on performance tasks, rubrics, and the electronic portfolio. Providing clear examples of performance tasks was one strategy that faculty found useful. A sample performance task that meets FEAP 10 (Planning) is an assignment in an early field experience in the Core Teaching Strategies course, which is taught in the second semester of the junior year (see appendix E). The performance assessment rubric used to evaluate the quality of the instructional lesson plan is contained in appendix F.

In this example, the performance task is grounded in one course and its related field experience. There also are performance tasks that integrate across courses. For example, in the first semester senior year students take courses in math methods, science methods, and technology. The field experience portion of this semester focuses on nontraditional experiences in which students have an opportunity to consider how areas outside the traditional school setting can become avenues for curricular exploration and interdisciplinary teaching. The hallmark of this semester is the microteaching and self-reflection profile that all students prepare as a performance assessment. It demonstrates the Florida Educator Accomplished Practices 3, 10, and 12. Figure B provides a brief description of this assignment.

In the Math/Science/Technology (MST) block, microteaching is used as an instructional strategy to not only facilitate the students' use and application of strategies and skills, but also to create practice situations in which deliberate attempts are made to integrate technology in science and mathematics lessons and to encourage reflection on the experience. The purpose of the microteaching assignment is to provide opportunities for the preservice teachers to plan and practice the instructional strategies developed in the methods courses during the semester in a risk-free environment. Students develop and teach a 30-minute lesson that integrates math, science, and technology. The lesson is developed for a grade level of their choice and correlated to the state's curriculum standards. The preservice teachers are responsible for all facets of the teaching and learning activities, submitting the written lesson plan to the instructors on the day of their teaching session and making the necessary arrangements to acquire the technologies needed. These lessons are taught to their peers and observed by the math, science, and technology instructors who provide feedback on the students' lesson development (from introduction to closure), use of content

---

Figure B: Math, Science and Technology Microteaching Performance Task

Directions
- Develop and teach a math, science and technology integrated lesson for 30 minutes.
- Submit a written lesson plan to the instructor on the day of microteaching.
- Make all the necessary arrangements to acquire the technologies needed to successfully implement the integrated lesson.
- Each individual will submit a completed reflection profile four days after the microteaching.

Organization for microteaching occurs in the science methods class. The mathematics methods, science methods, and technology instructors observe each teaching pair. Each assesses the teaching and assigns a grade (50 points maximum) based on (1) structure, (2) meaningfulness, (3) effectiveness, (4) content, (5) application of state and /or national standards, and (6) professionalism. The three grades will be averaged and the result is the grade the student receives in each of the three courses for this component assessment. If one of the instructors/professors cannot participate in the observation, a substitute from the same subject area and from a different cohort will complete the observation.

---

knowledge, delivery of and response to questions, implementation of classroom organization strategies, and the appropriate application and integration of the technology. Guided by questions posed during the feedback session, students are required to reflect on their practice during the microteaching experience and suggest alternative actions toward improvement. The feedback from each instructor is compiled into one document and students receive one common grade for each of the three courses (on this one assignment).

PERFORMANCE ASSESSMENT IN THE PRE-INTERNSHIP AND GRADUATE INTERNSHIP

Prior to completion of the bachelor's degree, students complete a one-semester pre-internship field experience (15 hours per week for 14 weeks). During the pre-internship, student teachers are placed in dyads in an elementary classroom where they collaborate to plan for and teach young students. The student teachers take courses in Language Arts and Social Studies methods and complete integrated assignments for the two content areas. They also take an Integrated Teaching course that emphasizes the development of accommodations for special needs learners. Students complete course-based performance tasks associated with these experiences. As in the other undergraduate semesters, selected performance tasks are placed into the electronic portfolio. By the conclusion of the baccalaureate degree, each successful student has developed an electronic portfolio, which includes at least two pieces of instructor-approved, course-related evidence of successful performance on all 12 FEAPs. (Note: In most cases students accomplish this by providing less than 24 separate pieces of evidence as one source of evidence can document several FEAPs). Although this provides important evidence of student progress, faculty also wanted a comprehensive classroom observation protocol to document the ability of each student to demonstrate the FEAPs within the classroom context during the pre-internship and the graduate internship.

Some faculty were already familiar with Educational Testing Service's Pathwise Observation System (ETS, 1995). Faculty repeatedly argued for a comprehensive system that reflected the complexity of teaching and regularly suggested the Pathwise System as the appropriate solution, but cost was a recurring barrier. Nevertheless, the Pathwise System was selected as the best solution by faculty because of the underlying conception of teaching and the structure of the observation system.

Six principles underlie the Pathwise conception of learning and teaching: 1) Learning is an active process. 2) Learning builds on knowledge, experience, skills, and interests. 3) Learning is a highly individualized process. 4) Teaching must be adapted to the context. 5) Teaching involves complex decisions as well as actions. 6) Teaching draws on a large repertoire of techniques. These six principles are evident in the four domains of the observation system, each of which describes a distinct aspect of teaching.

Domain A: Organizing Content Knowledge for Student Learning includes a focus on the way in which teachers decide on learning goals for a lesson based on their knowledge of students and subject matter. "Domain A is concerned with how the teacher thinks about the content to be taught. This thinking is evident in how the teacher organizes instruction for the benefit of her or his students" (Orientation Guide, Pathwise Classroom Observation System, Educational Testing Service, 1995, p. 7).

Domain B: Creating an Environment for Student Learning, is founded on the notion that at a minimum, the social and emotional components of learning form the basis for academic achievement. A sense of community, fairness and rapport, belief in students' abilities to learn and meet challenges, and acceptable standards of behavior are elements of Domain B.

Domain C: Teaching for Student Learning, focuses on helping students connect with the content being taught. In this domain, learning goals and instructional procedures are made clear to students, students are encouraged to extend their thinking, teachers monitor students' understanding of content, and teachers use time effectively in order to help students learn the subject matter of a discipline. Just as in Domain B, the teacher's ability to teach for student learning is assessed through classroom observation (Orientation Guide, Pathwise Classroom Observation System, Educational Testing Service, 1995).

Domain D: Teacher Professionalism rounds out the four domains of teaching in the Pathwise Classroom Observation System. Teacher reflection on the extent to which learning goals were met, teacher efficacy, building professional relationships with colleagues, and communicating with parents and guardians are the elements of the fourth domain. Interestingly, both written and verbal responses are focused on student learning goals, a candidate's acceptance of responsibility for student learning, the candidate's ability to work with, not just coordinate or cooperate with parents, and the difference between notification and real communication with parents.

Grant funding from the Florida Department of Education provided the resources for an initial group of faculty and local teachers to be trained in the use of the Pathwise Classroom Observation System (Pathwise) protocol. Response to the protocol was uniformly positive. In order to contain the cost of continued training for observers, three faculty members became "certified" as Pathwise trainers for the purpose of delivering training to other University of Florida supervisors and cooperating teachers. These three trainers then developed a model for training that incorporates adapted observation and data collection forms. Having solved the funding dilemma, the program adopted the Pathwise System for use program wide.

Training for supervisors provided participants with 1) an understanding of the domains and criteria of successful teaching, 2) enhanced skill to evaluate teacher performance based on the criteria, and 3) strategies for providing constructive feedback based on teacher performance tied to the criteria (Danielson, 1996). Operationally, the domains are contained in a four-page document that allows the observer to gather evidence for each criterion through note taking prior to, during, and following the observation. A candidate must supply the observer with a class profile, an instruction profile, and a reflection profile. The class profile provides demographic information about the class makeup and class setting. The instruction profile, similar to a lesson plan, requires detailed description of learning goals, methods and materials to be used, relationship of content in this lesson to previous or future lessons, differentiated learning experiences, and assessment strategies. The candidate's reflection profile, completed following the classroom observation, includes identification of aspects of an unsuccessful or a successful lesson and specific reasons for lack of success or support for a successful lesson. A critical component of the reflection profile is the candidate's analysis of who learned and did not learn and how he/she knows who and what was learned.

COORDINATING PATHWISE WITH THE FLORIDA EDUCATOR ACCOMPLISHED PRACTICES

The faculty believed the Pathwise System provided a comprehensive assessment of the competence of student teachers; however, learning the observation system was only one step in the development of classroom-based performance assessment. The UF accountability system was linked to the FEAPs. Although the four Pathwise domains seemed logically related to the Practices, the specific connections between the domains and indicators and the FEAPs were not clear. In addition, it seemed important to the faculty to develop critical performance benchmarks for the pre-internship experience so that students would receive feedback and faculty could make judgments about whether students were ready to begin the graduate internship experience.

The UESEP faculty, again using funding from the Florida Department of Education grant, invited ETS to review the 12 FEAPs in order to determine the specific relationship between the Practices and the indicators for the four domains of the Pathwise Observation Protocol. A matrix was created by ETS staff that links the Pathwise indicators with the FEAPs (see Appendix G). To develop benchmarks, the faculty, along with representative cooperating teachers from the local school district, met as an advisory panel to review the observation/feedback protocols and to determine the criteria for adequate demonstration of the FEAPs. The Pathwise instrument, the student teacher reflection form, and the observer's feedback form were revised and adapted to reflect the input from the advisory panel. Benchmarks for satisfactory completion of the pre-internship were developed and included on the observation form so that student teachers, cooperating teachers, and university supervisors would be reminded of the criteria each time the forms were used. Each key criterion for completion of the pre-internship was printed in bold typeface to ensure clarity about program expectations. The advisory panel decided to require all student teachers to demonstrate a few key indicators for each of the 12 FEAPs prior to the completion of the pre-internship in order to advance to the internship phase of the UESEP program. At the completion of the graduate internship (final student teaching) the cooperating teacher and university supervisor must rate the student on all indicators of the 12 FEAPs as a final evaluation (See appendix H). This assessment is based on Pathwise observation data and judgment of the cooperating teacher and university supervisor.

It is important to note that the real value of the Pathwise Observation Protocol is not the final evaluation but the formative evaluations. University supervisors uniformly note that the Observation Protocol improves both their feedback to student teachers and the nature of the conversations about teaching and learning. That is, the Pathwise system creates a professional development sequence that scaffolds student teachers to successful performance. Even with this scaffolding, some pre-interns or interns experience performance concerns. In these cases, the student is placed on a Performance Improvement Plan and must remediate the specific FEAPs before moving forward to the summative evaluation. Interns with a score of two or lower on a four-point scale are required to remediate the FEAP to the satisfaction of the UESEP faculty in order to be considered "safe to teach."

CHALLENGES AND STRATEGIES

Training: The Ongoing Challenge

Optimally, a teacher education program would have a stable core of supervisors and, in fact, at the internship level, there is a strong ongoing cadre of supervisors. However, pre-internships are supervised by graduate students. At best these graduate students serve as field supervisors for three or four semesters, but many fill this role for only one or two semesters because they desire variety in their teaching responsibilities as part of their doctoral preparation. Consequently, new observers must be trained each semester and finding time for a two-day training at the beginning of every semester is a challenge. In addition, "maintaining our edge" has become a challenge. We have not yet created a follow-up to the training for observers in order to check

ourselves for accuracy and agreement. Creating a follow-up and facilitating ongoing conversation about observation is a task we have ahead
of us.

Securing "Buy In" From All Constituents

As with any new way of doing things there is some reluctance on
the part of faculty and cooperating teachers to abandon "what has been
working" and adapt to a new set of expectations. Faculty resistance has
been the greatest in regard to the use of rubrics. Faculty have expressed
concerns that rubrics place boundaries around student thinking and creativity. Although rubrics are useful in establishing expectations, the concern is that tightly specified expectations may limit student performance
in some cases. On the other hand, some faculty argue that rubrics
enhance performance by making the criteria for excellence public and
therefore more attainable. Using a broad definition of "rubric" has
enabled faculty to find ways to create rubrics that meet their needs, students' needs, and the needs of the accountability system.

In addition, there have been challenges in communicating the
Pathwise Observation system to all parties involved. Even though the
Pathwise protocol is an integral part of the pre-internship and final
internship semesters, communicating the expectations to all parties is
fraught with opportunities for miscommunication. So far we have met
this challenge by offering training workshops and by developing collaborative partnerships with local teachers and administrators in an effort
to disseminate the assessment system to school-based practitioners. All
university supervisors are trained in the Pathwise system; however, the
size of the teacher education program and the number of cooperating
teachers needed means that only a small (though growing) number of
cooperating teachers and school administrators have been trained.

Coordinating Data Collection and Review

Faculty in the UESEP determined that students should have ultimate responsibility for creating their portfolio of performance assessment evidence. Therefore, students were instructed to select two
documentation examples for each of the Accomplished Practices as
defined in the electronic portfolio matrix (see appendix I). Selected
assessment items were to be chosen from those that an instructor had
graded as a "B" or better and had identified as evidence that would be
appropriate for documentation. However, to date, only one individual
reviews completed portfolios. Faculty have not yet been involved in

assessing the total package to determine whether the FEAPs are comprehensively demonstrated in the portfolio. Instead, the strategy currently in place is a summative demonstration where students in their pre-internship showcase for faculty the performance assessments for two randomly selected FEAPs. If the student has not provided adequate documentation, then the complete portfolio is reviewed. In fall 2002 faculty began a review process of randomly selected portfolios to determine whether the portfolio system as currently constructed enables students to provide a comprehensive demonstration of the FEAPs. This review has raised some concerns that students (and possibly some faculty and/or teaching assistants) have an incomplete understanding of a few of the FEAPs. Faculty are working together to review the portfolio system with an eye toward revision, however, this is a challenging process. From a faculty perspective, program graduates are perceived by all external indicators (e.g., employer evaluations, certification test pass rates, initial hire and rehire rates) to be highly skilled and competent. Clearly, not all program graduates are equally skilled, but the program has clear procedures in place to determine whether a candidate is "safe to teach" and each semester a small number of students are counseled from the program. The issue for faculty is not whether it is their responsibility to uphold appropriate standards for the profession. They clearly accept this responsibility and have evidence that they are meeting it. For them, the issue is whether quality is likely to improve through increased attention to documentation of FEAPs. Portfolios are time-consuming to review if done correctly and faculty wonder about the cost-benefit ratio. Will comprehensive revision of the portfolio system lead to better prepared graduates? How much accountability is enough? What kinds of documentation have a robust enough connection to teacher quality to be worth the investment of faculty and student time? These are critical questions not only for teacher educators but for state officials who make decisions about state-level requirements for documentation that influence all teacher education programs.

CONCLUSION

The traditional assessment practices described at the beginning of this chapter are still in place at UF. Students still take basic-skills tests as required by the state. Faculty continue to monitor students' course-based performance and their overall grade point averages. Some students are still placed on probation. We still collect follow-up data about their performance on licensure tests and surveys of graduate and employer satisfaction. However, clear documentation of performance using course-based performance tasks and the Pathwise System provide much more specific information about what UF's graduates are able to do. More importantly, the performance assessments provide a focus for faculty conversations about program impact and for faculty/student conversations about student competence that have the potential to positively influence the learning of student teachers in the program. These conversations have enabled us to make more public our "professional consensus about the knowledge and skills that teachers must have to engage in responsible practice" (Porter et al., 2001, p. 259).

REFERENCES

Campbell, D. M., Melenyzer, B. J., Nettles, D. H., & Wyman, R .M., Jr. (2000). *Portfolio and performance assessment in teacher education.* Boston: Allyn & Bacon.

Danielson, C. (1996). *Enhancing professional practice: A framework for teaching.* Alexandria, VA: Association for Supervision and Curriculum Development.

Darling-Hammond, L., Diez, M. E., Moss, P., Pecheone, R., Pullin, D., Schafer, W. D., & Vickers, L. (1998). The role of standards and assessment: A dialogue. In M. E. Diez, (Ed.), *Changing the practice of teacher education: Standards and assessment as a lever for change* (pp. 7–9). Washington, DC.: American Association of Colleges of Teacher Education.

Darling-Hammond, L., Wise, A. E., & and Klein, S. P. (1995). *A license to teach: Building a profession for 21st century schools.* Boulder, CO: Westview Press.

Diez, M. E., Rickards, W. H., & Lake, K. (1994). Performance assessment in teacher education at Alverno College. In T. Warren (Ed.), *Promising practices in liberal arts colleges* (pp. 9–18). Lanham, MD: University Press of America.

Dwyer, C. A. (1994). *Development of the knowledge base for the PRAXIS III: Classroom performance assessments assessment criteria.* Princeton, NJ: Educational Testing Service.

Dywer, C. A., & Stufflebeam, D. (1996). Teacher evaluation. In D. Berliner & R. Calfee (Eds.), *Handbook of educational psychology* (pp. 765–784). New York: Macmillan.

Educational Testing Service. (1995). *Praxis III: Classroom performance assessments—Rating assessor proficiency.* Princeton, NJ: Educational Testing Service.

Grover, B. W. (1991). The teacher assessment dilemma: What is versus what ought to be! *Journal of Personnel Evaluation in Education, 5*(2), 103–119.

Haertel, E. H. (1991). New forms of teacher assessment. In G. Grant (Ed.), *Review of Research in Education, 17,* 3–29.

Haney, W., Madaus, G., & Kreitzer, A. (1987). Charms talismanic: Testing teachers for improvement of American education. In E. Z. Rothkopf (Ed.), *Review of Research in Education, 14,* 169–238.

Interstate New Teacher Assessment and Support Consortium. (1995). *Next steps: Moving toward performance-based licensing in teaching.* Washington, DC: Interstate New Teacher Assessment and Support Consortium and Council of Chief State School Officers.

National Council for Accreditation of Teacher Education. (1998). *Program standards for elementary teacher preparation.* Washington, DC: Author.

National Professional Board for Teaching Standards. (1996). *National board certification portfolio sampler.* Southfield, MI: Author.

National Professional Board for Teaching Standards. (2002). *NPBTS home page.* Retrieved from http://www.nbpts.org.

Peterson, K. D. (1995). *Teacher evaluation: A comprehensive guide to new directions and practices.* Thousand Oaks, CA: Corwin Press.

Porter, A. C., Young, P., & Odden, A. (2001). Advances in teacher assessments and their uses. In V. Richardson (Ed.) *Handbook of research on teaching,* (4th ed., pp. 259–297). Washington, DC: American Educational Research Association.

Stiggins, R. J. (1996). Keeping performance assessment in perspective. In R. E. Blum, & J. A. Arter (Eds.), *Student performance in an era of restructuring* (p. 2). Alexandria, VA: Association for Supervision and Curriculum Development.

Tellez, K. (1996). Authentic assessment. In J. Sikula, T. J. Buttery, & E. Guyton (Eds.), *Handbook of research on teacher education* (pp. 704–721). New York: Macmillan.

CHAPTER 15

The Electronic Portfolio Project

GAIL RING, SEBASTIAN FOTI, AND COLLEEN SWAIN

In this chapter we describe a model for the implementation of an electronic teaching portfolio program within the Unified Elementary Special Education Proteach (UESEP) program. We present the history and design of a systemic electronic teaching portfolio initiative, the key points of the change process, an example of its implementation in a specific course, the strengths and weaknesses of the program, and future directions of the electronic portfolio initiative. The Electronic Portfolio Project may be viewed at: http://www.coe.ufl.edu/school/portfolio/index.htm

DEFINITION OF AN ELECTRONIC PORTFOLIO

A teaching portfolio can be defined as a container for storing and displaying evidence of a teacher's knowledge and skills (Bird, 1990; Johnson & Rose, 1997). However, a portfolio is more than a container; a portfolio also represents an attitude that assessment is dynamic, and that the richest portrayals of teacher (and student) performances are based upon multiple sources of evidence collected over time in authentic settings (Wolf, 1991). An electronic portfolio is a Web-based or software-based organic, evolving collection of a student's work (Foti & Ring, 2000). While the research on using portfolios in preservice teacher education varies widely, most researchers agree that the act of constructing a portfolio contributes to the development of reflective practitioners (Freidus, 2000; Lyons, 1988; Shulman, 1988). In addition, Arter and Spandel (1992) contend that the instructional power of portfolios comes when students use criteria and self-reflection to make decisions about what they want to communicate about themselves.

BACKGROUND OF THE ELECTRONIC PORTFOLIO PROJECT

In the late '90s an important shift took place in the focus of accreditation procedures for teacher education programs. In the past, accreditation agencies determined what was being done in an educational institution by examining course materials such as syllabi and lists of objectives. When UF faculty and administrators learned that future accreditation committees would examine student performance rather than faculty materials, we envisioned faculty offices full of file cabinets, student projects, and videotapes. How would we manage all of the student work collected during the years between accreditation visits? We decided to teach students to manage their own materials by building a portfolio of their best practices and reflections on learning.

Although the electronic portfolio project was first suggested as a response to the requirements of accreditation procedures, it also was viewed as having the potential to benefit students. The planning team decided the portfolio should be organized according to the state of Florida's Accomplished Practices for educators. To document their competence on the Florida Educator Accomplished Practices (FEAPs), students would be required to reflect upon their teaching and classroom experience to identify instances that illustrated their accomplishments. We hoped that thinking about "best practices" would help the students make connections between their courses and their teaching, thus preparing them for job interviews and their teaching careers. Perhaps more importantly, we anticipated that portfolio development would inform student learning (Krause, 1996) and help students develop a rationale for their teaching practices (Shulman, 1998). That is, portfolio development has the potential to help students construct and revisit their knowledge and beliefs about teaching. In order for this to occur, we had to view portfolio development as an ongoing process in which students were actively engaged.

According to Barton and Collins (1993) the first and most significant act of portfolio preparation is the decision about the purpose of the portfolio. Many instructors look at a portfolio as a product, a way to evaluate their students at the end of the semester. By viewing the portfolio as product, the portfolio becomes merely a new way to evaluate students, usually using the same criteria used in the past. However, we believe portfolios must be more than evaluation tools. Instead we view the portfolio as a tool that enables students to think about their work and how to represent their work to the world. Portfolios can provide a new way of learning, and ultimately, a new way of teaching. Krause (1996) states that portfolio development allows numerous opportunities for the learner to think flexibly about how and to what degree learning and change have occurred over time.

All students majoring in Unified Early Childhood Education, Unified Elementary Special Education, and Secondary Education at the University of Florida are required to develop and maintain an electronic portfolio. The purposes of the electronic portfolio are to:

- present illustrations of competency in the 12 FEAPs
- assist students in making connections between theory and practice
- effectively use and integrate technology in the educational experience at UF
- develop and present a professional vita over time
- provide a forum for connecting a student's university experience to personal and professional insights
- assist the student in coming to a better understanding of professional requirements for certification beyond the University of Florida, such as National Board Certification (Ring & Foti, 2001).

DEVELOPING THE ELECTRONIC PORTFOLIO SYSTEM

The electronic portfolio model requires that instructors make connections between course assignments and the Accomplished Practices. During the design phase we created a matrix (appendix I) placing all of the courses on one axis and all of the FEAPs on the other. The completed matrix provided a picture of the extent to which the Accomplished Practices were being addressed throughout the program. When we recast the matrix by year, we discovered that some years focused on Accomplished Practices more intensively than other years. This analysis provided faculty a new way to think about the structure of the program and the substance of the courses within the program.

Convinced that we were engaging in a worthwhile project, we continued the design of the electronic portfolio program. Several ideas guided the design:

1. The College of Education (COE) administration must support and promote the program. This program requires

manpower and the cooperation of students, faculty, and staff. We needed all the support we could get!

2. While faculty had to be informed and play a role in the project, they did not, at least initially, have to be able to actually create an electronic portfolio. We believe that much technological innovation is stymied by the belief that, "before you can teach the students, you have to teach the teachers." We viewed the faculty's role as developing course connections with the FEAPs and mentoring students in portfolio development. In particular, faculty should guide students' decisions about what artifacts to include in their portfolios, not how to include artifacts in their portfolios.

3. Our portfolio system would be situated on the Web. After examining a number of programs suitable for portfolio building, we decided that the Web was the only truly universal access and dissemination mechanism.

4. The students need a great deal of support. It is important to note that many of our students have little or no technology experience before entering our program. We recognized we would need to help them overcome their anxieties regarding technology as well as their lack of skills. Consequently, we planned to offer human as well as Web-based support structures to assist them.

5. The college should furnish students storage space on our college server for their portfolios. Doing this allows students to keep their portfolios active indefinitely. We hope that students will continue working on their portfolios after they leave the college. Storage space provides a means of supporting their professional development as well as yielding data for teacher educators to study teacher learning.

In the summer of 1999, through a grant from the Florida Department of Education, we were able to involve a cadre of faculty in the initial planning of the portfolio project. The goals of these summer sessions were to give the faculty time and support to:

• Restructure their syllabi by adding the FEAPs, describing how they are addressed in each course
• Develop Web-based syllabi for the elementary education portfolio matrix

- Restructure their assignments so that they were more closely aligned with the FEAPs.

Through our preliminary work with the faculty, we hoped to develop faculty commitment to the electronic portfolio initiative, thus generating greater support for our efforts. The conversations with faculty prior to program implementation allowed for faculty input and gave us time to make changes based on their suggestions. We also hoped that these conversations would help us think about potential barriers to the implementation of the portfolio program. We now view these preliminary sessions as an essential component of the portfolio process.

Armed with the belief that our students were responsible enough to develop and maintain a record of their own achievements and understandings, we set forth to create an infrastructure to support their efforts. Portfolio content must be somewhat defined, but remain flexible and open-ended. As Wolf (1991) explains, "Standardizing the contents to some degree makes it easier for others to interpret each individual portfolio as well as make comparisons across many different portfolios" (p. 8). Consequently, we decided to ask each faculty member to create examples of assignments that would illustrate Accomplished Practices. We believed that rather than using the examples as fill-in-the-blank templates, students should use the examples as guides to help them start building their own illustrations.

We further standardized the portfolio by defining the structure of the first page. The opening page of the electronic portfolio is divided into two categories: academic- or university-related entries, and personal entries (i.e., pertaining to the student). The academic or professional category contains links to University of Florida and COE Web sites, a student created menu addressing the FEAPs, a coursework page with links to courses, and the student's professional affiliations and teaching philosophy. The personal category contains links to student information pages (here, students can be as creative as they wish using photographs, animated gifs, fonts, etc.), and a favorite links page, containing links to articles and Web sites that the students find interesting. Although research stresses the idea of flexibility and creativity in student portfolios (Krause, 1996; Paulson & Paulson, 1994), we insisted that students use our first page template. This was done so that our faculty and staff would know what to expect when they went into any student's portfolio. By standardizing the content and format of the portfolios, we were attempting to support the faculty as they embarked on the complex and potentially labor intensive endeavor of integrating electronic portfolios into their curriculum.

Key Contextual Variables

Two contextual factors were critical to the development of the electronic portfolio model. Although these factors were outside of the department in which the development effort was housed, they significantly affected its direction and outcomes.

The support of the COE administration had immediate consequences. The college hired an Assistant Director of Educational Technology to head up the electronic portfolio project and spearhead a general technology faculty support initiative. The new position helped open communication between the head of the portfolio project and the faculty. Faculty wanted help with a variety of technology projects. In the process of helping them with their projects, the Assistant Director of Educational Technology was able to inform them about and encourage them to participate in the electronic portfolio project. Whereas many faculty had little involvement with the portfolio project in the first year, by the second year, they were beginning to discuss portfolios with their students and seeking ways to integrate their course work with the electronic portfolio.

Another key contextual variable was the university's computer policy. The university established a policy that every student must have access to a computer. This policy has no doubt affected the portfolio project. The problems associated with student resistance to mandatory computer use do not exist in our college as all students on campus are expected to use computers and computers are readily available.

IMPLEMENTING THE ELECTRONIC PORTFOLIO SYSTEM

Students are admitted into the UESEP program in their junior year of college, and the portfolio is introduced to them at their orientation to the College of Education. During the first few weeks of courses the director of the electronic portfolio project conducts a hands-on workshop in which students learn about the electronic portfolio project, the FEAPs, and the support structures that have been put in place to assist them. The development, maintenance, and revision of the portfolio are discussed on editorial and technical levels. Students begin developing their portfolios while becoming familiar with Web editors, browsers, and the technical aspects of building, linking, and publishing Web pages. After the initial workshop, 10 hours per week of lab support are available. Understandably, it is difficult for students to comprehend the FEAPs, develop a portfolio, and face the prospect of developing Web pages, so supporting them through each step of this complex process is essential.

We believe that it is possible to build an infrastructure that attends to students' needs and simultaneously instructs them. To assist students we developed an online student support center. As we noted, in our model, the instructor of each course delineates how the course assignments integrate with FEAPs and/or curricular goals. To provide samples for students, we asked each faculty member to provide sample illustrations of assignments or assignment descriptions. These illustrations or descriptions were then converted to Web-based documents and added to the portfolio matrix. In addition, based on feedback and questions from students and faculty, additional online support systems were developed. Support pages include information sheets; tutorials related to a specific skill; descriptions of the FEAPs; external links to pertinent references; video clips showing examples; a list of frequently asked questions, misconceptions, and problems students encounter; and other helpful information. Brown-bag seminars, workshops, and question-and-answer sessions are held to provide additional support. The goal of the support infrastructure is to help students improve their performance without making decisions for them. Using portfolios as a forum to demonstrate mastery of the FEAPs transfers a great deal of responsibility to the students. Decisions about how to best demonstrate their competence, such as which information channels to use (e.g., video, audio, photographs, text-based anecdotes), should remain with the students. Portfolio development increases the number of decisions students have to make about specific assignments, goals, and/or tasks. It is demanding work. Putting together innovative and representative portfolios—the kind that really tell who students are becoming as teachers—requires a serious commitment of time and energy (Arter & Spandel, 1992).

Lessons From Pilot

As part of the electronic portfolio development process, we conducted a pilot study to learn how faculty members' instructional strategies influence student construction and use of an electronic portfolio. In the pilot, one of the authors (Colleen Swain) documented the strategies she used to integrate the electronic portfolio into a course she teaches in the Secondary Proteach program. Although this course was not part of the UESEP program, the pilot study about the implementation of the electronic portfolio can provide insight for other faculty members.

Swain's initial concerns were about how to seamlessly integrate the electronic portfolio into the course and have students accept the electronic portfolio as a long-term project instead of as an assignment for a single course. One of the goals of the course was for students to identify and internalize characteristics that excellent teachers possess and demonstrate on a daily basis. Swain wanted the electronic portfolios to enhance the students' learning of course objectives, and also enrich their reflection about and analysis of the learning events taking place during the course.

During the first semester of the pilot study, Swain's most important goal was that the students learn to appreciate the value of an electronic portfolio. She considered this a highly important goal because of the various constraints influencing the pilot study. The students who participated in this first pilot study semester were completing a secondary education minor and obtaining a baccalaureate degree from the College of Liberal Arts and Sciences. They were not part of an official teacher-education program but many of them would apply to the Secondary Proteach program after graduation. Most of the students in this course viewed themselves as "students" and not as future educators. The course met three times a week for 50 minutes and had a high enrollment. In designing the course, Swain carefully considered these constraints as well as her knowledge of adult learning theory (Knowles, 1984). Students in college courses frequently list relevance and the practicality of the material learned as important to them. Therefore, Swain decided to present the electronic portfolio as a tool that would benefit students in their future and enable them to document their growth as educators using the FEAPs as the central focus.

Through readings, videos, case studies, class discussions, and the presentation of sample portfolios, Swain represented portfolios as an important tool for students. Class activities provided students with opportunities to see that portfolios provided them with opportunities to reflect on the fundamental characteristics teachers should possess and demonstrate, think about their possible future career, and be evaluated in a more well-rounded manner. Swain also stressed that the skills they were developing would provide them with an advantage when they entered the Secondary Proteach program. Although Swain recognized that many connections about teaching would not be made until students actually got into a classroom in the role of a teacher, it was hoped that the readings, videos, case studies, and examples would help students begin making connections between theoretical knowledge and practice. She hoped that through developing portfolios students would critically analyze their evolving knowledge about teaching and develop an explicit awareness of their growth over the semester. However, the students' electronic portfolios did not exhibit the growth and reflection that

Swain had expected. Students exhibited no obvious pride in their portfolios. Their selections of materials were haphazard, and their rationale statements explaining why illustrations were included were trivial.

For the next semester, Swain stressed the electronic portfolio but without the initial emphasis on the FEAPs. Instead, she focused on how the electronic portfolios would help students think about teaching. At the conclusion of each class discussion about a case study or assignment, students were asked to analyze their thinking about the assignments they had completed. Students again were exposed to readings, videos, case studies, and K–12 student projects while participating in discussions about how electronic portfolios could be used as an instructional strategy. Students began to see the power of reflecting upon the various developmental stages of the assignments they created in the class. Students also became more reflective and took pride in developing their educational philosophies. During the second half of the semester, the FEAPs were introduced as a strategy for organizing knowledge about the development of a teacher for the state of Florida. Students were asked to select assignments from this course and any of their other education courses in the secondary minor to document their growth and learning in the process of becoming a teacher. At the conclusion of the semester, Swain was pleased to see the great pride many students had in their portfolios. Although some students still viewed electronic portfolios as another assignment to complete, there were more students than in the previous semester who were interested in their electronic portfolios as a way to document their growth as educators. For example, some students used the portfolio to document their progressive improvement in creating lessons that challenge and accommodate all students.

For future semesters, Swain is striving to instill a sense of ownership in more students. Although nearly all of the students demonstrated a more reflective approach in making decisions about what to include in their electronic portfolios, it was clear that most were unlikely to update their portfolios and document their professional growth beyond the scope of the course. Swain and her colleagues in the electronic portfolio project recognize that the adoption of any innovation takes considerable time (Rogers, 1995) but the pilot indicates that students are unlikely to perceive a portfolio as an ongoing learning experience without substantial effort on the part of instructors and the program. This idea is one that must certainly be adopted by the culture surrounding the teacher education program, and Swain hopes to help this process by sharing her electronic portfolio experiences with her colleagues.

Swain's lessons from her pilot studies show that faculty members need to scaffold students' pedagogical thinking in the development of the portfolio. The technical aspects of producing an electronic portfolio were soon mastered but cognitive elements surrounding the electronic portfolios must be an integral part of courses in the teacher education program and within the teacher education culture. Swain concluded that it is not enough for students to view the electronic portfolios as a way to document illustrations of the FEAPs. Instead students must be helped to use their electronic portfolio to show their growth and mastery of the practices that exemplify good teaching. In this way, their potential as an educator is expanded.

CHALLENGES FACED AND ADDRESSED

The electronic portfolio project was introduced to students in our teacher education programs in the fall of 2000. Unified Elementary and Unified Early Childhood students were college juniors who would complete their portfolios as master's-level students. The secondary students were master's-level students enrolled in a one-year teacher education program. Consequently, the first group of teacher education students to complete electronic portfolios were students in our secondary education program. We learned from our work with the secondary education students that it is important to be clear and explicit about the portfolio requirement from the moment it is introduced. Although we expended a great deal of effort to build support structures for the students, students were not notified about this program requirement in writing, nor was it an official component of any one course. Instead the requirement was introduced orally during large group meetings. This lack of formality created problems. Early in the school year, students attended meetings about the portfolio project and completed surveys about their technological abilities. They entered their names on the surveys and we kept a record of who attended the meetings (there was nearly 100% attendance). Still, as the year passed, and some students fell behind on their portfolio work, they claimed they were never told about the portfolio requirements. Because we had not formalized the process, that is, notified students in writing about their responsibilities, it was difficult to deal with these claims. In spring 2001, we created and disseminated a manual to all teacher education students describing the portfolio project and the students' responsibilities. In addition, we suggested that every faculty member make reference to the electronic portfolio requirement on his/her syllabus.

In addition, the problems associated with evaluation continue to plague us. We want to encourage students to take ownership of their work and make decisions about the evolving product. Still, there is a need for institutional evaluation of the students' work. Using performance assessment and formative assessment, portfolios are evaluated on a number of levels: assignments are evaluated and deemed "portfolio-ready" by the course instructor; then, from this increasing collection of illustrations, the students select multiple appropriate illustrations for each FEAP. Throughout the semester, the director of the Office of Educational Technology examines the portfolios. However, we strongly believe that students must be actively engaged in discussing and examining their own portfolios. We are working to give students multiple opportunities to present their portfolios to faculty, peers, and incoming teacher education students. We have found that these opportunities contribute to increased pride, reflection, and ownership on the part of the student. These presentations have also contributed to increased faculty interest and participation in the project. As they observe students' pride in their efforts and increased reflection on their course work, faculty become more active participants in the portfolio project.

It is essential that the portfolio program be designed so that all stakeholders have a say in its development. It is in the best interests of students, teachers, and district/state staff to work together to (1) preserve the instructional power of portfolios and (2) see how the potentially rich sources of information from portfolios can be summarized to show others what students are learning (Arter & Spandel, 1992). We continue to wrestle with the kind of staff development required at each level of implementation. Our feeling at this point is that individual faculty members are ready to innovate at different times, and that a high degree of individual support is required. If professors do not believe that the portfolio is valuable to students and their education, they probably will not promote it in their classes. In an attempt to address these concerns, the director of the portfolio project meets with individual faculty members to share ideas and alleviate their concerns about various aspects of the project. In addition, retreats are being scheduled to provide faculty with an opportunity to learn more about the program and share strategies for integrating the electronic portfolio into courses.

CONCLUSION

Rogers (1995) and others have demonstrated that innovation diffusion takes a great deal of time. The electronic portfolio program will surely prove to be no exception. We have learned that we must promote the use of portfolios to preservice teachers and their instructors. If we expect instructors to teach differently, then we must show them how to do so. By modeling a complex, student-centered model, we are teaching students about real-world complexity and problem solving. As we watch our students create portfolios, we notice the collaboration and sharing of ideas among students. As students begin to reflect on their work, as well as their learning experiences, they will begin to ask deeper questions such as: "What information is useful?" "What is my vision of teaching?"

As we proceed with the project we continue to have many questions about portfolio development such as: What factors in the development process contribute to richer student learning? How will developing a portfolio contribute to students' ability to reflect about their own work and their own progress? How does developing a portfolio contribute to the students' perceptions of themselves and their own abilities? As we continue to work with our students and their portfolio development, we hope to address these issues. It is our goal that the portfolio becomes a tool to stimulate students' abilities to reflect, reason, and develop intellectually (Sizer, 1984).

REFERENCES

Arter, J. A., & Spandel, V. (1992). Using portfolios of student work in instruction and assessment. *Educational Measurement: Issues and Practice, 11*(1), 36–44.

Barton, J., & Collins, A. (1993). Portfolios in teacher education. *Journal of Teacher Education 44*(3), 200–210.

Bird, T. (1990). The schoolteacher's portfolio: An essay on possibilities. In J. Millman, & L. Darling-Hammond (Eds.), *The new handbook of teacher evaluation* (pp. 241–453). Newbury Park, CA: Sage.

Foti S., & Ring, G. (2000). Portfolios: Beyond assessment. *Teaching & Learning: The Journal of Natural Inquiry, 14*(2), 18–22.

Freidus, H. (2000, April). *Fostering reflective practice: Taking a look at context.* Paper presented at the meeting of the American Educational Research Association, New Orleans, LA. (ERIC Document Reproduction Service ED 227–073).

Johnson, N., & Rose, L.M. (1997). *Portfolios, clarifying, constructing and enhancing.* Lancaster, PA: Technomic Publishing Company, Inc.

Knowles, M. (1984). *The adult learner: A neglected species* (3rd ed.). Houston, TX: Gulf Publishing.

Krause, S. (1996). Portfolios in teacher education: Effects of instruction on preservice teachers' early comprehension of the portfolio process. *Journal of Teacher Education, 47*(2), 130–138.

Lyons, N. (1998). Reflection in teaching: Can it be developmental? A portfolio perspective. *Teacher Education Quarterly, 25*(1), 115–128.

Paulson P. L., & Paulson, P. R. (1994, April). *Assessing portfolios Using the constructivist paradigm.* Paper presented at the annual meeting of the American Educational Research Association, New Orleans, LA. (ERIC Document Reproduction Service ED 376209).

Ring, G., & Foti, S. (2001). *Electronic teaching portfolios.* (Student Manual) Gainesville, FL: University of Florida, College of Education, Office of Educational Technology.

Rogers, E. M. (1995). *Diffusion of innovations* (4th ed.). New York: Free Press.

Shulman, L. S. (1988). The dangers of dichotomous thinking in education. In P. P. Grimett, & G. I. Erickson (Eds.). *Reflection in teacher education* (pp. 31–46). New York: Teachers College Press.

Sizer, T. R. (1984). *Horace's compromise: The dilemma of the American high school.* Boston: Houghton Mifflin.

Wolf, K. (1991). *Teaching portfolios: Synthesis of research and annotated bibliography.* San Francisco, CA: Far West Lab for Educational Research and Development. (ERIC Document Reproduction Service No. ED 343890).

PART 5

The Reform in Context

CHAPTER 16

A Special Educator's Reflections on Teacher Education Reform

LINDA BLANTON

Working for more than 30 years in teaching and teacher education, first as an elementary teacher and later as a special education teacher and teacher educator, I have often reflected on the similarities and differences in general and special education, with a special interest in the differences found in teacher education. In a paper I coauthored (Blanton, Sindelar, Correa, Hardman, & McDonnell, 2002), we overviewed the history of research on teaching and teacher education in general education and traced the gradual entry of special education into these already established arenas. Clearly, the fields of general and special education have very different research and development histories in teaching and teacher education. Although the general education community had flourishing programs of research on teaching and teacher education in the 1960s, '70s, and '80s, special educators were often consumed with advocacy and assuring the rights of students with disabilities. This fact alone is a large contributor to the delay on the part of special educators to explore alternative teacher education models and, more specifically, for the fields of special and general education to work together on common teacher education reform issues.

Another factor contributing to the delay of special and general educators working together on common teacher education reform issues is the nature of the reforms suggested in reports of various national commissions and partnerships. The emphasis on teacher education reform since the mid 1980s has kept most teacher educators focused on making changes such as the addition of more content knowledge to their curriculum. As noted in a recent American

Association of Colleges of Teacher Education (AACTE) white paper (2002), teacher education leaders have only more recently "been challenged to connect renewal efforts among and within university departments and units" (pp. 3–4). Since the mid 1990's, however, teacher education in special and general education has begun to intersect, with several factors influencing this trend.

The focus on inclusion (with earlier terminology and conceptions such as least restrictive alternative, mainstreaming, and the regular education initiative) brought general and special education closer together. In teacher education, inclusive school practices influenced some schools and colleges of education to develop dual, merged, or blended teacher education programs—programs to prepare preservice general and special education teachers together (Blanton, Griffin, Winn, Pugach, 1997; Stayton & McCullum, 2002). In addition, the changing requirements in federal laws (e.g., the 1997 Amendments to the Individuals with Disabilities Education Act) and a continuing emphasis on standards (i.e., accreditation, beginning teacher, and advanced certification) created a context for greater collaboration among general and special educators. As one example, the development of the INTASC (Interstate New Teacher Assessment and Support Consortium) standards engaged both general and special educators in the task of deciding what all teachers need to know and be able to do to work with students with disabilities (Interstate New Teacher, 2001). Another example is the initiative by many states to unify the personnel standards for the fields of early childhood education and early childhood special education into a single set of certification requirements (Stayton & McCollum, 2002).

Since the early 1980s, the special education literature has contained more and more examples of teacher education reform. Since its beginnings in the 1980s, the journal of the Teacher Education Division of the Council for Exceptional Children, *Teacher Education and Special Education (TESE)*, has been a primary source of teacher education issues, research, and reform initiatives in special education. *TESE* editors have used theme issues to focus specifically on various aspects of teacher education reform. Some examples include the spring issues in 1992, 1996, and 2000, and the 2002 summer issue. In the spring 1992 issue, authors focused on the topics of essential knowledge for effective special education teachers, the role of field-based experiences in the preparation of special education teachers, among others that dealt with assuring the preparation of effective special education teachers. The entire issue in spring 1996 was devoted to teacher education development and research in one special education department. In the spring 2000 issue, the topic of standards dominated with authors addressing high standards for special educator preparation, the process and impact of standards-based reform, and the development of portfolios and their effectiveness as an assessment tool in teacher preparation. The summer 2002 issue addressed personnel preparation for inclusive settings, focusing on blending teacher education in early childhood education and early childhood special education.

Although *TESE* is not the only outlet in the special education literature for topics related to teacher education reform in special education, it is a good example of the landscape of this work. In general, a fair summary of this landscape would be that special education teacher educators have begun to (a) write more in the literature about their teacher preparation programs; (b) do more research on components of their teacher preparation programs; and (c) focus on the same reform topics (e.g., standards-based reform) as their colleagues in general education. Also, like their colleagues in general education, special education teacher educators have yet to provide an adequate research base for most of their approaches to, and the overall structure of, teacher education.

Even with the growing body of literature on teacher education reform appearing in special education, very little is available to chronicle the intensive work it takes to achieve major reform in teacher education programs. Far fewer address what it takes to engage in teacher education reform when several university departments are involved, and when these departments include faculty from different fields (e.g., general and special education). Even fewer focus on how to inquire into the reform process by conducting research throughout their work. This book, therefore, is an important addition to the teacher education reform literature.

THEMES AND LESSONS LEARNED

The following key words capture the heart of the themes that thread throughout the current book: mission, collaboration, inquiry, accountability, reform. The University of Florida faculty, students, and colleagues heeded external and internal forces and responded with a mission to reform teacher education. Moreover, they depended on collaboration among faculty, students, and school partners to achieve their mission and goals; they engaged in regular inquiry to dig deeply into their work and assure understanding and continual growth; they held themselves accountable through performance systems and by writing about and reporting on their efforts, and; they accomplished early stages of reform in teacher education. The program renewal work undertaken at the University of Florida corresponds to many of the key elements noted in the literature on organizational change (e.g., Bolman & Deal, 1991) as being necessary ingredients in the change process: external mandates and conditions, clear vision, periodic successes, and buy-in by members of the organization.

The teacher education reform work at the University of Florida offers many lessons for those of us attempting to accomplish similar renewal. Pugach and Clift offer their perspectives on different aspects of the University of Florida's reform efforts, and both identified the lessons they believe will help others who engage in similar work. Taken together, these include:

- Expect teacher education reform to take time and to include many obstacles.
- Understand that higher education institutions, and education colleges within them, will need to establish structures and supports that enable participants to work well together even when they disagree.
- Commit to continuous improvement and use data to inform this process.
- Understand the importance of learning from students in the teacher education program.
- Understand how essential it is to engage in teacher education research as reform is undertaken.
- Accept that collaboration offers many learning opportunities.
- Create strong partnerships with schools to assure that field experiences align with the needs of the reform effort.
- Seek adequate resources to support teacher education reform.

These lessons are important to both general and special education teacher educators. As noted earlier, general and special education have different teaching and teacher education histories. Given this, it is easy to see how difficult it could be for the two fields to work together to change their programs. With this in mind, I would add the following lessons to what special education teacher educators and researchers might take away from the University of Florida's reform journey:

- Understand that special education's teaching and teacher education history needs to be understood among general education teacher educators. Similarly, special education teacher educators need to understand the history in general education. Openly sharing the histories of the fields may enhance understanding and create a better context for collaboration. An earlier publication by University of Florida faculty shared their attempts to bridge these differences in backgrounds (Bondy, Ross, Sindelar, & Griffin, 1995).

- Understand that special education's history includes a strong bias by many for a behavioral orientation toward teaching and learning. Since general educators have often focused on different orientations, it means that discussions about learning theory and subsequent teaching approaches are essential. Although this is only briefly discussed in the present text, the article by Bondy et al. (1995) offers some insight into how to bridge these differences.

- Consider the use of many methods to inquire into teaching, learning, and teacher education. Being steeped in particular theoretical orientations, special education teacher educators and researchers may overlook methods that would contribute to a greater understanding of their programs. Several chapters in the current book call on methods that others might consider in early stages of their reform efforts.

RECOMMENDATIONS FOR SPECIAL EDUCATION TEACHER EDUCATORS AND RESEARCHERS

Building on the lessons learned from the University of Florida's teacher education reform work, I would make a number of recommendations to teacher educators and researchers in special education:

- Teacher educators and researchers in special education must become as central to teacher education reform agendas as our colleagues in other fields of education. The dialogue within special education should reflect a greater focus on teacher education reform. In addition, the voices of more special educators need to become prominent in the larger teacher education reform community. Unfortunately, only a small portion of the special education community views themselves as teaching and teacher education researchers. Instead, many special educators continue to narrow their research to focus on student learning and classroom interventions within their specialty area (e.g., mental retardation). It goes without question that we need both.

- Special education teacher educators must conduct research on the nature and effectiveness of teacher education programs.

Even with the growing literature in special education on teaching and teacher education, most of this literature consists of program descriptions and evaluations (Brownell, Ross, Colon, & McCallum, 2001). In their recent review of the teacher education literature, Brownell and her colleagues note that "special education teacher education is a less established area of inquiry and we found no solid synthesis of available programs and the features exemplifying those programs"(p. 6). Their review revealed that some of the features of effective teacher education programs found in general education are also found in the special education literature. However, some other features (e.g., programmatic vision and heavy emphasis on subject matter pedagogy) are generally absent from the special education literature. The reader is referred to the Brownell et al. (2001) review for their recommendations for future research.

- Special education teacher educators must engage in collaborative research with general educators on the nature and effectiveness of teacher education programs. In this text, the University of Florida sets a good example for collaborative research. Although one can find some examples of collaborative research among general and special educators, few examples exist on the nature and effectiveness of teacher education programs. One example is the review by Stayton and McCullum (2002) of research on unified general and special education programs. These authors point out, "There is no research other than brief accounts of individual program evaluation data, that investigates program outcomes or that relates program outcomes to specific program characteristics" (p. 215).

- Teacher educators and researchers in special education must call on a broad array of methods in their inquiry of teaching and teacher education. The use of multiple research paradigms is critical to a deep understanding of the effectiveness of teacher education programs. A recent review of teacher preparation research by Wilson, Floden, and Ferrini-Mundy (2002) makes a strong case for "rigorous research in multiple traditions" (p. 202). It is essential that special educators respond to this need.

CONCLUSION

Despite many challenges, the University of Florida College of Education engaged in systemic teacher education reform. The faculty and administrators are to be commended for their accomplishments, especially when considering the current sociopolitical climate and the structures of higher education. Throughout their work, University of Florida faculty and administrators faced the same two major sociopolitical challenges the rest of us face: the ongoing attempt by policymakers to control teacher education curricula and the tension in teacher education programs to produce sufficient numbers of teachers while maintaining rigorous standards to assure a high-quality graduate. In addition, the higher education culture at the University of Florida and its College of Education is not likely to be different from that in most other large research universities. The traditional reward structures, focused on individual accomplishments, prevail in most research universities. Regardless, the faculty and administration in the College of Education at the University of Florida moved forward with major teacher education reform. In short, this book offers insights into a long journey, and all of us in special education teacher education have much to learn from it.

REFERENCES

American Association of Colleges for Teacher Education. (2002, February). *Preparing teachers to work with students with disabilities: Possibilities and challenges for special and general teacher education.* Washington, DC.

Blanton, L. P., Griffin, C. C., Winn, J. A., & Pugach, M. C. (Eds.). (1997). *Teacher education in transition: Collaborative programs to prepare general and special educators.* Denver, CO: Love Publishing Co.

Blanton, L., Sindelar, P., Correa, V., Hardman, M., McDonnell, J., & Kuhel, K. (2002). *Conceptions of beginning teacher quality: Models for conducting research,* Unpublished Manuscript. University of Florida, Center on Personnel Preparation in Special Education. Retrieved February 1, 2003 from www.copsse.org.

Bolman, L. E., & Deal, T. E. (1991). *Reframing organizations: Artistry, choice and leadership.* San Francisco: Jossey-Bass.

Bondy, B., Ross, D., Sindelar, P., & Griffin, C. (1995). Elementary and special educators learning to work together: Team building processes. *Teacher Education and Special Education.* 18(2), 91–102.

Brownell, M. T., Ross, D. D., Colon, E. P., & McCallum, C. L. (2002). *Critical features of special education teacher preparation: A comparison with exemplary practices in general teacher education.* Unpublished Manuscript. University of Florida, Center on Personnel Preparation in Special Education. Retrieved February 1, 2003 from www.copsse.org.

Interstate New Teacher Assessment and Support Consortium. (2001). *Model standards for licensing general and special education teachers of students with disabilities.* Washington, DC: Council of Chief State School Officers.

Stayton, V. D., & McCollum, J. (2002). Unifying general and special education: What does the research tell us? *Teacher Education and Special Education, 25*(3), 211–218.

Wilson, S. M., Floden, R. E., & Ferrini-Mundy, J. (2002). Teacher preparation research: An insider's view from the outside. *Journal of Teacher Education, 53,* 190–204.

CHAPTER 17

A General Teacher Educator's Reflections

ALAN R. TOM

Over my career I have been involved in the rethinking of a number of elementary and secondary teacher education programs. These programs have had as few as 15–20 students and as many as 125 students and were located in private as well as public universities, all of which were research oriented. Redesign issues in preservice teacher education have been a major strand of my scholarship (Tom, 1997).

When I first considered how to respond to this interesting account of the University of Florida's Unified Elementary Special Education Program (UESEP), I was easily attracted to redesign issues. This case study has implications for how other teacher educators think about and approach the reform of preservice programming, particularly in research-oriented institutions but also in other types of institutions. After speaking to redesign issues embedded in this particular case but also present in many other instances of teacher education reform, I address several redesign issues that have a special twist for those interested in developing unified general and special education preparation programs. While doing this analysis, I draw upon the findings and perspectives of various chapter authors. I conclude this chapter by offering some design ideas for consideration by teacher educators in other institutional settings.

PROGRAM REDESIGN: WIDELY SHARED ISSUES

My first reaction after reading the initial chapters is a sense of wonder that the Unified Program was ever created and implemented. The account in Chapter four of the development of the University of

Florida program is a dramatic story: a thoughtful period of conceptualization, the involvement of all units of the College of Education (including several not typically involved in teacher education), faculty opposition to the first program design, subsequent creation of four designs whose most promising elements were synthesized into a single design, the acceptance of a curriculum framework but not until the fourth faculty retreat, a two-year process in which course content and syllabi were redefined for every course and field experience in the entire program, and, in the midst of this course development, a state mandate that all state teacher education programs include an endorsement in English for Speakers of Other Languages (ESOL). In the end, more than four years passed between the dean's charge that the faculty create the new program (spring 1995) and the first cohort's initiation into professional study (fall 1999). The original target date for beginning the first cohort of students had been the fall of 1996.

One prominent lesson from the University of Florida case is that it takes a lot of faculty work and personal commitment to achieve basic change in teacher education. Though obvious, this lesson is very important; education faculties often lack the initiative and energy to pursue fundamental program reform. However, beneath the whirl of events lie implications that may be more telling for teachers educators than the admonishment that program reform entails hard work. In the following discussion I identify several design issues lodged in the University of Florida case but also frequently present in other reform settings. Connections to the University of Florida experience are made where appropriate. These design issues are grouped into two categories: the structure and culture of Colleges of Education and design parameters. The latitude a teacher education faculty has in dealing with a particular design issue varies by category.

Structure and Culture of Colleges of Education

Design issues connected to the structure and culture of Colleges of Education are often treated as "givens" around which teacher educators must navigate. The following discussion concerns the low status of teacher education, the presumed superiority of specialized knowledge, and the pivotal importance of course approval. With teacher educators having little apparent latitude in addressing these issues, they often treat considerations under this category as constraints which channel redesign efforts.

Low Status of Teacher Education. One of the most troubling properties of teacher education for teacher educators is the low status of this field, both within research-intensive universities and within each College of Education (chapter 2). Markers of this low status are peppered throughout the University of Florida case, despite the strong tradition of teacher education at that institution. During the planning process, for example, faculty members worried about the extent to which college resources and support would be available to them for developing and teaching courses in this time-intensive program (chapter 4). Even though grant funding supported aspects of the development and evaluation of the program, ultimately no additional hard-money budget was allocated to those who implemented the program (chapter 7). Similarly, the Dean of the College of Education was unable to get the Regents of the State University System Board to recognize work in the PreK–12 schools to be part of a teacher educator's official workload (chapter 4). Furthermore, the mandate by the Florida Department of Education of ESOL coursework (chapter 4) is something not likely to occur in programs for the preparation of professionals in higher status fields.

The teacher educators at the University of Florida were keenly aware of the ramifications of the resource starvation associated with low status. For example, each team was restricted to team planning of courses and class sessions but did not include team teaching for course delivery. Team teaching by full-time faculty was recognized as "costly and unrealistic within a large teacher education program" (chapter 6, p. 101).

Presumed Superiority of Specialized Knowledge. As indicated in chapter 2, "university structures value specialization and theory over integration and practice" (p. 40). Rare is the university faculty member whose primary commitment is to the institution, its goals and programs; allegiance tends to be to the academic specialty and to the academic department that houses that specialty. No less than other university colleagues, faculty members in Colleges of Education participate in this pursuit of specialization. In addition, education really is a confederation of subspecialties, each having (or desiring) its own departmental status.

The dominance of specialization has substantial implications for teacher educators at the University of Florida because they aspired to create "a practice-driven program that was unified, cross-departmental, and interdisciplinary" (chapter 2, p. 40). The findings in this book indicate mixed results in neutralizing the norm that each faculty member should be free to teach that person's specialized knowledge. For example, it is unclear the extent to which program themes are distributed over the professional curriculum (chapter 7), since faculty collaboration generally centered on the content of a particular course. However, course-level collaborative planning did, in part, overcome initial faculty skepticism that each professor would use the norm of instructional autonomy to justify a highly personalized view of specialized knowledge (chapter 6). Yet two of the three teaching teams examined in chapter 8 ended up negotiating arrangements to limit the scope of their collaborative course planning. Renee Clift (chapter 13) suggests that instructional autonomy can insulate faculty members from one another and thus limit the professional growth that often results from the surfacing and reconciling of diverse views.

Pivotal Importance of Course Design and Approval. If specialized knowledge and the departments into which this knowledge is organized are the building blocks of university structure, course development is central to the university process of curriculum decision making. Course approval can be viewed as the governance mechanism by which discipline-based faculty members control the content of majors and professional programs, including teacher education. The course approval process in a College of Education brings out the central concerns of specialized faculty members, ranging from the protection of content turf to adequate provision for detailed content.

Perhaps in response to the enormous importance faculty members typically attach to the design of individual courses, the focus of curriculum development for UESEP seemed to devolve to course design. While teacher educators at the University of Florida initially did attend to the design of the overall program, more than half of the planning time between 1995 and 1999 was devoted to the development of individual courses and securing approval from the college and university curriculum committees. Course design concerns often reflected the perspective of specialists. Faculty members, for example, worried that "course compression" might lead to "packing too much content into too few hours" so that "their own disciplines would get short-changed" (chapter 4, p. 78). Concurrently, *program* coherence increasingly seemed to focus on the consistency of content, assignments, and teaching materials across the multiple sections of a *single course* (chapter 6; chapter 8). Once focused on course design, the University of Florida faculty seemed to lose track of program design issues.

Since faculty members in large colleges of education—at the University Florida and elsewhere—are specialists, they typically are more at home with course redesign than with program redesign, since the latter requires a holistic view and an interest in what holds together the parts (courses) of a program. Even in the case of course design, specialist faculty members are often unwilling to collaborate for fear of compromising instructional autonomy. Programmatic themes or other integrating mechanisms can easily be ignored, and even the relatively straightforward task of preventing overlapping content across the courses in a program becomes problematic.

Design Parameters

Borrowing the term "parameters" from chapter 4, I use the idea of "design parameters" to indicate that decisions critically important to the design process are made even before this process begins. Several such design parameters were explicitly recognized by participants in the University of Florida reform effort. Most obviously, the new program was to merge special and general education. In addition, the new program was to continue to be a five-year effort, and this program was to involve several units not currently part of teacher education. Adopting these parameters no doubt made the program more complex to plan and implement. However, I want to focus on several other design parameters that had a major impact on program redesign and seem not to have explicitly been recognized as design parameters: program size, a single curriculum or multiple curricula, and coherence as an unquestioned good.

Program Size. The University of Florida has a large program, with more than 200 students entering each year. Large programs create a special bind for teacher educators in research-intensive institutions. On the one hand, graduate faculty in other areas in education typically are happy to see large numbers of teacher education students, particularly if this credit-hour production can be used to cross-subsidize graduate programming (a motivation rarely made public). On the other hand, these same graduate faculty worry, as did the University of Florida faculty (chapter 4; chapter 7), that a large innovative program, well designed and provided with adequate human and financial resources, will divert resources away from graduate programming.

Teacher educators in research-intensive institutions are internally pressured, therefore, to maintain large programs, with the extra effort coming from such places as larger workloads for teacher educators, greater reliance on graduate students and part-time adjuncts (Shaffer & Striedieck, 1999), or the increased use of clinical (non-tenure-line) appointments in teacher education. Each of these solutions presents threats to tenure-line teacher educators, either for their research productivity and/or for their association with a program whose quality might be imperiled.

From the description and analysis provided in this book, I cannot tell whether the commitment to large program size at the University of Florida has led to any of the threats just enumerated. It is not clear, for example, if the teaching load of the teacher education faculty is the same as other education faculty. Teacher education faculty do receive modest load recognition for serving as a "team leader" (chapter 4), and a pilot program, "Professor in Residence," provides .25 FTE to recognize faculty work in a specific school (chapter 4). Certainly, graduate students play a major role in the new program. As earlier mentioned, no additional hard-money budget was allocated to those who implemented the new program (chapter 7). The pressures of conducting a large, innovative program would seem to be affecting the tenure-line teacher educators at the University of Florida.

A Single Curriculum or Multiple Curricula. One decision made by teacher educators working in large programs is whether to use a single curriculum or to employ multiple curriculum models (Barnes, 1987; Book, 1983). Typically, teacher educators easily settle on a single professional curriculum, perhaps, as is the case at the University of Florida, because they lack sufficient tenure-line faculty to staff alternative models. However, this choice entails potential difficulties.

A large teacher education program, in which each course has numerous sections that can be staffed by graduate students or adjuncts, naturally leads a faculty to give substantial attention to achieving consistency of content across sections of a course. Thus at the University of Florida early and extensive attention was given to standardizing all sections of a particular course in terms of content, assignments, and teaching materials (chapter 6; chapter 8). The horizontal consistency of course content appears to have been given priority over the vertical integration of themes over the life of the professional curriculum, although this preference is understandable in the context of a large-scale program with interchangeable parts.

Choosing to run a large program in which each cohort represents a distinctive curricular approach turns a faculty's attention, from the beginning, to issues of vertical integration. Typically themes provide this integration (e.g., Peterson, Benson, Driscoll, Narode, Sherman, & Tama, 1995), and without such integration a program runs the risk of becoming a disconnected chain of courses. Since a relatively small faculty team tends to be responsible for each thematic cohort in a multiple models approach, midcourse changes in program content are much easier to make than when a very large faculty grouping is responsible for a single overall program (Tom, 1988, 1999a). Using the structure of a small faculty team, usually with only one faculty member from each specialty area, can also blunt faculty opposition based on alleged intrusions into instructional autonomy. Instead, the attention of each specialist is redirected to how that person's ideas interconnect with the ideas of other specialists on that thematic-based team. Such discussions by a small faculty team should also identify overlapping content; the elimination of such content may even enable the faculty to shorten the professional curriculum.

A theme-based curriculum structure implemented by small faculty teams is not without its problems (Peterson, Benson, Driscoll, Narode, Sherman, & Tama, 1995, pp. 40–41). This model cannot be done on the cheap; graduate students and part-time adjuncts can play a role, but they are not really in a position to be full-fledged team members. The success of thematic faculty teams depends on continuity of team membership; there may be no established course of study to fall back on should a graduate student be given full course responsibility. Teaching in thematic programs requires faculty participation; faculty cannot "strike deals" (chapter 8) to limit their participation or even opt out of group planning as some did at the University of Florida. What does one do with faculty members uninterested in teaming when teaming is a necessity? Not all of the problems related to theme-based professional curricula revolve around staffing. Students lose some flexibility in their schedules since they must attend class when a particular cohort meets, a potential problem when the majority of students hold half-time or more jobs as was the case at the University of Florida (chapter 11).

Coherence as an Unquestioned Good. While coherence is not the focus for any particular chapter, this idea is discussed in several chapters (e.g., chapters 6, 8, & 11). Most commonly, coherence is connected to course design. The focus tends to be on achieving consistency across the content in all sections of a particular course, including the tension between the autonomy of individual instructors and the goal of course consistency. Whenever the idea of coherence does arise, coherence is presumed to be an attribute of high-quality programs.

Failing to consider the value of coherence in an explicit way may have led faculty members not to be careful in delineating what they meant by coherence. Even though coherence is presumed to be an attribute of the entire program, this idea typically is applied to a particular course—primarily attaining consistency of content across all sections—and not to whether the programmatic themes flow across all the courses in the program. As a result, discussions of coherence by University of Florida faculty members might more aptly be referred to as course coherence rather than as program coherence.

The tendency to implicitly equate coherence and consistency raises another issue. Coherence in teacher education is not without its critics. In particular, Buchmann and Floden (1991, 1992) argue for a limited view of coherence, a view that distinguishes between coherence and consistency. Instead of a curriculum based on predetermined outcomes, Floden and Buchmann (1990, p. 313) believe that prospective teachers should possess a "web of beliefs," which facilitate the "making of new connections to disparate events or information." Floden and Buchmann conclude that the desirable program helps teachers "build interconnections among the various areas of knowledge and skill" yet has "numerous loose ends, inviting a reweaving of beliefs and ties to what may be as yet unknown."

Such a view of coherence would alter the extent to which multiple sections need to have common assignments and teaching materials, perhaps placing the emphasis more on common intellectual perspectives and course goals. Program themes would also have been highlighted, to the degree that these themes help to build a web of beliefs. Last, the severity of the tension between professional autonomy and course coherence might well have been reduced. It is also important to note, however, that the emphasis on performance assessment by the National Council for the Accreditation of Teacher Education (2002) and the strong regulatory stance in Florida (chapter 4) are forces that support a view of coherence as consistency.

PROGRAM REDESIGN: UNIFIED TEACHER EDUCATION PROGRAMMING

As noted by Renee Clift (chapter 13), cross-departmental cooperation is rarely attempted by faculties of education. At the University of Florida, one complication in developing such cross-departmental cooperation was tension and conflict that existed between general and special education faculty members (chapter 8). Considering these fields overall, Linda Blanton (chapter 16) attributes such tensions primarily to the differing perspectives of general teacher educators and special educators. Blanton seems to suggest that these differing perspectives are rooted in the contrasting histories and traditions of general and special education. The authors of chapter 8 explore the specific differences in the perspectives of these two fields as part of their analysis of teaming and course development by general and special education faculty members.

However, a parallel set of conflicts and tensions has long existed *within* general teacher education among curriculum and instruction professors and faculty members in social foundations and educational psychology. Advocates of multicultural education also have frequently clashed with general teacher educators over how to relate multicultural education to general teacher education. Moreover, curriculum and instruction professors, who usually constitute the core group of general teacher educators, are themselves not of a single mind. Indeed, tensions often exist among the various curriculum areas over the relative importance of each subject area, a particularly important controversy when we consider a multisubject program such as elementary teacher education. Faculty tensions seem to have deeper roots than the histories and traditions of particular fields.

Sources of Faculty Tensions: General and Special

With so many instances of tensions among subfields of general teacher education, including the curriculum and instruction areas that often share epistemological orientations and views of desirable approaches to teaching and learning, I believe that fully understanding the basis for tensions between special education and general education requires us to look beyond the specific histories and traditions of these two fields. Such faculty tensions are much more than a result of the historical evolution of these two fields and their contrasting intellectual orientations.

One way to grasp the deeper significance of these tensions is to highlight how specialized knowledge helps foster distinctive collective identities. Specialization, moreover, is the basis for departmentalization, a governance structure that embodies and defines the various realms of academic specialization. These two factors are briefly discussed below as they pertain to sources of tensions between general and special educators.

Specialized Knowledge and Collective Identities. I have already considered the priority given to specialized knowledge, particularly how the tension between instructor autonomy and interdisciplinary faculty teaming is rooted in the presumed superiority of specialized knowledge. Giving priority to specialized knowledge, however, goes beyond creating a boundary around an individual faculty member, either general teacher educator or special educator. The boundary is around a

ALAN R. TOM

collective of specialists, and these specialists do share a set of perspectives, perspectives that differ from those held by other collectives of specialists. In relation to general and special education, the authors of chapter 8 note that the literature suggests that "faculty from general and special education tend to have strikingly different views of teaching, learning, and discipline" (pp. 129–130).

While these differences in perspective do help explain tensions among special and general education faculty members, the impact of collective identities on faculty tensions tends to be overlooked. That is, chapter authors took for granted that the faculty members who are centrally involved in planning the unified program were either "general teacher educators" or "special educators." I refer to such identities as "topic-centered" and are easily gauged by how one introduces oneself to others (Tom, 1999b). "I am a professor of literacy" or "I'm a social studies person" are examples of relatively narrow topic-centered identities. "I teach in the elementary program" reflects a somewhat broader sense of identity, but that level of identity tends to be contrasted in this book with another limited identity: "I am a special educator." Little evidence exists that large numbers of faculty members saw themselves as what might be called "unified" teacher educators.

The importance of topic-centered identities is that such identities specify the range of responsibility a particular faculty member is willing to assume for teacher preparation. Accepting program-planning responsibility beyond one's self-designated identity requires the individual faculty member to see value in cross-identity dialogue and planning. Such valuing occurs, I believe, when programmatic collaboration is positively viewed, as someone might do when saying, "I am a 'unified' teacher educator." One thereby comes to believe that a faculty member coming from a differing area of expertise has important ideas to contribute to the task at hand. And, to some extent, the limits of specialized knowledge are being acknowledged. As planning at the University of Florida progressed, an increasing number of faculty members seemed able to broaden their identities to embrace responsibility for the development of the overall UESEP.

Departments and Specialization. At the University of Florida—and many other institutions—the collective identities of general teacher educator and special educator are insulated from each other by the departmental structure of the College of Education. Typically, such departmental structures are the basis for hiring, promotion, and merit considerations, all factors that tend to reinforce identity differences and make it difficult to span the boundaries of the collective identities.

The decision at the University of Florida to try to bridge the general education and special education departmental boundaries and their embedded collective identities was a bold one. This attempted spanning seemed to both succeed and fail, with the full story yet to be told. The reliance on using a single professional curriculum to overcome the effects of specialized identities appears to be a strategy with limitations. Is it possible that a better boundary-spanning strategy would have been a multiple curriculum models approach, with its intensive conversations and development activities among multiple small groups? Also, might the effects of departmentalization have been addressed more directly?

Structural Nature of Other Design Issues

Obviously, faculty tensions are not the only design difficulty revealed through the story of the development of UESEP. There were problems involving several dimensions of program development, especially in relation to course coherence and the need for added faculty resources. Yet these problems most likely would have occurred in any large field-oriented program. It is just that these problems were a bit more severe for the University of Florida program, which added to elementary teacher education the obligation to instruct special needs children and provide ESOL instruction. The nature of these program difficulties, however, does not differ in kind, only in degree. Thus, I will not comment further on such program development problems, although I will return to programmatic issues when I discuss alternatives that might overcome the faculty tensions and programmatic complications that seem to have accompanied the development of the University of Florida's UESEP.

ADDRESSING DESIGN BARRIERS: IDEAS FOR TEACHER EDUCATORS

The reform experience of the University of Florida faculty exposed a variety of design issues, many of which became substantial barriers to the development of UESEP. Since other teacher educators may want to consider developing a merged special and general teacher education program, I conclude by suggesting several ideas that might help address particular design barriers. These ideas acknowledge the importance of structural and governance considerations, as well as acknowledging the significance of specialized knowledge, and vary only in small part from

page

ideas that might be directed to reforming large teacher education programs which do not merge general and special education.

Consider Small Faculty Groupings

If we consider program development to entail a long-term conversation among faculty members, then that conversation is easier to do in small groups than large ones. Multiple curriculum models, each under the authority of a faculty team, is one avenue to achieve the advantages of smallness. Another way is the blocking of courses by semester (Tom, 1998), a structure the University of Florida employs. The blocking of courses for a particular semester places a cohort of students in a common set of courses, and facilitates coordination among the instructors of these courses.

Confront the Negative Effects of Specialization

From what I have argued earlier, one might assume that I see little value for specialized expertise in teacher education. That is not necessarily the case, since the negative effects of specialization can be overcome though dialogue and collaborative planning without sacrificing the advantages of specialized knowledge. However, a faculty must be alert to the ways that faculty specialization may sustain narrow faculty identities and divert attention from the thematic integration of a teacher education program.

Foster a Broadened Sense of Faculty Identity

I have suggested that faculty identity vis-à-vis teacher preparation is more focused on the range of responsibility one is willing to assume and on the value one attributes to working with other faculty members than on the specific beliefs held by a collective set of faculty members. Few mechanisms exist for deliberately broadening faculty identities, but I can suggest several possibilities: accepting a new teaching assignment, participating in cross-disciplinary team teaching, working on an interdisciplinary planning team (used at the University of Florida). The key to broadening faculty identity, based on those who have achieved it, may be assuming a broadened responsibility, although it is hard to know whether a broadened sense of identity precedes or follows the exercise of broadened responsibilities.

Try Staged Program Development and Approval

Early specification of the details of course content is understandable in light of the priority faculty typically give to course design and approval. However, premature emphasis on the details of course design can turn a faculty's attention away from program design, and few teacher educators are able to predict, for the totality of a program, the precise content prospective teachers will need in order to develop into skilled and reflective teachers. The piloting of a new program is one way to test out program ideas on a small scale, as well as to develop the program content as the trial effort unfolds (Tom, 1997, pp. 176–185). Full-scale implementation of a large program can profit from this staged program development, as long as the initial approval of the program/courses recognizes that content revisions can be made in process. Once in place, a large teacher education program is hard to change in a major way; a faculty needs to make sure the reformed version is sustainable for a period of time.

Take Little for Granted

Our tendency is to focus on the visible parts of program reform, ranging from the content to be taught to how the reform will be planned. Certainly, such activities are key to teacher education reform. However, attention also needs to be directed to the impact of the structure and culture of the workplace and other systemic considerations. In addition, each reform effort carries its distinctive set of assumptions; we need to listen carefully when a colleague raises issues that question these assumptions.

CONCLUSION

I have used the opportunity to explore the creation of the Unified Elementary Special Education Program as a way to identify issues that arise when a program is redesigned. By no means have I conducted an evaluation of the reform efforts of the faculty at the University of Florida. Rather, I have made suggestions for consideration by other teacher educators interested in fundamental program reform.

There remains the question of whether my ideas—indeed the ideas in other chapters—will be pertinent to those in institutions less research-oriented than the University of Florida. I believe that faculties in most large institutions, particularly public ones, will find relevance in the design issues from the University of Florida experience. Such faculties must also have the initiative and commitment to reform exemplified by general teacher educators and special educators at the University of Florida.

270 ALAN R. TOM

REFERENCES

888ion programs. *Journal of Teacher Education, 38*(4), 13–18.

Book, C. L. (1983). Alternative programs for prospective teachers: An emphasis on quality and diversity. *Action in Teacher Education, 5*(1–2), 57–62.

Book, C. L. (1996). Professional development schools. In J. Sikula, T. J. Buttery, & E. Guyton (Eds.), *Handbook of research on teacher education* (2nd ed., pp. 194–210). New York: Macmillan.

Buchmann, M., & Floden, R. E. (1991). Program coherence in teacher education: A view from the USA. *Oxford Review of Education, 17*, 65–72.

Buchmann, M., & Floden, R. E. (1992). Coherence, the rebel angel. *Educational Researcher, 21*(9), 4–9.

Floden, R. E., & Buchmann, M. (1990). Coherent programs in teacher education: When are they educational? In D. P. Ericson (Ed.), *Philosophy of education 1990* (pp. 304–314). Normal, IL: Philosophy of Education Society.

National Council for Accreditation of Teacher Education (2002, edition). *Professional standards for the accreditation of schools, colleges, and departments of education.* Washington, DC: Author.

Peterson, K. D., Benson, N., Driscoll, A., Narode, R., Sherman, D., Tama, C. (1995). Preservice teacher education using flexible, thematic cohorts. *Teacher Education Quarterly, 22*(2), 29–42.

Shaffer, L. B., & Striedieck, I. M. (1999, February). *Segregating and synergizing factors within one research-based teacher education program: Fostering shared decision making.* Paper presented at the meeting of the Association of Teacher Educators, Chicago, IL.

Tom, A. R. (1988). The practical art of redesigning teacher education: Teacher education reform at Washington University, 1970–1975. *Peabody Journal of Education, 65*(2), 158–179.

Tom, A. R. (1997). *Redesigning teacher education.* Albany: State University of New York Press.

Tom, A. R. (1998). Three fanciful recommendations for teacher education. *Teacher Education Quarterly, 25*(4), 139–143.

Tom, A. R. (1999a, April). *Bigger isn't always better, and small can be very beautiful.* Paper presented at the meeting of the American

Educational Research Association, Montreal, Quebec, Canada. (ERIC Document Reproduction Service No. ED 430924).

Tom, A. R. (1999b). How professional development schools can destabilize the work of university faculty. *Peabody Journal of Education, 74*(3–4), 277–284.

CHAPTER 18

The Unified Elementary Program: Response from a School-Based Perspective

DIANE W. KYLE AND GAYLE H. MOORE

We have been asked to respond from a school-based perspective to the teacher education reform exemplified in the development and implementation of the Unified Elementary Special Education Proteach (UESEP) program. In preparing our response, we decided on a different format than those of the previous chapters. What you will read is a "conversation" about the book, mostly with Diane W. Kyle asking questions of Gayle H. Moore about her reactions from her perspective as a recently retired elementary teacher.

Before beginning the conversation, we thought it would be helpful to introduce ourselves so you know a bit about who we are, why and how we have worked together for almost 12 years, and what has influenced our thinking about teaching and learning. After our introduction, we will explain the organization of our conversation.

Moore recently retired after 31 years as an elementary teacher, mostly in Oldham County, Kentucky. In 1991 she requested a transfer to LaGrange Elementary because the school was piloting the nongraded (K–3) primary program mandated as part of the 1990 Kentucky Education Reform Act (KERA), and she wanted to be a part of the new initiative. That move ended up being quite a significant decision in Gayle's professional life.

Kyle is a professor in the Department of Teaching and Learning in the College of Education and Human Development at the University of Louisville where she has taught general curriculum and teacher education courses since 1980. In 1991, Kyle and a colleague, Ellen McIntyre, designed a research study of teachers' development and implementation of the newly mandated KERA primary program. Through a contact with the LaGrange Elementary principal, she connected with Moore's team of teachers, and a decade-long research collaboration began, most recently as part of a five-year study funded by the Center for Research on Education, Diversity and Excellence (CREDE). Kyle spent a great deal of time observing in Moore's classroom, went with her on many family visits to the homes of children in the research project. With others on the research team, she and Moore have coauthored articles, book chapters, and books and presented at state and national conferences.

Paralleling this time was the reform of the teacher education program at the University of Louisville and the establishment of Professional Development School (PDS) sites and relationships. Already having a research project and connection with teachers well-established, LaGrange became one of the first PDS sites. Kyle became the liaison, working with elementary Master of Arts in Teaching (MAT) students, and Moore became a mentor teacher. This provided yet another opportunity for professional collaboration. With other mentor teachers and principals across PDS sites, Moore participated extensively in designing, reflecting on, and revising the program. In addition, we have presented about aspects of the program at professional conferences and coauthored an article about the role of a mentor teacher.

Our perspectives about teacher education, teaching, and learning have been informed by what we have lived, read about, and studied during the experiences outlined above. Knowing a bit more about the lenses through which we read this book may help explain the questions asked, the responses given, and the lessons we learned. Obviously, this is a somewhat constrained conversation, not as free-flowing as a casual talk between two friends and colleagues. Although Moore didn't know ahead of time the questions Kyle would pose, we did discuss organizing them in categories to make sure we responded from a variety of viewpoints. And, we revised and edited for better readability.

We begin with Moore's responses based on her own preparation and experience as a teacher, then follow with responses based on her perspectives as a mentor teacher, as a participant in a statewide reform initiative, and as a research collaborator. Throughout, we address themes across the book's chapters and raise questions for teacher education research and practice. We end by sharing lessons learned.

RESPONSE BASED ON OWN PREPARATION FOR AND EXPERIENCE OF TEACHING

Kyle: You've taught for 31 years and have spent a lot of time thinking about teaching, helping others learn to teach, and so on. Based on all of that, what do you think teachers today most need to know and be able to do?

Moore: The need for knowing content is a given, but teachers needs to be prepared to teach ALL children who could be in their classrooms no matter what diversities are represented—language, race, culture, disabilities, and so on. Teachers need to understand how children learn, know how to figure out each child's needs, and then how to connect the appropriate instruction. It seems to me that this is the main theme of what I read—teachers need to know how to teach a great diversity of children, and teacher education needs to make sure they're well prepared to do that. The book talks about both constructivist and explicit instructional approaches. My experience as a result of KERA and our CREDE work, and my learning in graduate classes and as a mentor teacher, certainly put me in the constructivist camp. However, I believe, too, that teachers need a repertoire of skills, including those that reflect a more traditional view of explicit teaching. Teachers today also need to know a lot about the communities and families of their children and how to use that knowledge in their teaching. I definitely want to talk more about what the authors of chapter 10 wrote about. I found myself responding a lot to that chapter.

Kyle: Yes, we'll be sure to get to that. Maybe first it would help to put some of your reactions in perspective as far as your background and experience. Having read this book about preparing teachers, I wondered how you reflected on your own preparation for teaching. What was that like, and how was it different from this example?

Moore: Everything was university based and focused on theory mostly, with very little practice. I had the typical methods courses and observed for a few hours in an elementary classroom during my junior year. Student teaching in my senior year involved eight weeks in sixth grade and eight weeks in third. I was responsible for teaching a unit but expected to teach what the teacher normally taught. My college advisor observed my teaching once or twice in each placement. So, it's pretty obvious that my preparation differed in lots of ways from the experiences of those in the UESEP program. UESEP students have a wonderful chance to learn about the connections of theory and practice, to be involved with children in many different settings throughout their program, to learn how to work as part of a team, to get lots of support from the faculty, and so on. I think they are very lucky, even though the ones who saw themselves as guinea pigs had some criticisms.

Kyle: Did you teach children like yourself or not?

Moore: Very much like myself—small town USA. My culture shock came the next year in my first year of teaching when I taught in a rural school, but still there was no racial diversity. Again, I think the

University of Florida students benefit so much from working with children in different kinds of situations.

Kyle: How about your own preparation for teaching children with special needs?

Moore: We didn't identify children as having special needs. They were just children who were "slow learners." In both student teaching placements, one of my jobs in the classroom was to take the low reading group aside and work with them.

Kyle: How did you know how to work with them?

Moore: I didn't. I just followed the manual the way the teacher did. Certainly not how they're being taught in the Unified Elementary Program, is it? In my first years as a teacher, we were given books and manuals and expected to get the students to the end of the books by the end of the year. I felt like anyone who could read a manual could teach, because that was all you did.

Kyle: A few years later you were asked to teach a learning disabilities (LD) class. How did that happen, and what was the experience like?

Moore: This was the first time in my district that students were labeled as having learning disabilities. The special education coordinator was trying to figure out what to do with the many children who by third grade were not reading on grade level and not learning like the other children. She asked if I'd be interested in teaching a class of these children, and I agreed. Every child who wasn't keeping up was considered LD. I got no special training. I did the best I could, just trying to figure out what each child needed and how to work best with him or her. I loved the kids, but it was frustrating. Two years later, I moved from that district and from then on taught in regular elementary classrooms. Certainly, I had many children in my room over the years who had similar needs to those in that early class. I guess that's why I think the idea of unifying elementary and special education makes so much sense to me. Reading this book helped me see what a benefit that could be. I would have been so much better prepared to help all of my children if I'd had that kind of preparation. I worked with some wonderful collaborative special education teachers in recent years, but I would have been better at collaborating with them if my own preparation had been unified.

Kyle: Given everything you've said about your own preparation and experiences, what else can you share about your reaction to the Unified Elementary Program?

Moore: I think they are on the right track and seem to be providing learning experiences that will prepare their students well for the realities of today's classrooms. I particularly appreciated how they emphasized collaboration in so many ways—teams of faculty working across disciplines, pairs and triads of students working together, teams of university and school faculty designing the program, and so on. From my experience, collaboration is so key in schools today, and I think the graduates of this program will be so ready for that. Also, as I've already said, the extensive preparation for teaching general *and* special education is so impressive. Another thing—the Florida students are being taught as if they will be professionals—capable of making decisions, being reflective, studying and learning from their own teaching, and so on. That's so important. I was so glad KERA happened before I retired, because I not only got to teach the way I thought was best, but it also seemed as if teachers were more respected and viewed more as professionals. It helps if you've been prepared that way and expect it.

Kyle: So the collaboration, the unified general/special education focus, and the professionalism are particular strengths. What other strengths of the program did you identify?

Moore: Two things. First, I think it's wonderful that the students have the ESOL preparation. That's not something our MATs have, and yet more and more they have children in their rooms who speak little or no English. The other teachers and I needed to know more about this, too. This is a change that has happened so fast it seems. In the past 10 years in Kentucky, the student population in many schools has changed dramatically, and the language differences are amazing. It's not just teachers in states like Florida, Texas, and California anymore who need this preparation. What they are doing at the University of Florida can help other teacher education programs learn how to improve in this area.

The second thing I mentioned earlier. I wanted to comment on chapter 10, the one written about the involvement of the school counseling faculty. Our work with CREDE caused us to think so much about how to make learning meaningful for students—how to "contextualize" teaching—and we spent so much time visiting families and getting to understand their "funds of knowledge." So, when I read this chapter about this component of the program, I was so impressed. I agree with the authors that we need to change from "blame and judgment" to "collaboration and co-ownership" in our work with families. We need to see families as caring about their children and wanting better for them, and we need to see it as the responsibility of school people to reach out, learn from, and work with those caregivers. We will never help children succeed in school if we don't focus our efforts like this. And, so, we need to prepare those coming into teaching to value who their students and families are and to discover what they know and want. That will happen when preservice teachers and counselors have the kinds of experiences outlined in chapter 10. They are likely to develop a commitment to family involvement, recognize potential barriers, and develop strategies for overcoming those barriers. I also appreciated the authors' realization that they should be practicing what they were preaching. That's probably a good lesson for all of us to think about!

Another strength of the program, I think, is the close partnership between the university and school faculty. But, maybe that's more appropriate to talk about when you ask about my response based on my role as a mentor teacher.

Kyle: Ok, good idea. Before we leave this section, though, what questions would you ask if you had a chance to talk with those who designed the program?

Mooe: Well, this is an ongoing concern, and I know it from both my own experience and from working with MATs. The people who developed the Unified Elementary Program obviously had a clear vision of the kind of teacher they wanted to prepare—the kind of teacher they thought would provide the best learning for all children who might walk through their classroom door. They created the program based on the current best thinking and research. However, how do you prepare students this way and at the same time prepare them for the realities of teaching where so many influences can keep them from teaching the way they've been prepared to teach? That is such a challenge. It's not new, but I've seen some of my best MATs struggle in their first years of teaching with just this issue. Strong field-based programs help, but I wonder how else we can help prepare them to face these challenges and not give up or give in.

RESPONSE BASED ON ROLE AS A MENTOR
TEACHER IN A PDS

Kyle: Public school partners worked collaboratively with university faculty to develop the Unified Elementary Special Education Proteach program. This process is discussed in detail in chapters 4 and 5. As a teacher who worked in a similar way in developing our elementary MAT program, how did you respond to these chapters? What are the strengths and limitations of working in this kind of partnership?

Moore: What I read rang true with my experience. Our mentor teachers worked side by side with the university faculty to read about teacher education reform and create what we considered a model MAT program. For example, I remember one summer when the mentor teachers and university faculty met to plan how to assess students in their field placements. Also, we met across sites each semester to reflect and talk, and at the end of the year, we shared ideas about what to keep and what to change for the next year. Knowing our views mattered was so important and made working with the MATs so much easier. We were all on the same page about the program. As teachers, we really felt as if we were viewed as teacher educators as well. I feel sure that has been true for the teachers who helped design the Unified Elementary Program.

The issues they identified and the challenges they faced were true for us as well. For instance, we also had grant funding to support teachers who contributed their time and effort to the design, implementation, and revisions of the program. The grant provided money for release time, materials, and for specific work like developing the MAT Handbook. So that raises the question, "How can such partnership work happen if such support is not available?" As the authors mention, everyone—university and school faculties—have so many demands on their time. Everyone already has so much to do.

Another partnership issue has to do with being partners in ways other than developing the program. Think about going to conferences, for example. University faculty are expected to do that, and sometimes get travel support. But, school districts may not see that as useful professional development for teachers or, if they do, may not have the money to send teachers. I did have that support and know how meaningful it was for me as a classroom teacher to go to (and present at) conferences like AERA or Holmes. I learned so much that made me a better teacher. The student teachers who helped write this book are getting another kind of professional experience that many teachers don't have. Maybe they're going to present about what they've written as well. I hope so. But, I think the issue of how to broaden professional development opportunities for teachers—to see research, writing, presenting, and so on as legitimate ways of learning as a teacher—is one we need to address in school districts and schools. And, of course, we need to prepare new teachers so that they see themselves getting involved in such activities. The students in the Unified Elementary Program seem to have the kinds of experiences that will help them see the importance of research and of teachers being reflective about what they do.

Also, another issue—maybe not a limitation, but definitely a challenge—is how you get new people involved in the partnership. Those of us who helped work on creating the program shared so much. We understood why things were the way they were. With a changing cast of characters in schools and universities, how do you get new people to have that kind of involvement or feel that kind of commitment? I remember we talked about matching up new and experienced mentor teachers, but I don't think that ever got off the ground. Anyway, I think that's an important issue.

Kyle: As a mentor teacher who worked with our MAT students from the beginning, how did you respond to the students' views described in chapter 11?

Moore: This chapter brought back lots of memories! The theme of our program was, Teachers as Learners and Leaders, and sometimes it was hard when we got what we wanted! We empowered the students and then had to deal with them when they challenged us, asked for changes, expected that they'd have a voice, and so on. In the early years, there was a lot of ambiguity and figuring things out as we went along. I'm sure our students also felt like guinea pigs. But, many also let us know how well prepared they felt the next year in their own classrooms.

Our students tended to open up to their mentor teachers about their concerns. Like the University of Florida students, they wanted their learning to be "practical;" for example, they never wanted to leave the classroom to go to university classes. They thought the "real" learning was with the children. This was when it was important for the university faculty and classroom teachers to be on the same page. We learned that we had an important role in helping the students understand the usefulness of theory and to help them see that it's there in what we do, even if we don't always talk about it. Without a theory as a base for good teaching, you can easily get led astray. The university faculty and teachers had to work together so that we weren't "bad-mouthing" the university about being an ivory tower, and the university faculty weren't "bad-mouthing" teachers about just doing "cutesy" activities.

Our students also raised concerns about things being confusing and stressful and about personal concerns. We worked on that, just as they did in the Florida program. We made changes based on feedback, and we tried to help with students' personal concerns such as travel, child care, and so on as we made school placements. But so much more is expected of teachers today, and becoming well-prepared to teach means it's going to be a very demanding experience. There's just no way around that.

RESPONSE BASED ON ROLE AS PARTICIPANT IN
A STATEWIDE REFORM INITIATIVE

Kyle: The chapters of this book describe various aspects of an extensive change effort. You spent 10 years being involved in such an effort as a

result of KERA. The authors of chapters 6 and 8 address new faculty roles and ways of working, something KERA teachers faced as well. How did you respond to their findings?
Moore: I think I related most to the discussion about teaming—how great it can be if it works yet how hard it is. I realized as I read that some of the same issues that were true for us were true for the university faculty. We worked at my school to arrange the schedule so we would have common planning time. Like the authors, we didn't necessarily team teach, but we did work as a team to plan. We found many of the same advantages they found. We had people to brainstorm with about ideas for teaching, ways to present a lesson, and so on. We discovered new things about one another as we each contributed. I think our children benefited because we were creating lessons built from what a group of people knew, not just one. I imagine this is true for the students in the Unified Elementary Program as well.

However, I could relate to many of the challenges the authors identified, too, either from my own experience or what I heard from friends. It's very hard if you're on a team with people who don't have the same beliefs you have about education—or at least aren't willing to find a common ground. It takes time to work through the compromises. It takes a long time at first for the team to gel and learn how to work together. In the long run, if it works well, you can end up saving time because everyone contributes and shares. If it doesn't work, though, you find yourself planning with the team and then going off and doing your own thing—double planning. And, of course, there are the more personal kinds of challenges—dealing with someone who always wants to be in charge or someone who doesn't contribute much or wants to spend the whole time socializing, and so on. The university faculty faced the challenge of having to meet other responsibilities like writing articles or working on grants. At the school level, now that we have more site-based responsibilities, teachers also have lots of other demands that can get in the way. I think this is when you have to have the person in charge—like the principal—figure out how to make teaming happen if it's supposed to happen. In my school, for example, our principal made sure no other committee meetings were scheduled on team planning day. I'm not sure what the parallel is at the university level, but I know that our principal worked hard to remove the barriers and excuses that could get in the way of teaming and collaborating.

RESPONSE BASED ON ROLE AS RESEARCH COLLABORATOR

Kyle: In the past few years, we've worked together to study teaching and student learning. In these chapters, the study of the Unified

Elementary Program has involved university and school faculty as well as students in the program. How has your experience with research shaped your reading of this book?

Moore: If I hadn't had the experiences you mention, I wouldn't think I knew enough about research to understand a book like this. But, my experience in being on a research team for so long helped me understand more about things like what affects change, the hard work involved in reform efforts, and the importance of documenting what happens and trying to make sense of it. I think I have developed more patience about change and come to appreciate how complicated it is. I know better now that if change is going to happen, it's going to require the time to do it right—to help people come together, develop understandings, work through the rough spots, and celebrate the little victories along the way. I read this book and the experiences the various authors described feeling as if I could truly understand. My involvement with CREDE and research came close to the end of my career, but it helped me discover that teachers can be informed by research and also inform research. The people writing this book have been informed by and also have now informed the research on teacher education.

Kyle: I think this is a good place to stop and try to capture what we think our "lessons learned" have been from reading this book and talking about it together. Let's close by sharing a few that occurred to us.

LESSONS LEARNED

Value of Collaboration

Even though challenging, professional collaboration has many benefits and is worth the effort. By involving the whole faculty, working in teams, developing school partners, and engaging students, the program ended up being better understood and owned by more people. The same is true for teachers in schools trying to implement school reform. Working together and sharing expertise can be a powerful way to make sure you're meeting the needs of all the students.

Importance of Authentic Learning

We know how important it is for classroom teachers to make learning real and meaningful for children. It's encouraging to see throughout this book the attempts being made to make learning authentic as well for those hoping to become teachers. The faculty involved in the program are working to prepare teachers for the kinds of students they will have in their classroom and the kinds of roles they will be expected to play in a school. It's also encouraging to see university faculty using the same methods and strategies they want their students to use in their own classrooms.

Challenge of Reform

Let's face it. Reform isn't easy. This book certainly shows that, and it's a lesson that classroom teachers can understand. Whether at the school level or university level, trying to bring people together across areas or disciplines (especially disciplines often assumed to be too different to collaborate), is an awesome job. And, it takes time. It's messy, and unpredictable, and full of starts and stops and starting again. People come and go, so you always have new people to get on board—and maybe that's a new leader. But, as those writing this book have shown, it is possible. It takes people who sacrifice to make it happen, who feel passionate about the work, and who have a clear sense that the ultimate goal makes it worth the effort. That goal is helping more children be successful in school. Whether we're already teachers or preparing those who will be, do we really have any other acceptable choice?

Epilogue

ELIZABETH BONDY AND DORENE D. ROSS

This text captures a snapshot of the Unified Elementary Special Education Proteach program during its development and early stages of implementation. During 2001–2002 when the chapters were written, the program had 14 cohorts; now, all of those cohorts have completed the program and 21 more are working their way toward graduation. Yet the program is a living, breathing entity that continues to change for a variety of reasons, not the least of which is that faculty continue to study student learning as part of their work and thus are constantly modifying what they do within courses and in the program at large. Therefore, it seems appropriate to end with a brief description of where we are now in the ongoing development of this program.

PROGRAM TINKERING AND REFORM

Our program, like every other teacher education program in the nation grapples constantly with external mandates from state and federal governments. Many of these mandates impact curriculum, however, the most intrusive mandates (i.e., limiting the undergraduate curriculum to 120 hours, highly specific course prescriptions for the first 60 hours of coursework, an English Speakers of Other Language [ESOL] mandate of 15 semester hours or the equivalent) were established prior to or during our program development work and were built into the new program. Beyond that, the curriculum of this program is comprehensive enough that few of the subsequent mandates have had substantive impact on the curriculum, yet these mandates do create dilemmas for us that we have yet to resolve. Two are particularly difficult.

First, the ESOL mandate continues to challenge us. Though few faculty members question the importance of preparing our graduates to teach second language learners, Gainesville is a community with very few ESOL students; this makes it challenging to provide students with authentic experiences with ESOL students. A recent internal review of our infused program also created concerns for us. While faculty members are willing to infuse ESOL content and most do, the content with which faculty are most comfortable relates to diversity and culture and developing the attitudes and values of prospective teachers. They are less comfortable with and thus devote significantly less time to issues related to language and ESOL pedagogy. Based upon this review, we are in the process of creating individualized staff development plans for faculty to help them more comprehensively infuse ESOL content, particularly pedagogical content, into their coursework.

A second issue we are grappling with is performance assessment, required by our Florida Department of Education (DOE) and by NCATE. As we noted in chapter 14, we built performance assessment into the program using an electronic portfolio system and the Pathwise Observation System because of these requirements and because faculty members believe it is the right thing to do. In the fall of 2002, faculty conducted a review of student portfolios that suggested several problems. The major concern was that students' entries did not uniformly demonstrate excellent work, or even the best work a particular student was capable of creating. Many students fail to value the electronic portfolio and see it as a program requirement rather than as an assignment with any inherent value. A second concern was that the electronic portfolio is a very time-consuming activity for students, and faculty worried that students might develop negative attitudes about portfolio assessment that might discourage them from using it as teachers. Third, if faculty were to complete a comprehensive review of each portfolio as is suggested by DOE and as many faculty believe is necessary to make portfolio creation a learning experience for students, the demand on faculty time would be monumental. Faculty in a research I institution see this as an insurmountable barrier to research productivity. Finally, faculty are not certain that the complex and time-consuming tasks of creating and reviewing portfolios of performance-based work really increase our knowledge of what our students know and are able to do. They wonder if class grades, along with Pathwise documentation of the Florida Educator Accomplished Practices (FEAPs) are not sufficient documentation of the performance of student teachers who ALL pass state certification tests, are ALL judged as eligible for rehire, and who are widely sought by districts in Florida and outside Florida because of their competence. Faculty wonder if the state and NCATE are demanding faculty and students spend countless hours in needless documentation. Do we have evidence that course-based performance assessment is an important factor in the preparation of highly skilled teachers? In addition, given the current level of teacher shortages and the state and national emphasis on alternative routes to certification, we face a situation where a student might leave a teacher education program because of unsatisfactory performance on performance assessments, only to become eligible for certification through alternative certification programs like the American Board for Certification of Teacher Excellence, which judge teacher competence solely through performance on tests.

Nevertheless, faculty members recognize that there is a mandate for performance assessment and that there is tremendous (though unrealized) potential for student learning in a portfolio system. As a result of their review of portfolios, faculty made several decisions. First, faculty have more carefully reviewed the FEAPs to make certain that each course documents only a small number of them and that any FEAP that is addressed and assessed in a course is assessed comprehensively. Second, faculty have determined that conversation about the electronic portfolio and entries into the portfolio must become part of every course so that students see it as connected to the curriculum rather than external to it. Third, faculty have determined that, in addition to reviewing with students the performance task(s) assigned for a particular course, the faculty member might also help students understand the linkages across the task, the FEAP, and the student reflection section as the review clearly suggested these components were weak. Finally, faculty members acknowledge that the electronic portfolio system is not accomplishing its intended purpose (i.e., documenting student competence on FEAPs and helping students develop reflective capacity and ownership of their professional development). Consequently, they plan for the future a more careful review of the system in order to modify it or to develop an alternate strategy.

A second source of influence on the program is state impact on K–6 education. Florida, like many states, is placing more emphasis on high-stakes testing. The reading curriculum in schools is becoming more prescribed, schools are graded based on student test scores (among other factors), and districts have been mandated to retain third-grade students who do not meet the criterion scores on the state reading test. Through partnerships with schools, faculty members continue to work to determine or refine effective strategies for working with struggling learners. Although the state context creates opportunities to work more closely with schools on issues related to student learning, it also creates great pressure on schools. Administrators and teachers often do not want student teachers working with students during high-stakes testing years or at least during the months immediately prior to the test. Thus, issues related to finding placements and creating contexts for learning to teach have been exacerbated. In addition, schools and teachers are now grappling with how to communicate to large numbers of children, their parents, and peers that students will or have been retained. We are working with our school partners to identify strategies for working with all constituents in school communities to try to mitigate the possible negative effects of school retention and keep students and parents engaged in school. This work is just beginning.

PROCESS AND OUTCOME RESEARCH

We are amazed and thrilled by the enthusiasm with which our colleagues approach the systematic study of the UESEP program. In fact, the faculty and graduate students are working on more projects than we have been able to catalogue. Also, although some of their efforts are in press, most are not that far along, having been recently presented at conferences and still undergoing revision. Nevertheless, we are confident that concerted efforts to study student learning in the UESEP program will promote continuous improvement as well as provide insights helpful to teacher educators at other institutions. At this point, we have gained insight into the challenges of reform in teacher education (as outlined in chapters 1 and 2 and examined in more detail in many of the subsequent chapters) and the experience of participants (e.g., students, teachers, university faculty) in the reform effort. In order to contribute to the literature on the effectiveness of teacher education programs, however, we will need to examine closely the outcomes of our students' experiences in the Unified Elementary Special Education Proteach program.

Longitudinal Study: Learning to Teach Struggling Students

As UESEP was being implemented in the fall of 1999, several faculty from general and special education won a grant from the U.S. Department of Education/Office of Special Education Programs to prepare doctoral students for leadership roles in promoting inclusive practices in schools. In conceptualizing a unified graduate program, the faculty decided to involve the graduate students in a long-term study of students in the newly unified teacher education program. In particular, the study focuses on preservice teachers' beliefs and practices related to teaching students who are often described as "hard to teach" and/or "hard to manage." The doctoral students were assigned to one or two UESEP students whom they are responsible for interviewing throughout their semesters in the program and during their first year of teaching. During internship semesters, observation data are collected and discussed.

We are analyzing data following each year of data collection on the UESEP students. As of 2004, we have completed one study, Personal Epistemologies and Learning to Teach (Bondy, Ross, Adams, Nowak, Brownell, Hoppey, Kuhel, McCallum, and Stafford, submitted for publication). This study describes preservice teachers' beliefs about knowledge and how one comes to know as a means of explaining how they respond to the content and experiences they encounter. That is, personal epistemologies interact with other conditions present in classes and field experiences and influence what, how, and why students learn. Clearly, insight into preservice teachers' epistemologies has implications for teacher education pedagogy.

Additional studies based on the longitudinal data are in progress. Changes in Preservice Teachers' Conceptions of "Struggling" Learners, examines shifts in preservice teachers' thinking about learners who have difficulty and the strategies used to help them succeed. Follow up studies also are planned. In the fall of 2003 several of the 15 UESEP students in our study began their first year of teaching. We look forward to following them into their classrooms to help us determine the role of UESEP in mediating their beliefs and practices regarding struggling students. Until then, we will continue to examine the data for the stories they reveal about what and how UESEP students learn about teaching.

Other Studies of Teacher Education Processes and Outcomes

Faculty members and doctoral students are engaged in studying UESEP students' learning in courses and field experiences. The examples presented here provide a sense of the work being undertaken, but they are by no means comprehensive.

Some research teams are studying the ways in which UESEP students respond to innovative curricular and instructional arrangements, such as the integrated math, science, and technology semester (Dawson, Pringle, & Adams, 2003; Pringle, Dawson, & Adams, 2003). For instance, they study a specific element of pedagogy, such as microteaching, and the process of creating a culture in which the integration of technology and content areas is valued and embraced by preservice teachers. Similarly, faculty and doctoral students in the area of English Speakers of Other Languages are studying UESEP students' understandings of linguistic and cultural diversity and language learning based on the course and field experiences they have in the program (Harper, DeLuca, & Townsend, 2002). One study focuses particularly on cross-cultural and language learning in an innovative field experience in which UESEP students are "conversation partners" for university students who are learning English (Harper, DeLuca, & Bish, 2001).

Additional studies of innovative field experiences have focused on UESEP's students' learning about emergent literacy (Lamme, 2000) and cultural diversity (Adams, Bondy, & Kuhel, 2003). Another body of work uncovers the processes that support preservice teacher learning in a collaborative, integrated, school-based pre-internship called the Democracy, Diversity, Literacy Community (Silva, 2002). Each of these studies provides insight into adjustments teacher educators can make to strengthen the learning potential of field experiences.

Another kind of study, exemplified by Dawson and Bondy (2003), focuses directly on improving the practice of teacher educators through self-study of their teaching and their students' learning. In this study, a novice and an experienced teacher educator teamed up to study teaching and learning in a newly developed course. Both the process and outcomes of the self-study are proving helpful within UESEP and may be useful to other teacher educators.

Finally, it is exciting to watch doctoral students pursue research on the UESEP program for their dissertations. For example, one student studied interns' understandings of accommodations and their use of accommodations in the elementary classroom (Adams, 2003). Another is planning a study of UESEP students' experience with an assignment in which they are required to interview the primary caregiver of the student they are mentoring in a local public housing neighborhood. A third is planning a study of the connections between interns' racial identities and their implementation of differentiated instruction in elementary classrooms. We are particularly pleased to see our doctoral students pursue teacher education studies for their dissertations because it suggests that they will continue with this line of research after they have left us.

As the UESEP program continues to grow and change, we are cautiously optimistic about its future and the quality of the teachers we graduate. The national, state, and local contexts are such that often we are unsure of what lies ahead for us and who will make the decisions that affect our work with preservice teachers. We are grateful for the help we have received from teacher educators everywhere who share their research and writing in public forums. We are grateful for our UESEP students who patiently endure our endless questions and gladly complete our surveys. We are grateful for our colleagues who pursue their research with enthusiasm and determination. Together we can prepare excellent teachers for everybody's children.

REFERENCES

Adams, A. (2003). Elementary interns' knowledge and implementation of accommodations for diverse learners. Unpublished doctoral dissertation, University of Florida, Gainesville.

Adams, A., Bondy, B., & Kuhel, K. (in press). *Preservice teacher learning in an unfamiliar setting. Teacher Education Quarterly.*

Dawson, K., & Bondy, E. (2003). Reconceptualizing the instruction of a teacher educator: Reflective peer coaching in higher education. *Teaching Education, 14,* 319–331.

Dawson, K., Pringle, R., & Adams, T. (2003). Providing links between technology integration, methods courses and traditional field experiences: Implementing a model of curriculum-based and technology-enhanced microteaching. *Journal of Computing in Teacher Education, 20*(1), 41–47.

Harper, C., Deluca, E., & Bish, D. (2001, May). *Learning about another culture is E.E.S.E.E.!* Paper presented at the Sunshine State TESOL Conference, Tampa, FL.

Harper, C., DeLuca, E., & Townsend, J. (2002, May). *Exploring language and culture in an ESOL infusion program.* Paper presented at the Sunshine State TESOL Conference, West Palm Beach, FL.

Lamme, L. (2000). Project Booktalk: Future teachers bring library books to day care homes. *Journal of Early Childhood Teacher Education, 21,* 85–92.

Pringle, R., Dawson, K., & Adams, T. (2003). Technology, science and preservice teachers: Creating a culture of technology-savvy elementary teachers. *Action in Teacher Education, 24*(4), 46–51.

Silva, D. (2002, January). *Collaborative fieldwork: The democracy, diversity and literacy community.* Paper presented at the meeting of the American Association of Colleges of Teacher Education, New Orleans.

Appendix A
Unified Elementary Special Education Proteach Course of Study**

UNDERGRADUATE PROGRAM

Semester 1		Semester 3	
Composition	3	EDF 1005 Introduction to Education	3
Mathematics	3	Biological Science	3
Social and Behavioral Science	3	Humanities	3
Physical Science	3	Composition/Literature	3
Humanities	3	STA 2122 Statistics	3

Semester 3		Semester 4	
EDG 2701 Teaching Diverse	3	EME 2040 Intro to Ed. Technology	3
Populations	3	Mathematics	3
SPC 2600	3	Humanities	3
Humanities	3	Developmental Psychology	3
Physical or Biological Science with lab	3	General Education Elective	3
General Psychology			

Semester 5		Semester 6	
EDF 3115 Child Development for	3	EEX 3257 Core Teaching Strategies	3
Inclusive Education		EEX 3616 Core Classroom	3
EEX 3070 Teachers and Learners in	3	Management Strategies	
Inclusive Schools		SPA 3002 Communication Disorders	3
SDS 3430 Family and Community	3	EEC 3706 Emergent Literacy	3
Involvement in Education	3	TSL 3526 ESOL Language and	3
LAE 3005 Children's Literature in	3	Culture	
Childhood Education		HSC 3301 Health Science Education	
MUE 3212 Music for the Elementary	2	in Elementary Schools	
Child			
ARE 4314 Art Education for	2		
Elementary Schools			
Field Component: Bright Futures integrated into EEX 3070; Project Book Talk integrated into LAE 3005		Field component: Classroom observation and practice infused into EEX 3257, EEC 3706, and EEX 3616	
Total	16	Total	18

Semester 7		Semester 8	
SCE 4310 Elementary Science Methods	3	LAE 4314 Language Arts for Diverse	3
for the Inclusive Classroom		Learners	
LAS 3### Science elective	3	ENC 3254 Writing for Prof. Commun.	3
(3000 or above)		SSE 4312 Social Studies for Diverse	3
MAE 4310 Teaching Mathematics in	3	Learners	
the Inclusive Elementary Classroom		LAS 3###Social Sciences elective	3
LAS 3### Math elective (3000 or above)	3	(3000 or above)	
EME 4406 Integrating Technology	3	EDE 4942 Integrated Teaching in	3
the Classroom		Elementary Education	
Field Component: Integrated into SCE 4310 MAE 4310, and EME 4406		EDE 4942 involves Placement in elementary setting for 15 hours per week	
Total	16	Total	15

**This document describes the program for all students who entered from fall 1999 through spring 2001. Program modificatons to accommodate new state mandates were implemented for all students who entered fall 2002.

Appendix B
Unified Elementary Special Education Proteach Course of Study

GRADUATE YEAR/ Master's Program (36 hours)

Certification Options

During the graduate year, students may select from two certification tracks.

Option A: Dual Certification Track
- Confers Elementary and Special Education Certification
- 12 hours specialization coursework taken in special education

Option B: Single Certification Track
- Confers Elementary Certification
- Students select a 12–hour specialization in one of three areas
  A) Elementary Interdisciplinary: 3 hours each advanced pedagogy in literacy, math, science and social studies (technology infused)
  B) Elementary Specialist: 12 hours advanced content pedagogy in literacy, math/science, or technology
  C) ESOL Specialist: 12 hours advanced ESOL pedagogy

Coursework

EDE 6948/EEX 6863 Internship	12 hours
EEX 6786 Transdisciplinary Teaming OR EDE 6225 Practices in Child. Ed.	3 hours
EDF 5552 Role of Schools in Democratic Society	3 hours
EDF 5441 Assessment In General and Exceptional Student Education	3 hours
EDE TSL 5142 Curriculum, Methods, and Assessment for ESOL Learners	3 hours
Specialization (Includes 3 hr. Practicum for Special Ed. Only)	12 hours

Appendix C
Models of Collaboration

Model One	One faculty member from each of two departments teams in the coordination of the course. Together they work with three doctoral students from across the two departments. The faculty members each teach one section of the course. One faculty member will receive credit for coordination in the fall semester and one receives credit in the spring semester.
Model Two	One faculty leader works with four doctoral students. Doctoral students are drawn from across the two departments. The faculty member teaches one section of the course and receives credit for coordinating the course and supervising the doctoral students.
Model Three	The faculty leader works with a teacher-in-residence to plan and deliver the course. The teacher-in-residence represents an area of expertise not represented by the faculty member and is responsible for one section of the course. Doctoral students representing both departments teach other sections. The faculty member teaches one section of the course and receives one course credit for coordinating the course and supervising the other members of the teaching team.
Model Four	A faculty leader coordinates the work of four doctoral students from across the two departments. As part of instruction in this course, the faculty member and doctoral students use instructional modules. The faculty member teaches one section and receives one course credit for coordinating the course and supervising the doctoral students teaching the course.
Model Five	The faculty leader coordinates the course. Another faculty member (representing content from another area) receives credit for .25 FTE by serving as a consulting faculty member who delivers content to all the sections. Each section of the course has six extra students to fund this model. The faculty leader teaches one section and receives credit for coordination and supervision of doctoral students. The consulting faculty member assumes some responsibility for grading relevant aspects of student work.
Model Six	Two faculty members coordinate a course using a large auditorium or distance education structure. Three doctoral students (each at .25 FTE) lead six discussion sessions. One faculty member coordinates the course and supervises doctoral students in the fall and the other does so in the spring.

Appendix D
*Comparison of Authority-Client and Collaborative Approaches
to Family-School Relations*

Authority-Client Approach	Collaborative Approach
Purpose of Interaction: Solve the student's academic or social problem.	*Purpose of Interaction:* Foster a process of joint planning and problem solving between the family and school to maximize the resources for children's learning and social-emotional development.
Educator's Role: Expert who does "to" or "for" the family, serving as the central decision maker or problem solver.	*Educator's Role:* Professional working "with," not doing "to"; resource person who shares leadership and power with the family.
Student's Role: Often excluded from family-school interaction or has a passive role; assumed not to know what he or she needs.	*Student's Role:* Active role in all family-school activities and in determining own progress, problems, and solutions.
Caregiver's Role: Often passive recipient of "service" or "activity" that is defined by school professional.	*Caregiver's Role:* Active role in all family-school activities; seen as capable of deciding how to contribute to student's learning or solve student's problems.
Nature of the Relationship: Distant, sometimes adversarial; frequently with overt or covert blaming by each party.	*Nature of the Relationship:* Cooperative, nonblaming atmosphere created to promote problem solving.
Goal: For the two parties to have contact only when there is a problem to be resolved.	*Goal:* To design opportunities to get to know one another and establish a partnership to support children's learning and development.
Nature of the Activities: School staff assess the problem and prescribe the necessary cure; all are expected to be compliant with the school's decisions.	*Nature of the Activities:* Caregivers and students are seen as important resources for problem solving and learning; parents have a central role in problem solving.
Expected Outcomes: Crisis or problem is resolved.	*Expected Outcomes:* Increased family involvement in the student's school experience; improved academic performance; fewer "insoluble" discipline problems.

Appendix E
Performance Task Assignment

INSTRUCTIONAL STRATEGY ASSIGNMENT

Performance Indicator (Meets AP 10)
Working in groups of three, students will plan, teach, and evaluate one lesson plan using direct instruction and one lesson using cognitive strategy instruction. The focus for the lesson must be selected with input from the cooperating teacher and must fall within the expected curriculum for the grade level and school site, including Florida Sunshine State Standards. Successful lessons will demonstrate the following:
- Ability to write objectives appropriate for the students
- Ability to write lesson plans in an appropriate lesson plan format
- Ability to write objectives, lesson plans, and assessment strategies that link together logically
- Ability to design lessons that are likely to engage diverse students successfully in learning
- Ability to adapt instruction to meet the instructional needs of individuals within a group

Assignment description
For this assignment you will work in a group of three students. Your group will work together to plan, teach, evaluate and write a brief reflective report about two instructional strategies: direct instruction and cognitive strategy instruction. (Note: If your lesson plan focuses on the development of creative or critical thinking skills, it can also be used to met AP 4)

Planning and teaching the lessons
➢ Following presentation of the instructional model in class, each trio will consult with the collaborating teacher to identify a lesson topic appropriate to the model and the group of children and draft a lesson plan, which follows the model.
➢ Submit the draft to your course instructor for feedback.
➢ Revise the plan.
➢ Each trio teaches the lesson plan to a small group of children. During instruction the students play the following roles:
Teacher—teaches and collects any written products of the lesson
Observer 1—Observe to document classroom management strategies used/not used and to document use of all essential components of the lesson model using the rubric. Note all adaptations from the original plan. (NOTE: You must submit your notes!)
Observer 2—Keep detailed notes about what happens in the lesson. Record specific student comments (with student names). Specifically record evidence of engagement/nonengagement of students and any and all evidence of student learning. (NOTE: You must submit your notes!)

Appendix F
Instructional Strategy Assignment Rubric

Lesson Plan				
	Significantly below expectations	Slightly below expectations	Meets expectations for good work	A step above
Objectives	Learning outcomes are vague; learning outcomes are loosely connected to lesson focus; inappropriate for age/grade		Clearly specifies learning outcomes for the lesson; uses appropriate verbs; clearly linked to focus of lesson; appropriate for students;linked to Sunshine State Standards	
*Content	Omits components, inconsistent links between components, inappropriate for age/grade, problems in sequence, lacks sufficient interest to engage students		Includes all required components, clear links between objectives, appropriate for age/grade of students, clear and logical sequence; engaging high interest lesson, appropriate materials	
*Specificity and rationale	Lacks detail in description of materials, sequence, procedures; vague rationale		Sufficiently detailed that a substitute would have all required materials and could teach the lesson without seeking additional information; clearly specifies what the teacher will say and do; clear rationale for instructional decisions.	As de-tailed as model in course packet.

* These components will be counted double in assigning your grade.

Assessment	Assessment strategy is NOT systematic and/or not clearly linked to lesson objectives		Assessment strategy is systematic and clearly linked to learning objectives and appropriate for students	
Written Report				
	Significantly below expectations	Slightly below expectations	Meets expectations for good work	A step above
Analysis of student learning	Vague discussion of children's learning. Some links between intended objectives and student learning unclear.		Links between intended learning and student outcomes are clear. Provides summary of learning of all children in group; clear explanation of reasons for differing levels of student performance. Clear analysis of what was and was not learned.	
Conclusion	Confusing discussion of research findings.		Draws on research summaries to present clear conclusions about empirical support and limitations of the model.	
Comments				
Meets Accomplished Practice 10?		YES	NO	
Meets Accomplished Practice 4		YES	NO	

Appendix G
Florida Accomplished Practices Matched to Pathwise/Praxis III
Teacher Performance Assessment Criteria

Florida Accomplished Practices	Pathwise/Praxis III Teacher Performance Assessment Criteria
1. Assessment: Uses assessment strategies (traditional and alternate) to assist the continuous development of the learner.	Domain A: Organizing Content Knowledge for Student Learning A5. Creating or selecting evaluation strategies that are appropriate for the students and that are aligned with the goals of the lesson. Domain C: Teaching for Student Learning C4. Monitoring students' understanding of content through a variety of means, providing feedback to students to assist learning, and adjusting learning activities as the situation demands.
2. Communication: Uses effective communication techniques with students and all other stakeholders.	Domain A: Organizing Content Knowledge for Student Learning A2. Articulating clear learning goals for the lesson that are appropriate for the students. Domain B: Creating an Environment for Student Learning B2. Establishing and maintaining rapport with students. B3. Communicating challenging learning expectations to each student. Domain C: Teaching for Student Learning C1. Making learning goals and instructional procedures clear to students. C2. Making content comprehensible to students.
3. Continuous Improvement: Engages in continuous professional quality improvement for self and school.	Domain C: Teaching for Student Learning C4. Monitoring students' understanding of content through a variety of means, providing feedback *(Continued on next page)*

	to students to assist learning, and adjusting learning activities as the situation demands. Domain D: Teacher Professionalism D1. Reflecting on the extent to which the learning goals were met. D2. Demonstrating a sense of efficacy. D3. Building professional relationships with colleagues to share teaching insights and to coordinate learning activities for students.
4. Critical thinking: Uses appropriate techniques and strategies that promote and enhance critical, creative, and evaluative thinking capabilities of students.	Domain A: Organizing Content Knowledge for Student Learning A4. Creating or selecting teaching methods, learning activities, and instructional materials or other resources that are appropriate for the students and that are aligned with the goals of the lesson. Domain B: Creating an Environment for Student Learning B3. Communicating challenging learning expectations to each student. Domain C: Teaching for Student Learning C3. Encouraging students to extend their thinking. C5. Using instructional time effectively.
5. Diversity: Uses teaching and learning strategies that reflect each student's culture, learning styles, special needs, and socioeconomic background.	Domain A: Organizing Content Knowledge for Student Learning A1. Becoming familiar with relevant aspects of students' background knowledge and experiences. A4. Creating or selecting teaching methods, learning activities, and instructional materials or other resources that are appropriate for the students and that are aligned with the goals of the lesson. *(Continued on next page)*

Appendix G (Cont'd.)

	Domain B: Creating an Environment for Student Learning B3. Communicating challenging learning expectations to each student. Domain C: Teaching for Student Learning C3. Encouraging students to extend their thinking.
6. Ethics: Adheres to the Code of Ethics and Principles of Professional Conduct of the Education Profession in Florida.	Domain D: Teacher Professionalism D2. Demonstrating a sense of efficacy.
7. Human Development and Learning: Uses an understanding of learning and human development to provide a positive learning environment, which supports the intellectual, personal, and social development of all students.	Domain A: Organizing Content Knowledge for Student Learning A1. Becoming familiar with relevant aspects of students' background knowledge and experience. A3. Demonstrating an understanding of the connections between the content that was learned previously, the current content, and the content that remains to be learned in the future. A4. Creating or selecting teaching methods, learning activities, and instructional materials or other resources that are appropriate for the students and that are aligned with the goals of the lesson. Domain B: Creating an Environment for Student Learning B1. Creating a climate that promotes fairness. B2. Establishing, maintaining rapport with students. B3. Communicating challenging learning expectations to each student.

(Continued on next page)

	B4. Establishing and maintaining consistent standards of classroom behavior. Domain C: Teaching for Student Learning C3. Encouraging students to extend their thinking. C5. Using instructional time effectively.
8. Knowledge of Subject Matter: Demonstrates knowledge and understanding of the subject matter.	Domain A: Organizing Content Knowledge for Student Learning A2. Articulating clear learning goals for the lesson that are appropriate for the students A3. Demonstrating an understanding of the connections between the content that was learned previously, the current content, and the content that remains to be learned in the future. A4. Creating or selecting teaching methods, learning activities, and instructional materials or other resources that are appropriate for the students and that are aligned with the goals of the lesson. Domain C: Teaching for Student Learning C1. Making learning goals and instructional procedures clear to students. C2. Making content comprehensible to students. C4. Monitoring students' understanding of content through a variety of means, providing feedback to students to assist learning, and adjusting learning activities as the situation demands. C5. Using instructional time effectively.

(Continued on next page)

Appendix G (Cont'd.)

	[Knowledge of subject matter is best measured by Praxis II tests.]
9. Learning Environments: Creates and maintains positive learning environments in which students are actively engaged in learning, social interaction, cooperative learning, and self-motivation.	Domain B: Creating an Environment for Student Learning B1. Creating a climate that promotes fairness. B2. Establishing and maintaining rapport with students. B3. Communicating challenging learning expectations to each student. B4. Establishing and maintaining consistent standards of classroom behavior. B5. Making the physical environment as safe and conducive to learning as possible. Domain 5: Teacher Professionalism D2. Demonstrating a sense of efficacy.
10. Planning: Plans, implements and evaluates effective instruction in a variety of learning environments.	Domain A: Organizing Content Knowledge for Student Learning A1. Becoming familiar with relevant aspects of students' background knowledge and experiences. A4. Creating or selecting teaching methods, learning activities, and instructional materials or other resources that are appropriate for the students and that are aligned with the goals of the lesson. Domain C: Teaching for Student Learning C4. Monitoring students' understanding of content through a variety of means, providing feedback to students to assist learning and adjusting learning activities as the situation demands.

(Continued on next page)

	Domain D: Teacher Professionalism D1. Reflecting on the extent to which the learning goals were met.
11. Role of Teacher: Works with various education professionals, parents, and other stakeholders in the continuous improvement of the educational experiences of students.	Domain D: Teacher Professionalism D3. Building professional relationships with colleagues to share teaching insights and to coordinate learning activities for students. D4. Communicating with parents or guardians about student learning.
12. Technology: Uses appropriate technology in teaching and learning process.	Domain A: Organizing Content Knowledge for Student Learning A4. Creating or selecting teaching methods, learning activities, and instructional materials or other resources that are appropriate for the students and that are aligned with the goals of the lesson.

Appendix H
Teacher Education Intern Rating Sheet

Intern's Name:_____ ID# _____

Major Field:_____ Semester: Fall_____ Spring_____
(year)   (year)

SUBMITTED BY: Directing Teacher ( )   College Coordinator ( )

Other_____ ( )

Name: _____

Title & Dept. or Position _____

Address: _____

Signature: _____ Date: _____

INSTRUCTIONS: Please rate the intern at the level best representing *your estimate of competence and potential as compared to other interns.* Use the following ratings as a guide: **1** - Does not meet the expectations; **2** - Meets expectations at minimal level; **3** - Meets expectations at satisfactory level; **4** – Exceeds expectations. This information comes under the Board of Regents student records policy. As such, access (beyond required handling) will be limited to the intern and those designated by him or her on a need to know basis.

Rating Criteria	Not Observed	1	2	3	4
1. Uses assessment strategies (traditional and alternative) to assist the continuous development of the learner. Collects and uses data from a variety of sources.					
2. Uses effective communication techniques with students and all other stakeholders. Recognizes the need for effective communication in the classroom. Appropriate use of English, suitable voice quality.					
3. Engages in continuous professional improvement through lifelong learning, self-reflection, work with colleagues and teammates, and meeting the goals of a professional development plan.					
4. Uses appropriate techniques and strategies which promote and enhance critical, creative, and evaluative thinking capabilities of students. Is building a repertoire of realistic projects and problem-solving activities designed to assist students in demonstrating their ability to think creatively.					

(Continued on next page)

Appendix H (Cont'd.)

5. Uses teaching and learning strategies that reflect each student's culture, learning styles, special needs, and socio-economic background. Creates a climate of openness, inquiry, and support by practicing strategies of acceptance, tolerance, resolution, and mediation.				
6. Adheres to the Code of Ethics and Principles of Professional Conduct of the Education Profession in Florida.				
7. Uses an understanding of learning and human development to provide a positive learning environment that supports the intellectual, personal, and social development of all students. Students are actively engaged in learning, social interaction, cooperative learning, and self-motivation.				
8. Demonstrates a basic understanding of the subject field and is beginning to understand that the subject is linked to other disciplines and can be applied to real-world situations.				
9. Plans, implements, and evaluates effective instruction.				
10. Communicates and works effectively with families and colleagues to improve the educational experiences at the school.				
11. Uses appropriate technology in teaching and learning processes where available.				
12. Creates positive and productive learning environment; is able to care for students, motivate them, and show interest in them; adapts and changes instruction in unpredictable dynamic classrooms.				
13. Designs and implements an effective behavior management policy.				
14. Is punctual, uses mature judgment, provides accurate reports and records (professional responsibility).				
15. Demonstrates enthusiasm for teaching.				
16. Demonstrates responsiveness to supervision (ability to accept constructive criticism and incorporate suggestions into teaching performance).				
17. Presents a professional appearance in dress, grooming, attitude, and demeanor.				
18. Demonstrates initiative and self-reliance.				

SUMMARY: Please add any additional information you consider pertinent to your professional evaluation of this student.

Appendix I
Electronic Portfolio Matrix

Practices	AP.1	AP.2	AP.3	AP.4	AP.5	AP.6	AP.7	AP.8	AP.9	AP.10	AP.11	AP.12
Semester 1												
EDF 3115	X			X	X		X					
EEX 3070			X		X					X		
LAE 3005				X	X							
SDS 3430	X	X			X	X				X	X	
Semester 2												
EEX 3257			X	X						X		
EEX 3616									X			
EDG 3706	X						X					
TSL 3526	X	X			X		X					
Semester 3												
SCE 4310	X	X	X	X	X		X	X	X	X		X
MAE 4310	X	X	X	X	X		X	X		X		X
EME 4406	X	X	X	X			X	X				X

(Continued on next page)

Appendix I (Cont'd.)

Practices	AP.1	AP.2	AP.3	AP.4	AP.5	AP.6	AP.7	AP.8	AP.9	AP.10	AP.11	AP.12
Semester 4												
LAE 4314		X	X		X			X				
SSE 4312												
EDE 4942	Intern	Evalu	ation	Form								
Graduate												
EDF 5441	X			X								
EDF 5552										X		
EDE 6225 or	X	X	X	X	X		X	X	X	X		
EEX 6786			X								X	
EDE 6948 or	Intern	Evalu	ation	Form								
EEX 6983												
EDG 6931	X	X		X	X		X		X	X	X	

Contributors

Alyson Adams is the program coordinator for the University of Florida's Lastinger Center for Learning. She recently completed her PhD at the University of Florida, specializing in teacher education and collaboration. Her dissertation is an examination of student teachers' beliefs and practices related to making accommodations for diverse learners.

Ellen S. Amatea is a professor in the Department of Counselor Education at the University of Florida. She directs the marriage and family therapy training program, coordinates the delivery of a teacher education course on family-school involvement, and serves as a consultant to UF's laboratory school staff on developing family-school involvement practices.

Patricia Ashton is a professor and director of the educational psychology program at the University of Florida. Her research interests include teacher education and teacher and student motivation. She is coauthor with Rod Webb of *Making a Difference: Teachers' Sense of Efficacy and Student Achievement*.

Anne G. Bishop coordinates the Center on Personnel Studies for Special Education (COPSSE) at UF. She is also an instructor in the unified elementary program. Her prior experience includes 26 years as both a teacher and school/district level administrator.

Linda Blanton is dean, College of Education, at Florida International University. During her 30 years in education, she has been a teacher in both general and special education, a university professor, and she has served in numerous leadership positions. Dr. Blanton was the recipient of the TED/Merrill Excellence in Teaching and Teacher Education Award.

Elizabeth Bondy is a professor in the University of Florida's School of Teaching and Learning, codirector of a unified (general and special

311

education) doctoral program, and professor in residence at an urban elementary school. Her research interests include teaching and learning in underperforming schools and teacher education for diversity.

Mary T. Brownell is an associate professor in special education at the University of Florida. Her research interests focus on teachers' careers and development in special and general education. Currently, she codirects the Center for Personnel Studies in Special Education funded by the U.S. Department of Special Education.

Renee Tipton Clift is a professor in the Department of Curriculum and Instruction at the University of Illinois at Urbana-Champaign. Her research interests include the form and process of collaboration and partnerships, the appropriate uses of technology in initial and continuing teacher education, and the process of learning to teach secondary English in diverse contexts.

Vivian I. Correa is a professor in and past chair of the Department of Special Education at the University of Florida. Dr. Correa's areas of expertise are in teacher education, early childhood special education, multicultural education, and working with Latino families.

Zhihui Fang is an associate professor of literacy and language education at the University of Florida. He has published in the areas of literacy development, applied linguistics, and reading teacher education. He has also collaborated with university and public school colleagues to develop balanced literacy programs for inclusive elementary classrooms.

Sebastian Foti is a Fulbright Scholar currently developing software for K–12 schools. He received his PhD in Educational Technology from the University of Florida. His work with electronic portfolios at the K–12 levels served as the background for the University of Florida's Electronic Portfolio Project.

Rona Monique Frederick is a doctoral student in the Department of Curriculum and Instruction at the University of Maryland, College Park. Her research focuses on urban schooling, instructional computer technology, and critical race theory.

Cynthia C. Griffin is an associate professor of special education in the University of Florida's College of Education. Her areas of research interest include: 1) beginning special education teachers; 2) instructional strategies in math and reading; and 3) teacher education. She recently completed a federally funded research grant designed to study first-year special education teachers and their accomplishments and problems of practice.

Sharen Halsall is assistant director/elementary coordinator in the School of Teaching and Learning, College of Education. Before this she served as Coordinator of the Child Development program at Santa Fe Community College where she worked on articulation of programming between community college and university teacher education programs.

David Hoppey is a doctoral candidate in the Department of Special Education at the University of Florida. His interests include teacher education, inclusive school reform, and developing school-university partnerships to help prospective and inservice teachers effectively meet the needs of all students.

Joanna Jennie is a doctoral student in marriage and family counseling at the University of Florida where she is investigating white racial identity development in teachers and counselors. She has been a teacher, school-based therapist, educational audiologist, and consultant on hearing impaired children in the United States, France, and Israel.

Diane W. Kyle is a professor in the Department of Teaching and Learning and Co-Director of the Nystrand Center of Excellence in Education at the University of Louisville. She teaches curriculum courses and facilitates center initiatives with university and school partners to improve teaching and student learning. She recently coauthored a book about school-family connections.

Holly B. Lane is a member of the special education faculty at the University of Florida. She specializes in literacy intervention and preparing teachers to help struggling readers. Her current research focuses on developing the pedagogical knowledge and skills to teach reading in diverse classrooms.

Cynthia McCallum is a doctoral candidate in the School of Teaching and Learning at the University of Florida. Her areas of interest include diversity, women's studies, and inclusive teacher education. She is currently working on her dissertation, which will examine preservice teachers' racial identity and classroom practice.

James McLeskey is professor and chair of the Department of Special Education at the University of Florida. For the last 13 years he has worked with teachers and administrators in local schools as they have developed and implemented inclusive school programs. Dr. McLeskey's research interests include effective methods for achieving school reform, issues influencing teacher learning, and the translation of research-based methods into practice.

Gayle H. Moore recently retired after teaching elementary school for 31 years at grades K–8. She has collaborated on research studies related to Kentucky's nongraded primary program, participated as a mentor teacher in the University of Louisville's Master of Arts in Teaching (MAT) Program, and recently coauthored a book about school-family connections.

Virginia Mallini received her bachelor's and master's degrees from the University of Florida's College of Education in 2002. She is teaching elementary school in Colorado.

Angela Mott received her bachelor's and master's degrees from the University of Florida's College of Education in 2002. She is in her second year of teaching in an urban elementary school.

Rhonda Nowak is an assistant professor of literacy education at Loyola University New Orleans. She is a former special education and Reading Recovery teacher. Her research interests include literacy and teacher education.

Marleen C. Pugach is professor of teacher education in the Department of Curriculum and Instruction at the University of Wisconsin-Milwaukee and director of the Collaborative Teacher Education Program for Urban Communities. Her scholarly interests include building collaborative relationships between the preparation of special and general education teachers, the intersection of inclusion and school reform, and urban school-university partnerships.

Peter L. Rennert-Ariev is an assistant professor of teacher education at Loyola College in Maryland. His research interests focus on preservice teacher preparation, characteristics of teacher education programs, and performance-based assessment.

Gail Ring is the director of instructional technology in Bowling Green State University's College of Education and Human Development. She received her PhD in Educational Technology from the School of Teaching and Learning at the University of Florida. Gail's research interests include innovation diffusion and electronic portfolios.

Dorene D. Ross is a professor in the School of Teaching and Learning at the University of Florida. She served as a faculty leader in the development of the unified elementary program and codirector of *Recreating Teacher Education,* a grant from the BellSouth Foundation, designed to restructure the College of Education and facilitate implementation of the unified program.

Lynne Stafford is a doctoral candidate in teacher education at the University of Florida and a public school classroom teacher with 20 years of experience. Her research interests include field experiences, classroom management, and the cohort system for grouping students in teacher education courses.

Colleen Swain is an associate professor of educational technology at the University of Florida. She specializes in the integration of technology into the curriculum and classroom, the impact of educational technologies on student achievement, distance teaching and learning, teaching methodologies for secondary education, staff development, and computer applications.

Alan R. Tom is professor of education in the School of Education at the University of North Carolina at Chapel Hill. His teaching, program development, and research interests focus on the initial preparation of teachers and their career development. Tom is author of *Teaching as a Moral Craft* (Longman, 1984) and *Redesigning Teacher Education* (SUNY Press, 1997).

Linda Valli is an associate professor in the Department of Curriculum and Instruction at the University of Maryland, College Park where she works with preservice, inservice, and doctoral students. Her research interests include teacher learning, high-quality teaching, school improvement, and cultural diversity.

Theresa B. Vernetson is assistant dean for student affairs in the College of Education at University of Florida. She has been responsible for the coordination of student teaching placements since 1985 and has extensive experience in professional development training in the areas of effective teaching and clinical education.

Rodman B. Webb is professor and has served as associate dean at the University of Florida's College of Education. He is the author or coauthor of *The Presence of the Past, Schooling and Society* and *Making a Difference,* coeditor of *Qualitative Research in Education,* and founding coeditor of the *International Journal of Qualitative Studies in Education.*

Catheryn Weitman is the executive director of graduate education and research in the School of Education at Barry University where she has also served as chair of K–4 Teacher Education, director of field experiences/internship, director of graduate elementary education programs, and dean. Nationally, Dr. Weitman is known for her leadership and involvement with the ACEI/NCATE performance-based program approval process.

Index

academic autonomy or freedom,
39–41, 102–104, 110, 135–137,
197–198, 260
American Council on Education, 11,
13

Bellsouth Foundation, 46, 74, 119
Bright Futures, 85, 181, 182, 222

Center for Educational Renewal, 13
Child Development for Inclusive
Education, 85, 183, 222
Children's Literature for Childhood
Education, 85
coherence, 99, 115, 135–137, 260,
263–264
cohorts, 57–58, 268
collaboration
as a program theme, 277, 282
barriers/tensions, 52, 132, 140
benefits of, 140–141, 147–162,
200, 278–280
concerns and solutions, 75–76,
78–79, 102–112
with families, 168, 170–172,
277–278, 296
with liberal arts faculty, 60
with school partners, 59–60,
77–78, 94–96, 124–125
with teacher education
colleagues, 172–175,
197–198, 202–203, 265–268,
281, 295

Core Classroom Management
Strategies
content, 61
field experience, 86–88, 149,
153, 155–157, 181
Core Teaching Strategies
content, 61
field experience, 86–88,
148–149, 153, 156–157, 181,
184
course of study, 293–294

Educational Standards Commission,
220
electronic portfolio
and Florida Educator Accomplished Practice matrix,
308–309
and performance tasks, 213,
221, 222
concerns about, 286–287
development of the project,
233–244
Emergent Literacy, 61, 87–88, 149,
181
ESOL
program content, 57
program rationale, 53
state mandate, 80, 258, 259,
277, 285
ESOL Language and Culture, 61,
88–89, 93–94, 149, 181

317